Miracle-Gro®

BEAUTIFUL PERENNIALS

Simple Techniques to Make Your Garden Sensational

Meredith Books
Des Moines, Iow

FROM THE

Perennials are among the easiest of flowers to grow. They come back year after year in a dance of color that often lasts from spring until fall. All they ask from you is a spot to grow where they'll receive the right amount of sunlight, a weekly watering, and an occasional dose of plant food.

Tapping into all of the possibilities that perennials have to offer requires just a few things from you: a little imagination, a basic knowledge of growing plants, patience, and a copy of this book.

Miracle-Gro *Beautiful Perennials* shows you how to use a simple design process—known as backward design—that takes the fear out of perennial garden planning. Even if you've never designed a garden before, this method will help you create a gorgeous garden. Follow the step-by-step photos to see just how easy garden design can be.

In addition to learning the secrets to garden design, *Beautiful Perennials* teaches you the fundamentals of perennial gardening. You'll find advice on choosing a location and selecting

plants for your garden, and you'll gain the knowledge and skills you need to grow healthy perennials. The extensive encyclopedia will introduce you to know more than 280 perennials.

Since 1951, Miracle-Gro has been helping gardeners grow strong, healthy flowers, vegetables, and houseplants. Miracle-Gro books draw on the experience and expertise of the folks at Miracle-Gro to help readers become knowledgeable, confident gardeners. Learn their secrets and find success in *your* beautiful garden.

EDITOR

TABLE OF

CONTENTS

CHOOSE

Vistas of flowers gladden your soul, whether you're sitting on a deck overlooking the backyard, sipping tea in a screened gazebo, or peeling potatoes at your kitchen table. The pleasure of perennial gardening lies in nature's abundance and your ability to see and experience it.

You can grow a perennial garden just about anywhere, be it at the front, back, or side of your house. Wherever you locate it, a perennial garden brings beauty. Because of the plants'

THE SITE

versatility, it may also provide a solution to some of the challenges in your landscape. For example, you can use perennials to highlight changes in grade along stone steps, making the transition from top to bottom safer and more visible. Plant them on slopes where they beautify as well as prevent erosion. Or grow them as an accent among the rocks on the face of a dry-stone retaining wall.

In entry gardens, perennials' colorful flowers and handsome leaves welcome visitors to your home throughout the

growing season. Behind the house, the garden offers private pleasure for you and your friends and family.

Perennials don't have to be flashy to work on different sites and in different situations. Sometimes simply the shape and drape of the leaves make the perfect foil for a garden ornament or brightly colored blooms.

Although siting perennials may seem challenging, reading this chapter, learning the techniques, and assessing the results will give you the tools to find the perfect garden site for your needs, where the perennials will be as helpful as they are pretty.

assess space needs

Raised beds and a step up to the decking helps to visually enlarge this small garden. Richly textured plants, such as hosta, lady's mantle, and Japanese maple soften the straight lines and angles.

The site for a perennial garden can be any size. Whether you live in the city, the suburbs, or the country, a perennial garden will fit your space. It can be as small as a container on your deck or as big as the meadow beyond the back door. The size of your garden depends on how much space is available for a garden, the time you have to dedicate to gardening, and why you want a garden in the first place.

SMALL YARDS
No matter how small your outdoor space, you can create a garden with character and charm. A small garden often takes its cue from the buildings and walkways that surround it; small gardens tend toward the architectural in design.

In tiny areas, circular patios and lawns become garden focal points. Simple geometric shapes help organize limited space. Perennials with striking form and foliage emphasize the architecture of small gardens and add structural interest; plants with loose or rounded habits soften angularity and bring an appeal to hard features.

Several tricks with perennials can make a small yard feel larger. For example, creating changes in level—such as adding a step up from your patio to the garden, planting some perennials in raised beds and others in low borders, or combining perennials of varied heights—gives the illusion of greater size. Another trick is to arrange plants so that parts of the garden

are hidden from view. When you can't take in a whole space at once, your mind "sees" a larger space.

BIG YARDS
Similarly, suburban and country gardens look their best if they are sensitive to their surroundings and fit into the area and region where they grow. If river birch (*Betula nigra*), gayfeather, and black-eyed Susan are native to the land near your town, then they may thrive in your garden, depending on the site. Although gardens near the house frequently reflect the angular and architectural nature of the deck and walls, distant boundary plantings can have a wilder, more naturalistic character reflecting nearby open space.

Complex water gardens and elaborate perennial beds suit gardeners with plenty of time to maintain them. The results, however, are worth the effort.

Moreover, large lots bring opportunities for different garden areas for a variety of practical and ornamental functions.

SIZE FACTORS

time People often dream about having a lavish English-style garden full of monstrous delphiniums and masses of blooms. In reality, those palatial English gardens take hours to maintain, a staff to do the work, and an ideal—moist and mild—climate. Most Americans, however, live fast-paced, task- and errand-filled lives in fairly harsh climates. Multi-purpose gardens and landscapes that are easy to maintain are more our style.

To avoid taking on more than you can handle, mesh your garden with your lifestyle. Have you always dreamed of puttering in the garden and now actually have time to enjoy it? Do you spend hours commuting to work so that the only time available for gardening is limited to one weekend afternoon? Or, when you get home, would working in the garden help you recover from a stressful day and long commute? At home, do children take up most of your time and energy? The answers to these questions will ensure you have a right-size garden that satisfies your imagination and fits your schedule and abilities.

children Children needn't keep you from gardening. In fact, by including them in your projects you can boost the amount of time you have outdoors. Show your children how to nurture tough plants like

TIP YOU CAN ACHIEVE YOUR GARDENING GOALS ALL AT ONCE OR IN STAGES. IF THIS IS YOUR FIRST GARDEN, CONSIDER STARTING SMALL. GARDENING IS A PROCESS, AND EXPANDING YOUR GARDEN FROM YEAR TO YEAR MAKES THE WORK FUN AND GIVES YOU NEW PROJECTS TO DREAM ABOUT.

daylilies and coneflowers while avoiding sharp plants that may injure them.

This informal mixed bed combines ornamental grasses, salvia and other flowering perennials, roses, shrubs and small trees for all-year interest.

BEDS OR BORDERS

The ideal size and site for your perennial garden also depends on whether you want a bed or a border and on the garden's purpose in the landscape. Before you can decide upon a garden layout, it's important to understand the differences between beds and borders.

> **TIP** USE PERENNIALS WITH MULTI-SEASON INTEREST IN HIGHLY VISIBLE BEDS AND BORDERS. CATMINT, LAMB'S-EARS, SEDUM, GERMANDER, LAVENDER, CORAL BELLS, CRANESBILL, AND ORNAMENTAL GRASSES ARE GOOD CHOICES.

beds A bed is a stand-alone island planting surrounded by lawn, gravel, or other low, uniform surface. Beds can be geometrical—square, rectangular, circular, oval—or free-form, with kidney-shape being one of the most popular forms. Beds are typically planted in descending layers, with tall plants near the center, surrounded by medium-size plants, and short plants at the edge. Most modern beds are informal in style, but Victorian-era beds with their tidy, geometrical layouts frequently had a formal look. Beds can be either small or large, depending on their garden location and purpose, and work well around mailboxes and lampposts.

ABOVE: Although flowers in a mixed border often peak in summer, the trees and shrubs in it provide year-round structure.
LEFT: This lavish U-shaped border relies upon a dark background of evergreens to make it stand out in the landscape. Borders always have a "back," such as a fence or hedge.

borders Borders are beds with straight backs; unlike beds, they are never free-floating. They tend to be planted against a tall neutral backdrop like a brick wall or a dark green yew hedge to set off the floral drama. The front of the border edges a path or an expanse of lawn. Traditional borders are rectangular, about 5 feet wide, and varied in length. Modern borders have either straight or curvy fronts, depending on their location in the garden. Like beds, borders are designed in layers, but here the tall plants are at the back, mid-size plants are in the central layer, and short plants are in front.

Gardeners may use a single border along a fence or double borders on either side of a path or yard. In a formal design, the pair of borders would have identical designs, whereas a single formal border against a wall would look the same on either side of an imaginary central line running from front to back. The plants in an informal border are balanced asymmetrically down an imaginary center line from front to back.

There are two kinds of beds and borders: herbaceous and mixed.

herbaceous Herbaceous beds and borders contain only herbaceous perennials.

In herbaceous designs, perennials, ferns, and ornamental grasses grow in interlocking drifts, creating a mosaic of colors and textures. The architecture of an herbaceous border comes from perennials whose striking forms last beyond the growing season, such as ornamental grasses and perennials like bear's breeches, heart-leaf bergenia, and 'Autumn Joy' sedum.

mixed borders Mixed beds and borders contain woody plants such as conifers, small flowering trees, and shrubs as well as annuals, perennials, and bulbs. Mixed borders offer gardeners several advantages. Most importantly, they give gardens year-round structure and interest, compared with herbaceous borders, which tend to peak in early to midsummer. Where space is limited, well-sited and well-designed mixed borders create maximum appeal with minimal effort.

why a perennial garden?

Before you make a final decision on your garden's site and size, think about why you want a garden. Reasons for having a perennial garden can be aesthetic and practical. Whether you want to create a beautiful view or block an unsightly one, the garden's purpose should dominate the design. On the next few pages, discover the many roles perennials can take on and how they can fit into your property and benefit your landscape plan.

PRIVACY

Don't let the beauty of perennials blind you to their varied uses. Experience peaceful seclusion in your own backyard by carving a private sitting area out of a border. Groups of tall, dense perennials make excellent privacy plantings. Ornamental grasses such as 6- to 8-foot-tall maiden grass surrounding a garden seat can create a feeling of isolation. Similarly, a U-shaped mixed planting of

LEFT: Tucked in a lush border, a bench provides a refuge from the hustle-bustle of a busy day.
BELOW RIGHT: A mixed border screens the view of nearby buildings and a ratty old fence.
BELOW LEFT: The gaze focuses on a beautiful border instead of the unappealing shed behind it.
OPPOSITE: A bank of daylilies in a raised bed makes a wall of privacy around an Adirondack chair.

small to mid-size conifers and perennials may form a private meditation space or sunbathing area. Make sure the plants you choose form not just an intimate space but also a visual barrier between you and the hubbub outside.

SCREENING

Tall perennials are also perfect for blocking bad views such as a neighbor's boat, beat-up car, or basketball hoop. Although physical screens should be dense and at least 6 feet high, psychological barriers that distract the gaze from an eyesore can be shorter and less opaque.

TIP BEFORE PLANTING FOR PRIVACY AND SCREENING, CHECK THE PERENNIALS' MATURE HEIGHT AND WIDTH. REMEMBER THAT PLANTS TAKE A FEW YEARS TO REACH MATURITY, SO BE PATIENT. PLANTING TOO CLOSE TOGETHER REQUIRES MORE PLANTS AND CREATES EXTRA WORK WHEN YOU HAVE TO THIN THEM OUT LATER ON.

RIGHT: A large clump of black-eyed Susan flops over a flagstone path, slowing down foot traffic and softening the hard edge of the paving.
BELOW: You can prevent trespassing by blocking the way with a planting of prickly pear or other spiked perennials.
BOTTOM: Movement down a grassy path is controlled by the shape of borders flanking it.

TRAFFIC CONTROL

In addition to privacy and screening, you can use perennials to control the flow of foot traffic through your yard. Frame a strip of lawn with borders and both your gaze and your steps will be directed down the grassy path formed by the borders. Such a straight shot is generally a fast walk. If you want to move people quickly past a service area or along the front walk, this is the way to do it.

Similarly, curvy perennial beds that intersect or jut out into a walkway will slow a visitor's progress, because it forces a person to walk around the intrusion. Curved beds and borders look best when necessitated by the lay of the land and the presence of obstacles such as boulders or established shrubs. Perennials not only direct foot traffic, they may also transform obstacles into landscape accents.

Short or rounded perennials grown in masses along the edge of paths soften the harsh lines and tie paths into the natural landscape. Taller, bushier perennials help prevent access to forbidden places.

To reinforce a perennial bed's ability to manage traffic flow, think about natural paths that people follow on your property. If you want to channel visitors along those lines, edge the path with perennials or mixed beds. If instead you want to keep certain areas restricted, discourage visitors by blocking off space with a strategically placed bed.

Moreover, you can set spiked or prickly plants where you want to limit access. For example, when planted closely and in sufficient numbers, the sharp, swordlike leaves of yucca and the prickles of sea holly and globe thistle effectively deter rambling pets. One of the best perennials for traffic

control is prickly pear *(Opuntia* spp.), a type of hardy cactus. Beware of these plants, however, if you have small children who spend time playing in the yard on their own. Youngsters may not keep their distance and could come to harm. Yucca with its stiff, sharp-pointed leaves can be especially dangerous to eyes.

Perennials don't have to be planted in the ground to direct foot traffic. Grow them in pots to mark deck edges and along wide outdoor stairways to set the boundaries and prevent visitors from stumbling off the sides.

EASY MOWING

Perennial beds are ideal around lamp-posts, mailboxes, trees, and other obstacles in the lawn. As long as they have broad, smooth curves or straight edges that are easily groomed by the lawn mower, these beds will ease mowing. The perennials in the beds will add beauty to everyday objects, and they require less effort than annuals. These beds are especially helpful around trees because nicks and scrapes left on a trunk by an errant lawn mower make a tree susceptible to pests and diseases.

ABOVE: A perennial bed around a lawn ornament protects the ornament from damage by runaway lawn mowers and increases the ornament's impact in the landscape. Well-placed perennial beds can also protect your trees from injury.

ARCHITECTURAL TRANSITIONS

Perennials are the perfect plants to bridge the gap between architectural elements in a landscape. Plants that have a rounded form, such as 'Autumn Joy' sedum and false indigo, or ones with a lax habit, including catmint and 'Snowbank' boltonia, soften protruding angles and deep corners by breaking up straight vertical lines. Plants with spiky or upright forms, such as mullein and 'Lavender Mist' meadow rue, emphasize verticality and, in the right location, can help balance the strong verticals of a house or other building.

Ground cover perennials often have a bolder texture than the lawn and can form a decorative link from lawn to paving while keeping a low profile in the landscape.

TIP KEEP FOLIAGE OF MATURE PERENNIALS AT LEAST 1 FOOT AWAY FROM THE WALLS OF YOUR HOME TO PREVENT TRAPPING WARM HUMID AIR AGAINST THEM. DARK, MOIST CONDITIONS CAN CAUSE MILDEW TO FLOURISH AND POTENTIALLY DAMAGE THE HOUSE.

A swath of taller perennials mitigates harsh transitions, especially when changes of grade between the deck and lawn exist. Similarly, the area where the patio or porch touches the lawn also profits from a visual transition.

Another potential trouble spot is the angle between the front walk, the house, and the driveway. If the angle is acute, the area may be too cramped for lawn or shrubs. An herbaceous or mixed bed of plants adapted to the particular conditions of the site improves this transition.

Some architectural garden transitions are purely decorative. A parterre is a formal ornamental garden with a symmetrical design marked out by low hedges and filled with plants or gravel of contrasting colors. Usually sited near the house, this linear treatment can bridge the gap between a doorway and the street, a raised deck and a swimming pool, or an elevated terrace and the lawn beyond. Shrubby evergreen perennials such as germander and lavender work well as hedges in parterres; long-blooming perennials or those with colorful foliage make excellent fillers.

ABOVE: By continuing the theme of the entry gardens, perennials and ornamental grasses turn a curbside bed into an effective transition from the house to the street.
OPPOSITE: Curvaceous borders draw the gaze away from the angles of the ranch house and direct attention to the attractive front door.

ABOVE: A mixed border of shrubs, roses, and perennials such as daylilies, hostas, and lady's mantle creates a foundation planting with year-round appeal.

foundation plantings A foundation planting is a group of plants—typically evergreen shrubs—that covers the exposed base of a home's front wall. Foundation plantings are a popular way to hide this utilitarian feature of your property's public area. In modern and contemporary houses built after the 1940s, foundations have become less visible with the walls sheathed in clapboard, brick, or stone almost to the ground, making the traditional tall, bushy foundation plantings unnecessary. That hasn't stopped the popularity of foundation plantings, however, because another purpose for them is to serve as a transition from the solid, hard edges of the house to the softer surface of the natural environment.

Although shrubs are most often used in this role, perennials may be even better suited to it, especially in newer homes where exposed foundations may be just 1 foot tall. Masses of hosta, lungwort, or short lady ferns are often popular near the shady base of new homes. Massed daylilies and other tough long-blooming sun lovers with attractive leaves thrive on the sunny side of the house.

LEFT: A colorful mixed border incorporates the foundation planting into the surrounding landscape.
BELOW: Lush perennials soften the harsh transition between this rectangular house and the surrounding lawn.

Perhaps the best way to deal with the transition from construction to nature is by installing an entry garden. In an entry garden, plants may be far from the foundation. They encompass part or all of the public area and enhance the experience of moving toward and entering the house. For example, a modern ranch house on a flat narrow lot with a concrete entry landing merging with the driveway would lend itself to this treatment. An entry garden with a winding path lined by bermed shrubs and perennials would reduce the harshness of the concrete and asphalt expanse.

Perennials create architectural transitions for plants, too. Taller perennials cover up the base of leggy shrubs, while ground cover perennials carpet the earth under shrubs and trees.

Choose perennials to use as architectural transitions depending on the climate in your region and on your garden's style. Coral bells make ideal architectural transitions. The various cultivars bloom in pink, red, salmon, or white; their foliage colors range from green, purple, amber, and yellow to silvery garnet, frosted green, and blackish maroon.

Conditions in gardens next to north-facing walls are typically colder and shadier than those in gardens beside south-facing walls. Hydrangea, astilbes, hakone grass, and ferns flourish in this shady walled garden.

ECOSYSTEM TRANSITIONS

Most properties have several ecosystems or environments that vary in the amounts of sun, soil, and moisture, and the types of organisms inhabiting them. Perennials help bridge these areas and bring unity to the design of the landscape.

For example, if you have a pond in your yard, planting bold- and medium-textured moisture-loving perennials along the edge of the pond helps to integrate it into the landscape. In a new development, your yard may look out on countryside, such as woodland, meadow, or farm fields. Perennials will buffer the transition between carefully planted places around the house and the natural area.

Some construction practices create changes in an ecosystem. Drainage swales; hot, dry spots next to south-facing walls; and dark areas in front of north-facing walls create completely different planting environments. South-facing walls hold heat, which warms the adjacent soil, sometimes enough to grow perennials that may not be cold-hardy in your area. For instance, 'Moudry' fountain grass, a perennial hardy in Zone 6, could likely thrive next to a protected south-facing wall of a home in Zone 5.

North-facing walls provide growing conditions suitable for shade-loving plants like hosta, lady's mantle, heart-leaf brunnera, and hellebore. These areas, however, tend to be colder than normal.

Drainage swales bring opportunities to grow plants that like plenty of moisture, including foam flower, ligularia, Christmas fern, and woodland phlox.

BELOW: Moisture-loving perennials along the edge of a pond create an ecological transition between the water and dry land.
BOTTOM: A Mediterranean-style garden featuring lavender and grasses helps a patio and yard blend with the native California landscape beyond.

ABOVE: Seen through French doors, this perennial garden creates a peaceful impression because of its cool gray-green and blue-green foliage and violet, pink, and lavender blooms.

IMPROVE OR CREATE A VIEW

If you have a deck, patio, or picture window overlooking your yard, why not better the view with a perennial garden? A perennial garden is a changing tapestry of color, texture, and interest all year long. Perennial borders look especially attractive against tall evergreen hedges, fences, and walls, whereas beds are ideal for creating a focal point in a lawn.

Depending on sizes, colors, and forms, perennials can make a view stand out or recede. They can draw your attention to a distant prospect or away from an eyesore. Warm colors—intense reds, yellows, and oranges—are stimulating attention grabbers. Flowers and foliage in these hues shorten visual distances, especially when popping out of a far away dark or neutral background.

Blue, violet, and blue-green are cool colors creating restful effects, as are other hues with bluish or silvery tints. Gray- and gray-green-leafed plants, such as lavender, artemisia, and lavender cotton, along with light pastels such as pale pink and lemon, also are cool hues. Cool colors make far-off beds look even farther away because they appear to retreat.

ABOVE: This deck looks upon a planting of bear's breeches and sedum, which offer three seasons of interest. Cannas and daylilies supplement the planting with attractive flowers and foliage.

LEFT: Silver lamb's ear recedes into the background behind a bank of showy sulfur yellow and pink flowers. The combination creates a peaceful setting for a gazebo.

FAR LEFT: Whether seen from the house or from the road, eye-popping red and orange daylilies attract attention and shrink the distances in the landscape.

PUTTING A GARDEN WHERE IT IMPROVES OR CREATES A VIEW WILL INCREASE YOUR PLEASURE IN LOOKING AT AND BEING OUTDOORS. THE FOLLOWING METHODS WILL HELP YOU FIND THE PERFECT GARDEN LOCATION. START BY THINKING ABOUT YOUR HOUSE AND THE ROOMS IN REGULAR USE; JOT DOWN IN A NOTEBOOK WHAT YOU SEE WHEN YOU LOOK OUT YOUR WINDOWS. THEN GRAB YOUR CAMERA.

[1] Photograph your yard as you see it from indoors, shooting from the spot where you spend the most time viewing it. For example, if you look through French doors while eating breakfast, take pictures from there. Do the same outdoors, photographing sight lines from the deck, picnic table, porch swing, patio, and much-used benches or garden chairs around the yard.

TIP TAKE CARE NOT TO LOCATE YOUR GARDEN OVER BURIED PIPES OR CABLES. IF YOU CUT A WIRE, YOU COULD LOSE POWER, PHONE, OR CABLE SERVICE. EVEN IF YOU DON'T CUT THE CABLE, A NICK IN A WIRE COULD LEAD TO MOISTURE DAMAGE THAT EVENTUALLY RESULTS IN A SHORT CIRCUIT. PIPES MAY LEAK GAS OR OTHER SUBSTANCES INTO THE SOIL, WHICH COULD HARM PLANTS.

[2] Choose a key view, such as the one from your deck or patio or the one from the street as you enter the property and run off 8-by-10 color or black-and-white photos of that view. If working from snapshots, enlarge them on a copier to 8½ by 11 inches.

[3] Use small pieces of masking tape to attach the enlarged photo to your work surface; tape tracing paper over the photo. On the tracing paper, outline the dominant features visible in the photo including the outline of your house, shed, doors, windows, porches, and decks. Also draw in paths, any existing beds and borders, and established trees and shrubs.

[4] Roughly sketch a garden where you think it would look nice, not worrying about individual plants at this point but simply using shapes to represent future plantings. Repeat this step several times with several pieces of paper, shifting the garden's location and its height and shape. Choose the site that looks best to you and meets your goals.

[5] When you find a location that pleases you, go to the spot where you took the photograph and study your sketch. Then, mark out the bed with a garden hose, clothesline held down with garden staples, or landscapers spray paint.

MATERIALS NEEDED

- Camera
- Tracing paper
- Pencil
- Notebook
- Masking tape
- Plastic templates, optional
- Garden hose, landscapers paint, or clothesline and landscape staples

AFTER YOU DECIDE ON A SPOT FOR YOUR GARDEN, MEASURE THE AREA SO YOU'LL KNOW JUST HOW BIG THE GARDEN CAN BE. THIS PROCESS PINPOINTS THE LOCATION OF YOUR GARDEN WITHIN YOUR LANDSCAPE AND GIVES YOU A PERMANENT FRAME OF REFERENCE TO WORK FROM.

[2] You will need to establish two baselines at a right angle to each other. These lines allow you to establish the exact location of any object within your yard. Your house can make one of the baselines. Measure the side of the house that faces the area where the garden will go. Note the measurements on your drawing. You may find it helpful for the design to also locate doors, windows, porches, decks, and walks coming off of the house. Measure their size and their exact location, then note this information on your drawing.

[1] Make a rough drawing of your house and yard on the graph paper. With a compass, locate north, and mark that orientation on the drawing.

MATERIALS NEEDED

- Clipboard
- Pad of graph paper
- Pencil and eraser
- Magnetic compass
- 100-foot tape measurer or a distance roller, such as the Measure Meter, or a laser distance measurer
- String and stakes
- Garden hose

[3] The second baseline could be a fence, driveway, or other permanent structure running at a right angle to the house. However, you must be certain that the fence is straight along its entire length. Then you can simply measure from your house to the fence to establish the second baseline. Mark the line on your drawing.

[4] If there is no permanent line to work with, make one with stakes and string. Pound the first stake next to the corner of your house. To ensure the line is straight, follow the 3–4–5 method. From the stake, measure on your house 3 feet; mark this spot. Next, on the string, measure 4 feet from the stake; mark this spot. Now measure between the two marks. If the distance is 5 feet, the string is perpendicular to the house. (You can use any multiple of three, four, and five for this technique to work, such as 6–8–10 or 9–12–15.)

[6] Use a garden hose to mark out the general size and shape that you are thinking about for the bed or border. Measure the length and width of the garden. If the garden will be a border with a straight and a curved edge, make marks every 3 feet along the straight edge. From these marks measure out to the curved edge. For a bed, create a straight line down the center with stakes and string. Measure every 3 feet along this line, then measure out from this point to both sides of the bed. When you transfer the measurements to the graph paper, simply connect the dots to re-create the curved edge.

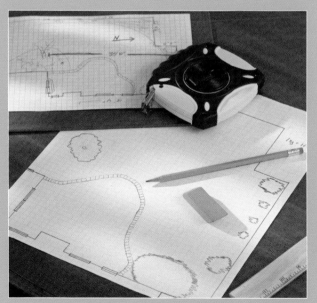

[5] To locate the garden space in your landscape, measure from each baseline to nearby trees, shrubs, and any permanent structures. Add these measurements to your drawing.

[7] Transfer all your measurements to a clean sheet of graph paper, carefully locating every object in the drawing. A scale of one box equals 1 foot should be adequate unless your lot is very large. Draw the baselines to the bottom and edge of the paper so you'll have more room to work with.

DECIDE ON

A STYLE

Now that you've located your garden and mapped the site, you're ready to start thinking seriously about how you want the garden to look. This is the time for thumbing through magazines and books and looking at the myriad ways other people have put together their gardens.

Like your home, your garden reflects who you are and shows off your interests in life. Cottage gardens, for instance, celebrate spontaneity using perennials that self-sow. Tropical gardens are exotic with jumbo foliage and dramatic flowers. Prairie gardens

sing Mother Nature's song, taking their cue from America's extreme inland climates. Drought-tolerant grasses and wildflowers dominate this garden style, which is one of the easiest types of gardens to maintain.

The style of your garden can reflect a hobby or a passion in your life. For example, if butterflies appeal to you, draw them to your yard with a butterfly garden planted with the spring- or fall-blooming perennials that attract them. If you and your spouse are considering a train garden, think about using dwarf perennials to create a miniature landscape around the tracks.

You will, of course, want to choose a style that meshes with the way you live. If you spend most of your time coaching, carpooling, or working, select a style that's easy to maintain. In cold

regions, that's probably not a tropical garden, which requires you to spend extra time each year in spring and fall planting and lifting tender perennials.

This chapter profiles several popular garden styles, both formal and informal. You'll discover the plants, decorations, and accents most appropriate for each style, learn how the style will fit with your existing landscape and with the architecture of your home, and find estimates on the amount of care each style will require. This section introduces you to the possibilities; now put your own spin on them.

finding a style

ABOVE: This informal perennial garden provides a welcoming entry to a traditional suburban lot. Close planting of abundant perennials discourages weeds and gives the garden a carefree, cheerful look, reflecting the owners' own outlook on life.

Although gardens are as diverse as the people who plant them, they have several aspects in common. Most have plants, ornaments, and furniture for seating or entertaining; the best gardens have style.

So what is style? Garden style is the individual way you arrange these elements to express your personality. Style may also convey a historical period— Romantic or Neoclassical, for example —by featuring certain characteristics that were popular during a specific era.

In successful gardens, plants, ornaments, and furniture show consistency and harmony. That doesn't mean that they come from the same historical period; rather, when seen together, they create a sense of unity that sets the garden apart from another one down the street. Style shows that there's a mind at work. How the garden looks depends on the effect you want to achieve.

A theme can give a garden a unifying purpose that has a positive influence on the garden's style. A theme directs the choice of plants and often their layout. For example, if you want a garden for fragrance, site the plants where you can best appreciate their scent. Weave paths through the garden so you can stop and sniff the flowers. Place a seat where the flowers' perfume can envelop you. Other popular themes include herb and edible-flower gardens, evening gardens, silver gardens, Biblical or Shakespearian gardens, and gardens attracting butterflies, songbirds, or hummingbirds.

The choices are exhilarating, so where do you begin? Gardening magazines and public and private gardens provide lots of ideas, of course. But so does just being out in nature and at home. Visit a nearby state or national park and see which kinds of plants grow in that environment and the color and texture of the rocks. Now sit down with a pad of paper and answer the following questions to help you focus on the look you want.

Where do you live? A garden that incorporates your area's natural landscape materials into the design looks right for its location. It also makes sense to use plants that thrive in your climate, whether they are native to the locale or have originated far away. A garden with colorful, drought-tolerant perennials and native fieldstone paths may seem ideal on the western plains, but it may not be appropriate in the Pacific Northwest, where moisture is more abundant. Is your house traditional or modern? House style can affect a garden's style, because buildings and gardens usually look best when they complement each other. If the facade of your house is stately, square, and boxy with a symmetrical layout of

ABOVE: In Southwestern gardens, drought-tolerant grasses and perennials with gray-green leaves not only make good sense, but they also complement stucco, gravel, and other local building materials.

windows around the front door, then consider a formal garden with symmetrical hedges and beds on either side of a central front path. If you're making an entry garden for a ranch house with a low horizontal facade, then keep plantings near the house short and informal.

Are you away from home during the day? If so, consider an evening garden planted with scented, white or pale colored flowers, which look luminous in low light. For example, pale yellow night-blooming citron daylily (Hemerocallis citrina) releases a powerful fragrance upon opening in the evening. Its flowers fade early the next day, but new blooms will greet you when you return from work.

are you formal or informal?

ABOVE: Clipped hedges and classical statuary are typical elements of formal garden style. Another formal feature is the garden's symmetrical layout with geometrical beds divided by stone pavers.
OPPOSITE: You don't need to live in a mansion to have a formal garden, nor does a formal garden need to include classical elements. Here, pruned potted boxwoods and identical plantings around a central fountain focus your attention on the symmetrical facade of the house.

Know yourself before choosing a garden style. Just as there are formal and informal gardens, there are also formal and informal people. It helps to know which one you are.

Formal people like everything in its place. They are often traditionalists who adopt conventional dress and behavior. They like wearing well-pressed suits to their workplace and enjoy slipping on a dinner jacket or an evening gown from time to time. Classical architectural styles hold a strong appeal to the traditional at heart.

Folks who lean toward informality prefer more casual clothes. Informal folks think that casual Friday is the best workplace innovation in years. At home they wear T-shirts soft from laundering and blue jeans with holes and frayed cuffs. When it comes to entertaining, they prefer backyard barbecues to black-tie

affairs. They think that gardens should fit comfortably into their natural surroundings rather than dominate nature with man-made, arty designs.

Many people, however, blend these two extremes in their homes and in the garden. They lead mostly casual lives, but a dressy night at the opera or a fundraiser isn't out of the question. Inside their homes, they place an elegant heirloom chair in the same room as a comfortable modern sofa. In the garden, they like to see nature's exuberance within an orderly framework.

FORMAL STYLE

Formal gardens resemble classical architectural styles that draw inspiration from ancient Greece and Rome. They are symmetrical in layout and may be richly patterned. Paths or walks form a clear central axis in the garden, which may be crossed by minor axes formed by straight hedges or narrower paths. Fountains, birdbaths, urns, or topiary may mark the intersections.

In a formal landscape, the garden can extend the boundaries of the house and create an architectural transition to the outdoor world. Formal gardens also complement the simple geometry of modern-style homes. In this case, the pattern could be as simple as a rectangular bed divided into four equal parts with a boulder in the center, or as complicated as a geometric grid with intersections marked by perennials that provide year-round interest in the landscape, such as lavender or Russian sage.

In formal gardens, the walks, beds, and borders link up with the residence or a nearby structure such as a shed or pool house. Geometrical shapes such as circles, squares, ovals, and rectangles dominate the garden design. Clipped hedges and topiaries—shrubs, trees, or woody perennials pruned into geometric or animal sculptures—are popular elements of traditional formal gardens. A formal garden requires frequent pruning to ensure that its structure does not change over time.

Parterres and knots are types of formal gardens. A parterre is an ornamental garden in which low-clipped hedges outline a symmetrical pattern, creating an intricate design. A parterre is best seen from above—from a high deck, a terrace, or the second story of a house.

Although boxwood is the most popular hedging material for a parterre, woody perennials such as lavender, germander, and lavender cotton sheared into thick low hedges are also used. Let short plants with colorful foliage carpet the space in between.

INFORMAL STYLE

ABOVE: Informal gardens have curved pathways for exploring. Shrubs and perennials balance off-center, and successive focal points lead you down the path.

Broad curves and flowing lines characterize informal gardens. Paths are winding and indirect. Beds and borders have curved edges, and plantings tend to be in masses and drifts. A large informal garden may be hard to take in all at once, often being a progression of charming scenes along a meandering path. Water features in informal gardens tend to be kidney-shaped or irregularly curved instead of geometrical in shape.

Informal gardens appear casual. Their layouts are asymmetrical and lack a central axis. For instance, in an informal garden,

a mass of perennials on one side of an off-center axis might balance a colorful piece of sculpture on the other.

Meadow, prairie, and woodland gardens are usually informal in character, whereas cottage gardens can be formal or informal in their design. Because perennials in these gardens sometimes sprawl and are more loosely planted, weeds can hide. Even so, maintaining such gardens takes less time than a formal design.

You can grow a variety of grasses and native wildflowers for season-long interest in an informal meadow garden, which suits a sunny slope. Narrow gardens are also good candidates for informal designs; a long, snaky path through lush plantings creates surprise and makes the garden feel bigger. Use tall dense grasses or shrubs to partially block the walkway from the main sight lines for the best effect.

Informal entry gardens suit split-level houses and the Prairie-style houses popularized by architect Frank Lloyd Wright, because these plantings complement the strong asymmetrical lines of their facades. By paying attention to the balance of plantings, however, you can make an informal landscape with any style of house.

A combination of formal and informal styles works for many gardeners. By including a strong geometric element such as a circular gazebo or a long rectangular arbor, you can bring a casual garden's twists and turns into focus. Likewise, you can add informal structure to a sunny meadow garden by mowing a path with gentle curves through the flowers and grasses. Or mow two straight paths, so that they form a cross in the center, and mark the intersection with a rusty iron urn planted with a drought-tolerant ornamental grass.

RIGHT: This informal perennial border set against a split rail fence suits a casual suburban setting. Large clumps of foliage and flowers on each end of the garden result in informal balance (see below).

BALANCE

In garden design, balance is an idea separate from but related to style. Balance works like an old-fashioned scale with a central fulcrum or pivot holding a horizontal arm that has plates at either end. When balanced, the scale's plates hold equal amounts of weight. A garden is balanced when its visual weight appears to be equally distributed. Because plants grow and gardens are always in flux, balance is dynamic, changing over time and from different points of view. The different types of balance relate to different styles.

■ **FORMAL:** A symmetrically balanced or formal composition is like a scale holding identical weights on each plate. Formal balance exists when the design on one side of a central dividing line mirrors the design on the other side. If vertical and horizontal lines divide the garden, each section is symmetrical from side to side and from top to bottom.

Formal style gardens typically have formal balance. Few home landscapes can carry off a totally symmetrical design. Yet a nearly symmetrical design—where the lines of the garden are geometrical but the plants within are random and focal points provide the balance—give similar structure and visual interest.

■ **INFORMAL:** Asymmetrical or informal compositions are akin to a scale with one long and one short arm. It takes more weight on the plate closest to the pivot to balance the weight of the longer arm; so the weights on the plates can't be identical. Informal gardens typically have informal balance. Their parts do not mirror each other, nevertheless all parts carry equal weight.

Informal or asymmetrical balance is more popular among gardeners but harder to achieve than the clear geometry of formal balance. One way is to contrast a small group of perennials that have a powerful visual presence with a much larger mass of perennials that tend to shrink back. For example, combine a few perennials with large, brightly colored flowers with a large group of perennials that have pale blooms.

a garden to match your style

TIP WHEN YOUR FLOWERS FINISH BLOOMING, AVOID CUTTING ALL OF THEM BACK. LET SOME GO TO SEED TO FORM NEW PLANTS, WHICH WILL OCCUR AT RANDOM, CREATING A CHARMING SPONTANEOUS LOOK.

ABOVE: This informal cottage garden romanticizes the simple life with its white picket fence, rose arbor, and profuse plantings of perennials.

Informal gardens come in many styles. Cottage gardens, tropical gardens, naturalistic gardens, and prairie gardens with flowing lines and lushly growing plants are just a few that lend themselves to an informal treatment.

COTTAGE STYLE

Irresistibly lavish, cottage gardens appeal to lovers of nature and beauty alike. Fruit trees mingle with herbs, annuals, perennials, and roses in seeming disarray.

Cottage gardens appeal to those romantic souls who admire old-fashioned good looks and a romantic sense of abundance. At first glance this type of garden may look like a jumble of plants, but on close inspection you discover that its joyful simplicity results from an inherent careful design.

Most cottage garden flowers are easy to grow. Many self-sow, which accounts for the cottage garden's spontaneous look. Popular cottage garden perennials include foxgloves, lupines (*Lupinus* spp.), roses, phlox, pinks, primroses, columbines, and hollyhocks.

Cottage gardens have humble beginnings in the Middle Ages, when peasants cultivated small plots of plants that fed the owners, cured their ailments, and freshened the air in their homes.

Today's cottage gardens idealize the past and romanticize those practical plots. Surrounded by a white picket fence and accented with rose-covered arbors, they look nostalgically to the simple, quiet life before computers and television sets.

Around every bend is an ornament. Birdhouses punctuate beds and borders, along with birdbaths, sundials, topiary table accents, and tipped urns spilling out flowers. Suitable furniture includes white wicker with plump cushions and elaborate French-wire or wrought-iron tables and chairs.

TROPICAL STYLE

Tropical gardens are like extroverts— they attract attention and stand out in a crowd. They contain plants with lush colorful foliage, dramatic architectural form, and exotic perfumed blooms in shocking hues. Densely planted and jungle like, these gardens thrive on extreme contrasts in texture rather than gentle transitions. Flower colors are intense, ranging from glowing pink and yellow to fiery orange and red.

Suitable furniture materials for a tropical look include rattan, teak, and bamboo. Cover cushions with bark cloth, a material that simulates traditional tropical fabric made from the soaked and pounded inner bark of trees. Tie a hammock between two trees. Build a tree house for kids or adults and a cabana for shade by a swimming pool. Let tiki torches light the garden at night, and install a waterfall for hypnotic splashing sounds.

If your garden is small, strive for a jungle effect. Plan a path that twists through borders thick with a few big-leaved or colorful shrubs and a coarse-textured tree covered with delicate vines and underplanted with masses of ferns and gaudy perennials. In bigger gardens, contrast a sweep of bright green lawn with bold-textured beds and borders of hot-hued blooms. Surrounding a hot tub with a tropical garden creates a sultry escape from the everyday world. Set it apart from the rest of your landscape with tall hedging or a wooden fence.

Tender perennials with bold textures such as banana and elephant's ear (*Colocasia esculenta*), bright-hued flowers such as canna and bird of paradise, and colorful structural plants such as New Zealand flax are the backbone of tropical gardens. Although they require night temperatures above 55°F, they will work in cold-climate tropical gardens as long as you plant them in pots that you bring indoors at night when temperatures drop, or lift them from the soil and store them in the basement over the winter.

Cold-climate gardeners can take advantage of hardy plants with the bold characteristics of tropicals. In consistently moist soil, umbrella plant (*Darmera peltata*), Zones 5 to 7, has coarse-textured 2-foot leaves, which turn red in fall. Ostrich fern grows up to 5 feet tall and spreads fast in moist soils. It has feathery 1-foot-wide fronds with a vaselike habit. Hardy to Zone 3, it grows in light to full shade. For a daring look, grow spiky Adam's needle (Zones 4 to 10) and hardy hibiscus (Zones 5 to 9), with its 10-inch red, pink, white, or bicolor flowers.

BELOW: Tropical gardens feature striking contrasts of shape and texture, from coarse bananas to fanned palmettos and the daggerlike leaves of other tropicals.

TROPICAL PLANTS

The following relatively tender perennials will lend your garden a tropical flair:

■ **Banana** (*Musa* hybrids) are grown for their gigantic oblong green or dark red-and-green leaves up to 2 feet wide and 9 feet long. Hardy in Zones 9 to 11. With protection, some will survive in Zone 5.

■ **Bird of paradise** (*Strelitzia reginae*) has birdlike orange-and-blue flowers emerging from a beaky green bract. It grows up to 5 feet tall. Hardy in Zones 10 and 11.

■ **Canna lily** (*Canna* hybrids) grows from 2 to 10 feet tall and is valued for its big leaves and red, pink, orange, or yellow blooms. Hardy in Zones 8 to 11, or Zone 7 if protected. 'Tropicana': 4 feet tall; striped green, yellow, and orangy-red leaves; orange flowers. 'Bengal Tiger': 3 to 4 feet tall; striped green-and-yellow leaves edged in red; orange blooms.

■ **Coleus** (*Solenostemon scutellarioides*) grows 1 to 3 feet tall. It is cultivated for its foliage, which comes in a spectacular array of patterns and colors ranging from pink, maroon, and purple to lime, yellow, and green. Hardy in Zones 10 and 11.

■ **New Zealand flax** (*Phormium* hybrids) has foliage colors ranging from maroon, purple, and bronzy green to green with rose, apricot, pink, cream, or yellow variegation. Sword-shaped leaves form an upright cluster 2 to 9 feet tall. Zones 9 and 10, but root-hardy in Zones 7 and 8 in a sheltered spot with winter protection.

NATURALISTIC STYLE

Naturalistic gardens take their cues from Mother Nature. This design style respects the lay of the land, using it as a guide for plants and planning. Naturalistic gardens integrate details drawn from local scenery into their design. Native plants form the core of these gardens, drawing bees, birds, and butterflies to them for food, perches, and shelter. For the basic garden structure, select trees, shrubs, and perennials native to your region, adding non-native plants from similar habitats and climates, if you like.

Like nature, these gardens are loose and curvy in outline. They change over time as trees grow and the light dims due to a growing canopy. Unlike a formal garden, where you control the growth, here you can let your perennials be what they are—some forming great swaths and others staying in smaller clumps.

Wilder-looking than many informal gardens, naturalistic gardens include a variety of trees, shrubs, perennials, ornamental grasses, and self-sowing annuals. Damp, naturalistic perennial borders in a lightly shaded New England backyard might include marsh marigolds, blue flag iris (*I. versicolor*), Jack-in-the-pulpit (*Arisaema triphyllum*), and cinnamon and sensitive ferns. In a sunny yard, Joe-Pye weed, butterfly weed, New England aster, goldenrod, wild geranium, wild columbine, and butterfly weed would be an appropriate combination.

Though naturalistic gardens are often lush, they're easy to maintain. Because native plants predominate, once established these gardens usually need no extra water, fertilizer, or pesticides. Birds may devour troublesome insects in naturalistic gardens and leave helpful ones alone.

If you choose this kind of garden, think about avoiding a high-maintenance lawn. Instead, choose low-maintenance, low-growing native grasses that, once established, need no extra water or fertilizer. Drought-tolerant buffalograss (*Buchloe dactyloides*), for example, makes a natural lawn that thrives in parts of the South, West, and Midwest where it is native.

Wood and other natural materials make the best furniture in naturalistic gardens. This is the place for rustic log furniture and Adirondack chairs. If you live where granite boulders or other types of stones prevail, use benches and birdbaths carved from these materials, or make sitting areas of flat-topped rocks.

Several types of naturalistic gardens exist, including woodland, meadow, and prairie gardens. Meadow gardens contain mostly low-growing, sun-loving perennial grasses, with wildflowers added for color and variety. Meadows can be dry, moist, or wet, depending on local conditions. Naturalistic gardens are suited to cities and suburbia, where a tallgrass prairie garden could overwhelm the site.

Woodland gardens grow below a canopy of deciduous trees. Their blooms peak in spring, often before the trees unfurl their leaves. In woodland gardens, you can play with light and shade, contrasting plants that thrive in dense shade with those that prefer sun and would thrive in sunny woodland gaps and along the dappled woodland edge.

RIGHT: Meadow gardens, typically composed of low grasses and wildflowers, look wilder than many informal gardens and are easier to maintain.

ABOVE: The luminous seedheads of ornamental grasses dramatize the autumnal beauty of a prairie garden. **LEFT:** A blue-glazed terra cotta bird bath makes the perfect accent in this prairie garden planted with lilies, cinquefoil, and tall spiky mullein.

PRAIRIE STYLE

Grown for bright summer wildflowers and pink, bronze, and tan fall grasses, prairie gardens are microcosms of the grand waves of grass and wildflowers that once grew on Western and Midwestern plains. Grasses ruled the first prairies, which were called short-grass, tallgrass, or mixed-grass prairies. As ancient prairies gave way to farms, housing developments, and shopping malls, botanical gardens began to tout their praises and reproduce them to keep visitors aware of this lost environment.

Revisiting your American roots with a prairie garden doesn't take much space. As long as your climate is cold in winter and hot in summer and receives some rain, you can grow a little bit of prairie from Maine to Montana.

Grow your prairie garden in full sun. Once established, prairie gardens are drought-tolerant (although they can stand wet sites) and low-maintenance. Like cottage gardens, prairie gardens excel when they look natural, although not unplanned in their layout and choice of plants. They look particularly good with low, informal houses such as bungalows and ranches.

With their abundant grasses, prairie gardens have a fine to medium-fine texture. Grasses are the ideal backdrop for native perennials such as purple coneflower, black-eyed Susan, blazing star, asters, penstemon, bee balm, butterfly weed, tickseed, and prairie smoke *(Geum triflorum)*. Skip fancy cultivars and plant straight species for copious seeds. Birds, bees, and butterflies will pack your prairie garden, which is an ideal habitat for them.

You can successfully grow a prairie garden of ornamental grass and prairie wildflowers in a container. The area inside a circular gravel drive is also a good spot; just plant the space with wildflowers and native grasses and mow once a year. If your lot is sunny and lawn care wears you down, replace the whole yard with a short-grass prairie. Or keep lawn and beds around your house but naturalize your lot's edges with loose, curvaceous, prairie-style borders. If you install a deep prairie border or convert your whole property to ornamental prairie, mow paths and spaces where you want to walk, entertain, or place a focal point.

MODERN STYLES

The best contemporary gardens combine sensitivity to the local environment with an appreciation of abundant nature and simplified form. They are often somewhat formal in appearance, but unlike formal gardens that you enjoy from afar, these new gardens fulfill a different function in harmony with today's busy technological world. They are for people who like being outdoors to entertain, to relax, to garden, or to contemplate. Many incorporate the latest in electronics, placing audio equipment, TVs, and DVD players in waterproof enclosures so the owners can enjoy all of their favorite activities while they enjoy the outdoors.

The basic structure of these modern gardens may be geometrical or loose, but the plantings are informal—to save on maintenance time and cost. In modern gardens, a sweep of one perennial or ornamental grass softens and humanizes the stark walls of a house or an outbuilding. To create an effect of simplicity in your garden, avoid complicated plantings involving just a few samples of many different perennials. Instead, develop a palette of a dozen or so perennials—or more if the plants have a similar appearance. Grow them in broad drifts across your landscape. Or use them in roles that other plants normally fill, for example, grow them as ground covers or as hedges. Grow perennials with foliage and flowers that complement your interior decor and vines that soften angles, fences, and walls.

Garden grids—alternating squares of paving and plantings—are popular con-

ABOVE: Modern gardens are often a mix of the formal and informal, with straight lines and hard materials, such as stainless steel, softened by free-ranging plants.

temporary garden features. A grid design is simple and works in different settings. They look best when they complement the architecture of a house. In rural areas, grids might repeat the rectangles of a house as well as contrast with the curves of the natural landscape. In cities, a grid design could turn the minuscule backyard of a townhouse into an extension of indoor living space with paved blocks for furniture and open blocks for plants. Avoid paving every section of a grid. Instead, make a pattern combining paved sections with plants that have multiseason interest, such as 'Elijah Blue' blue fescue.

THE NEW AMERICAN GARDEN STYLE

Part wild, part tidy, the New American Garden has Mother Nature as its muse. Drawing inspiration from American meadows and prairies, the style's creators, Wolfgang Oehme and James van Sweden, use lush plantings in a brand-new way. In residential landscapes, the designers frequently combine manicured lawns with layers of perennials in broad, sweeping beds. They plan their gardens carefully

ABOVE: The New American Garden is a modern take on naturalistic- and prairie-garden styles. They are colorful and exuberant and equally at home in formal and informal landscapes.

for multiseason interest, and every plant counts toward the final design. Their gardens are relatively low- maintenance, a boon in this busy world.

Well-edged beds keep the vast perennial swaths in check. Limbed-up trees provide dappled shade and an architectural presence in the garden. Many perennials are tough enough to tolerate drought, wind, and salt. Native and exotic plants mingle in this style. Hosta and ligularia bring coarse texture to shade plantings, whereas straight-edged sunny beds of Russian sage, spike gayfeather, and threadleaf coreopsis show up against a backdrop of tall miscanthus.

PLANTS FOR NEW AMERICAN GARDENS

Combine natives and exotics with ornamental grasses in sunny modern gardens. Here is a range of plants that work well together in the landscape.

■ **NATIVE GRASSES**
  Big bluestem
  Little bluestem
  Prairie dropseed

■ **ORNAMENTAL GRASSES**
  Feather reed grass
  Miscanthus cultivars

■ **PERENANIALS**
  New England aster
  Lanceleaf coreopsis
  Purple coneflower
  Joe-Pye weed
  Daylily
  Spike gayfeather
  Coneflower
  Sedum
  Adam's needle

DESIGN YOUR

GARDEN

A garden at peak bloom brings joy to all who see it. Although budding perennials may be attractive at close range, the impact of peak bloom draws and delights you from afar as well as close up. The loveliest perennial gardens coordinate plants by size, shape, and color. Plants harmonize and contrast in waves of colorful bloom. Foliage color and texture support the display of glorious flowers and sometimes steal the show.

A garden writer once described the way he designs his garden as "walking around with pot in hand, looking for a hole to plant it in." His is a collector's garden in which each individual plant is known and loved, and his technique is common among gardeners. Sometimes the resulting garden is enchanting; more often it looks like a hodge-podge.

Achieving great results in the garden has more to do with planning and practice than with magic. In this chapter, you will begin to gain an understanding of the visual aspects of perennial plants, including their height, form, shape, texture, and color. You'll learn how to work with those features and use perennial plants to your advantage.

The steps described in the exercises on the Techniques pages are part of a design technique known as the backward process. These steps help simplify planning because you work with geometric shapes that represent plant traits rather than with actual plants in mind. In this way, the decision about which specific plants to use doesn't interfere with the design process. Instead of fitting the design to the plant, you select plants for the design.

the secrets to good design

Working with characteristics such as plant size, shape, texture, and color is the key to making good plant combinations. These traits are consistent throughout the life of most perennials. However, some perennials change in size, shape, or texture while in bloom. Becoming familiar with a perennial's traits throughout the gardening year is important to understanding how the plant will fit in with the trees, shrubs, and other flowers in your yard.

PLANT SIZE

Size refers to a plant's height and width. Knowing the height helps you arrange perennials for best viewing in the bed or border. A perennial's mature width helps you figure out how far apart to space the plants and the number of plants you need to buy for a particular space.

Several factors affect the size of a perennial. Some plants may be much taller when they are in bloom than when

Similarly, in a bed seen from all sides, tall plants hold the center, plants of medium height take the middle ground, and short plants are on the edges.

The concept of tall, medium, and short is relative to a bed's width, with very tall plants—those more than 4 feet tall—looking best in wide beds and borders. Tall, medium, and short is also relative to the other plants in the garden. If the tallest plants in your garden are 3 to 4 feet tall, then 2-foot-tall flowering plants are fine for the midrange, and 1-foot-tall perennials fit the foreground. When 7-foot hollyhocks dominate the center of a bed, however, you need to raise the height of front and mid-tier plants. For example, a 3- to 4-foot middle ground would be more proportional to the 7-footers in the center.

scale You also need to consider the scale or relative size of your perennials to their location. Big yards need large beds and borders to suit the scale. These large beds and borders call for large, coarse-textured perennials such as New England asters or 5-foot-wide big-leafed hostas. Such plants would overwhelm a minute space. Instead, tiny backyards look best with small gardens filled with smaller clump-forming perennials such as Wherry's foam flower or pasque flower.

As in most matters of design, there are no set rules for combining plants by height. In fact, just as setting out plants in rows results in an uninteresting garden, having a garden in which all the perennials are the same height, forming flat layers in the front, middle, or back, is equally dull. To avoid this, some garden designers add variety to a garden by placing a taller architectural plant in the front or middle of the border. To pull this off, they select tall plants that are in scale with the short ones, making sure that the former are no more than three times taller than the shorter perennials.

OPPOSITE: A bold-leafed hosta and massive umbrella plant fit well in a large-scale border near a heavy Adirondack chair.
ABOVE: With tall perennials in back and short ones in front, all of the plants are in view. Notice that heights vary in each tier.

out of bloom. For example, fern-leaf yarrow consists of a low mound of leaves until it blooms, then 2-foot flat-topped flower stalks rise above the plants. A perennial's age also influences its size; a seedling or division will be smaller in both width and height than an established plant.

Garden conditions help determine a plant's size. Well-nourished, well-watered plants growing in ideal conditions tend to be fuller and larger than ones that grow in adverse conditions. Sun-loving perennials will become elongated and thin when light is insufficient. Similarly, drought may stunt the growth of a parched moisture lover.

combining plants by height In a border, arranging perennials by height means that tall perennials are typically at the back, medium-size ones are in the middle, and short plants are in front.

TIP CREATE AN ELEMENT OF VISUAL SURPRISE IN A GARDEN BED OR BORDER BY LOCATING A TALL, SELF-SUPPORTING PERENNIAL SUCH AS GREAT CONEFLOWER OR 'AUTUMN SUN' CONEFLOWER WITHIN A MASS OF SHORT PLANTS. AS LONG AS THE PLANTS ARE IN SCALE WITH EACH OTHER, YOU'LL HAVE A STUNNING ACCENT FOR YOUR GARDEN.

PLANT SHAPE

Another important design trait is form, which refers to a plant's mass and outline—its shape. The form of a perennial is three-dimensional and incorporates the growth pattern of the stems and their orientation in space. Most perennials have rounded forms. Some, however, are upright with vertical or almost vertical stems. There are also columnar perennials that have a tall narrow shape like a cylinder, and there are pyramidal ones, which are broader at their bases than at their tips.

ABOVE: A garden with many plant shapes is never boring. This planting contains mounds, fountains, creepers, and rosy flower spikes.

Other perennials have sprawling stems that spread irregularly over the ground or creeping stems with a distinctly horizontal growth pattern.

Plant mass also differs among perennials. Some perennials are densely branched, which gives the plant a solid look. Others may be fountainlike and graceful, or loose and airy with a light, spacious effect. A perennial's mass and shape often change over the years as it ages or grows larger.

flower shapes In addition to plant forms, there are flower shapes or forms that you can read, or distinguish, from a distance. Flower forms may further emphasize a plant's shape, or they may change the shape altogether. Common forms include spikes, plumes, stars, daisies, spheres, and flat or loose flower heads. Those that have the most effect on the perennial's overall shape are those that rise on sturdy stems above the plant.

Spiky blooms, such as those of perennial salvia and liatris, are long round spires, taller than wide and often with tapered tips. A plant may send up a lone spike or a group of spires that are uneven in height.

Plumes, such as those of astilbe, are upright feathery flowers made up of clusters of tiny blooms.

Starry flowers, like those of balloon flower, have pointed petals emanating from a small center. Daisies are similar except that the central point is a broad, round disk. Both stars and daisies may occur singly or in clusters.

Spherical flowers, such as those of blue globe thistle, are rare. Like plumes and spikes they are composed of many tiny flowers.

Flower heads are clusters of flowers. They may be flat, rounded, or irregularly branched.

using plant shapes By contrasting different plant forms, you can create garden harmony or chaos. The latter happens when too many shapes fill a given space. They compete for attention, making the garden look busy and cluttered. Using just a few forms throughout a garden builds harmony.

For example, spiky and other upright masses stand out against rounded forms. Imagine a planting of daylilies and nettle-leaved mullein. The mullein produces groups of tall white spikes emerging from a coarse clump of leaves on the ground. The daylilies, on the other hand, give rise to attractive fountains of strappy leaves. Their blooms held above the foliage are a colorful bonus.

The form of the daylilies enhances the garden all summer long; the mullein provides a short burst of interest while it is in bloom. Its vertical spires make the

Plant Shapes

MOUND
Hosta, Jacob's ladder, lungwort, 'Powis Castle' wormwood

FOUNTAIN
Daylily, maiden grass, perennial fountain grass

CREEPING
Goldenstar, moss phlox, pinks

SPRAWLING
Catmint, ornamental oregano

UPRIGHT
Obedient plant, smooth white penstemon, sundrops

perfect foil for the daylilies' large rounded to triangular blooms. While the mullein is in bloom, both flower shapes balance each other.

Because many perennials have different shapes and sizes in and out of bloom, you should consider both periods when planning a garden. For example, fern-leaf yarrow forms a gray-green carpet most of the summer. But in midsummer, its flower heads rise 1 to 3 feet above the ground, depending on the cultivar. If you were to plant yarrow at the back of the border, based on the flowering height, you would miss the wonderful effect of the foliage.

Similarly, a perennial such as coral bells belongs in the front of the border, even though it is 2 feet tall when in bloom. Its airy flower stems create a see-through haze above the plant; the low mound of leaves from which the flowers arise form its mass. Because nettle-leaved mullein is in bloom for just a few weeks and its foliage is not that interesting, it rightly belongs at the back of the garden.

Flower Shapes

SPIKES
Blazing star, cardinal flower, delphinium, foxglove, hollyhock, torch lily

PLUMES
Astilbe, goatsbeard, goldenrod, Joe-Pye weed

WANDS
Bellflower, blue false indigo, fragrant bugbane, gaura

DAISIES
Aster, boltonia, fleabane, shasta daisy, sneezeweed

SPHERES
Flat sea holly, globe thistle, ornamental onion

STARS
Balloon flower, goldenstar, toadlily

FLOWER HEADS
'Autumn Joy' sedum, butterfly weed, yarrow

LOOSE CLUSTERS
Hybrid anemone, lady's mantle, masterwort, meadowsweet

technique: working with size and shape

ABOVE: This tapestry of contrasting plant shapes relies on mounded, upright, and spiky forms for a balanced unified effect.

> **TIP** PLANTS WITH A LOOSE, OPEN HABIT HELP TO UNIFY A GARDEN BY WEAVING THROUGH OTHER PERENNIALS AS THEY GROW, THUS DRAWING TOGETHER DRIFTS OF DIFFERENT PLANTS. TRY VARIOUS WEAVERS, SUCH AS WHITE GAURA, BORDER CLEMATIS, AND CRANESBILL.

PLAYING WITH PLANT shapes helps you create a framework for your garden. At their most basic, plant shapes are either horizontal or vertical. Reducing plants to these simple forms lets you visualize how the structure of the garden will come together, without color and texture distracting you.

Most gardens succeed by using mostly horizontal forms of various sizes. Vertical forms serve two purposes. Interspersed among the horizontal shapes of the foreground, midground, and background, they bring a rhythmic flow to the design. Verticals also serve as accents or focal points in the design, giving the eye a place to pause.

Practicing on magazine photographs of gardens that you find appealing will help you to learn how to work with plant shapes. You'll need three, four, or more photos that show as much of the garden as possible, rather than just a snippet. Lay tracing paper over the photos, then outline the key plant forms. The following steps will help you create a unified, harmonious design.

PRACTICE TRY

[1] With your pencil, trace the plants in the picture, superimposing rectangles and squares over them. Study the contrast in shapes and sizes. Do certain shapes make a pattern in the garden? Do the shapes at either end of the garden look alike? Are they larger or smaller than the other plants?

CREATE YOUR OWN

MATERIALS NEEDED

- Garden magazines
- Pencil
- Writing paper
- Tracing paper

[2] Try sketching a garden on your own, using just rectangles and squares of varying sizes to represent plant masses. Draw the garden as if you were standing in front of it and from the most frequent points of view. Decide where you'd like the tallest plants and where medium and low plants would look the best. Study the drawing to decide whether the balance of horizontal and vertical elements is pleasing. Rearrange the forms until the composition works for you and the garden looks well-proportioned. Using the encyclopedia starting on page 118, develop a list of potential plants that work for each shape.

A dramatic interplay of textures arises through the contrast of the fine-textured hedges and arches that form a backdrop for the garden, which is composed of medium- and bold-textured perennials.

TEXTURE

Texture is an important plant characteristic because it affects the play of light and shadow in a garden and gives the garden visual interest.

When you talk about a plant's texture, you're mostly referring to visual characteristics of the foliage, whether the leaves are large or small, rough or smooth, dark or light. Tactile characteristics also affect the perception of texture because they influence how light reflects from the leaves.

Perennials with fuzzy foliage such as lamb's-ears and rose campion have a dull nonreflective surface, which gives the effect of coarseness. Bumpy, rough-to-the-touch, wrinkly leaves also look coarse. Leaves with toothed, jagged, or wavy edges such as rodgersia are coarser textured than leaves with flat, smooth edges.

A gloss to the leaves can tone down texture. For example, the large, glossy, leathery foliage of hellebore appears finer textured than it would without the

sheen. Similarly, smooth, turgid foliage also looks finer textured.

Texture may be coarse, medium, fine, or somewhere in between. On the one extreme are plants such as 'Desdemona' ligularia, which has large, wavy, heart-shaped leaves on long stalks; it is bold- or coarse-textured. Plants such as frothy baby's breath fall at the other extreme. Their tiny leaves and flowers are delicate, conveying a weightless quality. Extremely coarse-textured perennials

using texture When working with plant shapes and sizes, too much of one texture is detrimental to a design. Filled only with bold-textured plants, a garden will seem small. Use only fine- or medium-textured plants and the garden looks dull. A garden that is a jumble of different textures will appear hectic.

The prettiest combinations come together when you avoid big changes in texture among the plants. Contrast fine-textured plants with medium-textured perennials and medium textures with coarse ones. Then you get a smooth, gradual transition from one plant to the next without jarring contrasts. For example, coarse-textured perennials combined with medium-textured perennials and maybe a few other coarse-textured plants, such as big-leaved hostas, blend into a border rather than stand out.

However, you can include a few big textural contrasts in the garden to create a focal point. For instance, you can play up the attention-getting qualities of a coarse-textured perennial such as 'Sum and Substance' hosta by combining it with a fine-textured companion, such as tufted hair grass. Just take care to not overdo it.

Uses for fine-textured plants include acting as garden backgrounds and highlighting garden stars. Because fine-textured plants do not draw attention, they help neighboring perennials stand out beautifully. That is why when visiting historical English gardens, you often see fine-textured yew hedges backing a border or a sea of green lawn surrounding a bed.

Flowers make temporary texture contrasts in your garden. In a partly shady bed, for example, the feathery plumes of summer-blooming astilbe and meadowsweet combine well with the bold, shiny leaves of heart-leaf bergenia and with daylily's medium to coarse blooms and strappy leaves.

Avoid using too many coarse textures in a garden. One very coarse plant such as giant gunnera (*Gunnera manicata*), in fact, may be all that most gardens can handle. Giant gunnera grows 6 to 8 feet tall and wide, with leaves up to 5 feet across. The plant is so large and the texture of its leaves so coarse that more than one would overwhelm most average-size suburban lots.

tricks with texture Use plant texture to change how you perceive garden space. Coarse plants at the back of a large garden make it feel smaller because they draw attention back into the space.

make attention-grabbing garden focal points. Very fine-textured plants are good fillers. Most perennials are medium in texture, falling somewhere between these two extremes.

Foliage texture is most significant in garden design because leaves usually last through the growing season, or year-round in the case of evergreens. Although flowers add texture to a garden, the effect is temporary, fading when the flowers fade.

Plant Textures

FINE-TEXTURED PERENNIALS	MEDIUM-TEXTURED PERENNIALS	BOLD-TEXTURED PERENNIALS
Arkansas amsonia	Anise hyssop	Bear's breeches
Lady's mantle in bloom	Blue false indigo	Bigleaf ligularia
Lavender	Blue star	Heart-leaf bergenia
Maidenhair fern	Butterfly weed	Heart-leaf brunnera
Silver mound artemisia	Goldenrod	Hollyhock
Thrift	Lady's mantle in leaf	Hosta
White gaura	Siberian iris	(big-leaved varieties)

technique: working with plant texture

Bold-leafed hosta and bergenia draw attention to this bed's foreground, while fine- and medium-textured plants lead your eye into the distance.

JUST AS YOU tested how to combine various plant shapes in the previous technique, this exercise shows you how to work with a range of textures. Achieving the right textural balance in which all the elements come together in a pleasing combination adds harmony to a garden. For this exercise, you'll use the final drawing from the previous exercise on plant shapes.

Most plants are medium, medium-fine, or medium-coarse in texture. Use very coarse plants sparingly as accents. Fine-textured plants make excellent fillers or garden backgrounds, especially for plants that have distinctive shapes.

After finishing this exercise, check the encyclopedia starting on page 118 for plants with desirable forms and textures for your own design.

> **TIP** USE PLANTS WITH BOLD LEAVES TO CREATE A TROPICAL OR PRIMEVAL GARDEN EFFECT. LARGE LEAVES CAN ALSO FUNCTION AS A BACKDROP FOR INTRICATE BLOOMS.

PRACTICE TRY

[1] To get a feel for using texture in the garden, lay the tracing paper sketches you made in the previous exercise back over the garden photographs. Fill in each plant shape with the texture of the plant underneath, using light, thin parallel lines to show fine texture and broad, heavy stripes for coarse texture. For medium-textured plants, draw narrow, widely spaced stripes. After you've finished, study your sketches to see how these gardens' designers used texture to create interest and emphasis.

CREATE YOUR OWN

MATERIALS NEEDED

- Garden magazines
- Pencil
- Paper
- Tracing paper
- Copies of the final drawing from "working with size and shape," page 49

[2] Now try adding texture to your own garden plan. Lay tracing paper over your final drawing from "working with size and shape." Fill in each shape with a different weight stripe, trying different textures for different shapes. Study your drawings. Look for a pleasing balance of textures. If you are not happy with the textural contrasts, redo the sketch on another sheet of tracing paper, changing the textures but not the forms of the plants. When you have finally developed a composition that appeals to you, check the encyclopedia to find plants with the desired form and texture for your design, and make a list.

PLANT COLOR: FOLIAGE AND FLOWERS

Flowers take center stage when it comes to color. Blossoms of blue, purple, pink, red, orange, yellow, white, and their many variations are usually the main attraction for most people. With some perennials, however, color also comes from the foliage, which may be gold, red, purple, or shades of green from chartreuse to greenish black, or variegated.

So why care about color? It touches the heart and soothes or stimulates the soul. It turns you into an artist with a palette of leaves and flowers. Color is a magnet that turns your head and draws you into a landscape.

To create beautiful perennial combinations, it helps to know some color facts. First, color is reflected light, which we see as red, blue, yellow, and all the other hues of the spectrum in between. All col-

ors relate to each other, and you can see the relationship on a color wheel, which is nothing more than a circular diagram of the spectrum.

Red, blue, and yellow are primary colors. They are the building blocks of all other colors in the spectrum. Orange, violet, and green are secondary colors; they are created by mixing two primary colors together.

Red, yellow, and orange are warm colors. They convey energy, activity, and vigor. You can see warm-colored flowers from a distance more easily than ones that bloom in cool blue, green, or violet. Also, warm colors seem to advance toward you. For this reason, a garden of bright yellow, red, and orange flowers seems cozier and smaller than a garden of cool-hued blooms.

ABOVE: Green foliage and blue-, violet-, and pink- flowering perennials provide the basis for this cool-color garden, which rests the gaze and appears to recede into space.

Blue, green, and violet are cool colors. Green prevails in nature and has a calming effect. Blue and violet suggest peace and restfulness. Flowers in these colors recede from view so that a garden of cool-colored blooms has a more open, spacious feeling than a garden composed of hot hues.

If you feel claustrophobic in your backyard, one way to make it seem larger is to plant perennials with blue, lavender, or white flowers or silver and blue-green leaves. Cool colors are also less visible from a distance and in bright sun. Where they really shine is in intimate spaces and at dusk or on cloudy days.

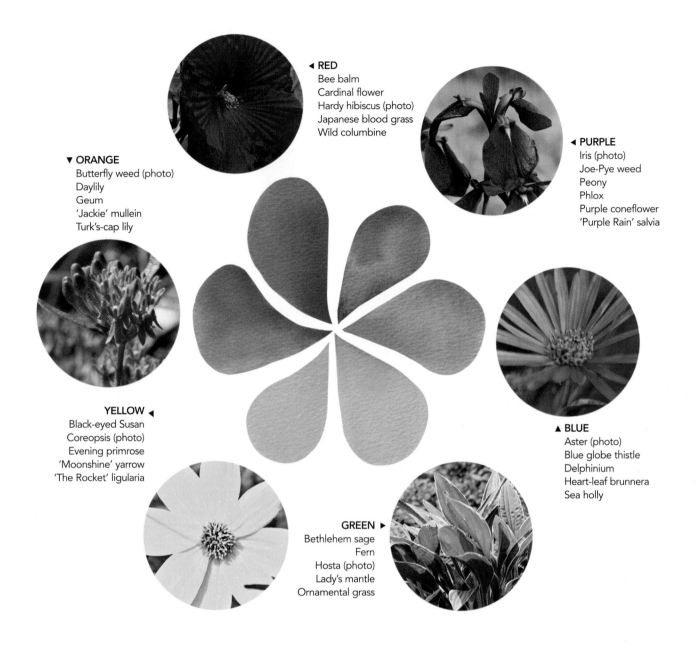

RED
Bee balm
Cardinal flower
Hardy hibiscus (photo)
Japanese blood grass
Wild columbine

PURPLE
Iris (photo)
Joe-Pye weed
Peony
Phlox
Purple coneflower
'Purple Rain' salvia

ORANGE
Butterfly weed (photo)
Daylily
Geum
'Jackie' mullein
Turk's-cap lily

BLUE
Aster (photo)
Blue globe thistle
Delphinium
Heart-leaf brunnera
Sea holly

YELLOW
Black-eyed Susan
Coreopsis (photo)
Evening primrose
'Moonshine' yarrow
'The Rocket' ligularia

GREEN
Bethlehem sage
Fern
Hosta (photo)
Lady's mantle
Ornamental grass

Two other qualities relating to color are important: the brightness or darkness of the color (its value) and the purity of the color (its intensity). Of the three primary colors, yellow has the brightest value. Yellow is brighter than orange, which is brighter than red. Green has a darker value than chartreuse (yellow-green), which is darker than yellow. The brighter the color, the more it stands out.

Intensity reflects the strength of the color. For example, pink and maroon are less-intense shades of red. Pastel blue and navy are less-intense shades of blue.

The purer the color, the more dominant it is in the garden.

A color wheel can be a helpful general guide for combining different colored flowers in beds and borders. As you can see above, warm colors are on one side of the wheel, cool colors on the other.

Colors that are opposite each other on the color wheel—red and green, yellow and purple, and blue and orange—are called complementary colors. Complementary colors are always a combination of a warm and a cool color and have maximum contrast. When you

combine perennials whose flowers or foliage are opposite colors in a bed or border, the colors seem to be intensified and the planting more varied and exciting. Consider pure red or magenta flowers against bright green foliage or a mass of purple-leaved coral bells next to golden hakone grass. Such combinations bring out the intensity of color in both plants and in neighboring plants.

Colors that are next to each other on the color wheel, such as red, orange, and yellow or blue, purple, and red, are harmonious and have a calming effect.

These are called analogous colors, but they sometimes are referred to simply as harmonious colors.

using color Color is a personal choice. You can break all the rules. You can even combine colors that don't really go together. However, for the most harmonious composition, it helps to plan for one dominant color scheme. As with the other plant characteristics, many unrelated colors crammed together look busy, whereas one unvaried hue may appear humdrum and uninspired.

Choosing colors for your garden is not much different from selecting a tie to match your shirt, a blouse to go with your skirt, a pillow for your couch, or paint for your kitchen. Start by selecting one dominant color, then accent or complement it with one or two other colors.

For example, you could decide to do a red garden, using perennials whose flowers or foliage come in varying intensities and values of red, from deep maroon to pale pink. This is a monochromatic color scheme. Such schemes create a restful effect in the garden.

For a more exciting yet harmonious scene, you could accent the red dominant color with three analogous colors, such as orange-red, yellow-orange, and yellow. A complementary color scheme could combine the red with green, orange, and blue for a striking yet agreeable composition.

When choosing a dominant color, be

aware that the darker or purer the color, the more dominant it will be. Brilliant, high-intensity colors also tend to dominate a garden. In small gardens, you may

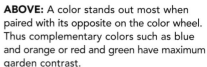

ABOVE: A color stands out most when paired with its opposite on the color wheel. Thus complementary colors such as blue and orange or red and green have maximum garden contrast.
LEFT: If hot spicy hues are your cup of tea, plant perennials with red, orange, and yellow flowers. These harmonious colors sit side by side on the color wheel.

want to use such colors only as accents.

If a pair of colors don't go together, for example an orange-red and a blue-purple, it's usually because they are too far apart on the color wheel. You can soften the contrast between jarring colors by separating them with a sweep of white flowers or silver-leaved plants.

Colors show up best against a contrasting background. Dark green hedges and dark red brick walls make excellent backdrops for flowers and for plants with variegated or silver leaves because of the strong contrast.

technique: working with plant colors

PRACTICE TRY

[1] Study the gardens in the magazine clippings for color. Analyze which colors and combinations work for you. Note whether one color repeats at intervals throughout the garden, or several colors make a repeating pattern. To help you see the patterns, lay tracing paper over the drawings you made while analyzing sizes and shapes. Then color in each box with colored pencils, markers, or crayons corresponding to the plant's flower or foliage colors.

CREATE YOUR OWN

MATERIALS NEEDED

- Garden magazines
- Pencil
- Paper
- Colored pencils, markers, or crayons
- Photocopies of the final drawing in "working with size and shape" page 49.

[2] Try the best of these color combinations on photocopies of your garden drawing. Consider weaving one hue around another. Use color accents. Make a pattern by repeating a few colors along the length of a bed or border. If you're not sure where to begin, keep a color wheel handy for reference. Check the encyclopedia for plants in colors that suit your design and make a list.

SCALE AND REPETITION
Purplish pink and off-white pair prettily throughout this garden, unifying the space through repetition.

A THEME AIDS UNITY
The classic details of an English-style garden are present in this design. They include clipped boxwoods, a stone column, a traditional garden bench and a piece of decorative garden sculpture.

RHYTHM
A sequence of clipped boxwoods along the borders draws you along the lawn path into the heart of the garden.

PRINCIPLES OF DESIGN

In order for shape, size, texture, and color—the basic traits of a perennial—to work together in the garden, you need to understand a few more principles of design. These principles are scale, emphasis, repetition, rhythm, balance, and unity.

scale Scale deals with size relationships—between you and your garden, between your garden and your yard, and between one garden element and another. Scale helps objects look right in their space. A ratio of 1:3 between objects will help avoid any one element from overpowering your garden. For example, in a 6-foot-wide border, the tallest plants are in scale with the garden when they are no more than 2 feet tall. Or a 30-foot-deep lot could handle a garden that is 10 feet wide; a 20-foot-wide garden would overwhelm the space.

emphasis Emphasis differentiates the important elements in a garden by creating visual accents or focal points. A well-placed accent adds variety to your garden and keeps it from looking dull. It leads people's eyes in the direction that you want them to look.

You can make visual accents by contrasting the size, shape, color, or texture of objects in a garden. A cluster of scarlet daylilies, for instance, is a focal point in a bed of erect feather reed grass; the bright red blooms and fountainlike form of the daylilies grab your interest because they are so different from the grass. Other ways to add emphasis include grouping several elements to give them more significance and using unusual or unexpected elements in the garden.

repetition Repetition is the repeated use of design elements, such as form, texture, color, and size, throughout a garden. Duplicating the same plant or plant grouping several times in a bed or in nearby beds and borders helps to cre-

EMPHASIS
The vertical trunk and vase-shaped branches of this small tree stand above the border, forming a focal point readily visible upon entering the garden.

BALANCE
Asymmetrical balance is evident in this garden. The side borders do not match but they carry equal visual weight, with the architectural features on the left balancing the heavier and more colorful planting on the right.

sequence draws you farther along the path and contributes to the overall garden experience.

balance Balance, discussed in depth on page 35, refers to the arrangement and visual weight of plants and objects in a garden when seen from a particular point of view. A balanced composition creates a feeling of stability and harmony and contributes to the garden's unity.

unity Unity is the last and most important design principle because it incorporates all of the other principles. A unified garden has a consistent design in which all the parts of the garden work together as a whole. Each part relates to the others in a coherent organization. A unified garden is a harmonious garden.

Having a theme for your garden, such as attracting butterflies, may help you create unity in your garden. A theme can clarify the garden's purpose, making it easier to choose appropriate plants and accessories for a consistent, unified look.

ate a unified design. For example, 'Autumn Joy' sedum planted at different points in a landscape adds consistent long-lasting color, form, and texture throughout the garden or throughout your landscape. Likewise you could pair 'Purple Dome' asters and 'Golden Fleece' goldenrod at intervals in a perennial border for a late-season splash of complementary colors.

rhythm Rhythm is the sequence in which the elements are repeated across the garden. It affects how your eyes move through the space, and it physically draws you forward along paths and around corners. Sometimes you can create a garden sequence through simple repetition of forms or colors; at other times, a sequence can involve a progression of focal points that are seen one at a time. A handsome urn filled with 'Gold Standard' hosta can draw you down a winding shady path to the next turn, where you see in the distance a bench inviting you to rest. Each step in the

technique: putting design principles to work

TIP CHOOSE A COUPLE OF TALL PLANTS WITH STRIKING FORMS FOR GARDEN STRUCTURE. SILHOUETTE THEM AGAINST GREEN FOLIAGE SO THEY POP OUT FROM THE BACKGROUND. PLACE THEM ON OPPOSITE ENDS OF THE BED TO ANCHOR YOUR PLANTING.

DESIGN PRINCIPLES are not just ideas. They are practical methods for making beautiful gardens. Scale, emphasis, repetition, and balance, combine to create unity. Unity brings harmony and pleasure, which is greater in scope than the other principles. Learning to apply the design principles gives you the ability to shape the garden for the effect you want.

In the previous exercises, you studied the use of color, size, shape, and texture in several gardens. Now, examine the gardens in terms of the design principles, especially unity. Look at the photographs for signs of the following:

scale How does the garden fit into the space? Does the height of the tallest plant seem proportionate to the width of the bed and to the plants growing nearby?

emphasis Spot accents and focal points by looking for sharp contrasts in color, texture, form, or size.

repetition Do colors, shapes, or textures appear and reappear throughout the garden or in nearby beds and borders? Repetition of perennials has a unifying effect on a garden design. You may want to circle each repeating element.

rhythm Do the repeating elements form a rhythmic pattern? Does this pattern draw you into the landscape or further into the garden?

balance Can you tell whether the garden is symmetrical or asymmetrical? Find elements of the garden that are in balance with each other.

theme Finally, can you discern a theme for the garden? Although not a design principle, themes help bring a garden into focus and ensure unity. Look for plants and decorations that support the theme. A bird-friendly garden, for example, should include perennials such as blazing star, columbine, great coneflower, sunflower, or hollyhock to attract birds. Look for birdhouses set at proper heights, birdbaths, and twiggy shrubs such as 'Chicago Luster' viburnum for nesting, perching, or shelter. Chairs and tables should be comfortable and informal or rustic in style to complement the informal plantings.

CREATE YOUR OWN

[1] Now relate what you learned from examining the photographs to a black-and-white photocopy of your final sketch from "working with size and shape." First, study it for symmetry. Do you need to add more visual weight (plants or accessories) to one area to balance the other side? Draw in boxes to add weight or white out lines between adjoining boxes to create one large mass.

[2] Lay tracing paper over the photocopy. Begin turning the rectangles and squares into actual plant shapes. The squares and rectangles may represent individual plants or groups of plants. Substitute spiky or upright perennials for vertical rectangles. Transform squares into mounds, fans, fountains, or round plant shapes. Low horizontal rectangles can become creeping or spreading perennials, or they may be a row of small mounded or spiky plants. Taller horizontals could be a broad group of vertical plants, which will appear as a horizontal mass. Remember that each square and rectangle represents not only a shape but a color and texture, too. Add lines or colors to differentiate the plant shapes. Refer to all of the plant lists you have created while doing the exercises in this chapter to help guide your thinking about which plants have the shape, color, and texture you are looking for. At this point, you are whittling down your plant list, but not making a final list.

[3] Step back and study your drawing. Have you gotten carried away? Remember, too much variety is . . . too much. You may want to place another sheet of tracing paper over your drawing and simplify the composition. Reduce the number of colors in the garden; rest your eye by leaving some areas green, filling them with foliage plants such as ferns or hostas. Reduce the number of different plants in the garden. For example, rather than sketching a different upright plant for each tall vertical box, use just one plant for all the boxes. When you are finally happy with the arrangement, you're ready to move on to the next step.

MATERIALS NEEDED

- Garden magazines
- Pencil
- Tracing paper
- Colored pencil
- a black-and-white photocopy of the final drawing from the exercise "working with plant size and shape," page 49

technique: from sketch to planting plan

Instead of growing perennials singly, plant them in drifts or tapering groups to increase the impact of their color and texture on the design.

MATERIALS NEEDED

- Pencil
- Graph paper
- Edited plant lists
- Final garden sketch from "putting design principles to work," page 61

IN THIS STEP of the design process, you turn your rough sketch into a final planting plan. A planting plan allows you to work out all the spacing issues in the design. Once all the plants are in place on the plan, you can then use the drawing to determine the number of plants to buy for the garden and to see exactly where each will go when you're ready to plant.

As you turned geometrical shapes into plant shapes in the previous exercise, it probably seemed as though each shape stood for one plant. In actuality, most perennials are planted in groups called drifts. Often they are planted in groups of three, five, seven, or nine, because odd numbers look more natural than even ones. Planting in multiples shows off plant texture and flower color. It gives the garden structure because each drift has more impact on the design than if the perennial were planted individually. Only the largest perennials or the ones with the strongest structural appearance stand on their own. Planting in drifts also helps a garden to look natural in its surroundings. Most drifts have irregular shapes, weaving in and around other drifts and echoing how plants grow in nature.

Before starting the planting plan, take your hose out to the site of the garden and mark out the bed. Make sure you have the shape of the bed just the way you want it, then measure the space.

You should also read the next chapter, "Choosing Plants," starting on page 66.

After reading that chapter, check the encyclopedia (page 118) and strike all the plants that won't survive in your garden from your lists. As you work, note the height and width of each perennial remaining on your edited list.

Next, redraw your final sketch from the previous exercise—don't groan; this is still a rough sketch. But this time you're drawing it to scale. On a sheet of graph paper, draw the length of your garden, letting 1/4 inch or one box equal one foot. Then re-sketch the plant shapes along this line, adjusting their sizes or numbers to fit the size of the garden.

CREATE YOUR OWN

[1] On a second sheet of graph paper, plot the outline of the garden space, referring to your measurements (see page 26). Draw the garden's length and width to scale, using the same scale as your rough sketch. Make sure curves and corners are in the right locations. Orient the garden so that its back is on the bottom and the front of the garden is on top.

[2] Tape the rough sketch, the one you drew to scale, to the top of your plot plan so that the fronts of the gardens face each other. You could also draw both gardens on the same sheet of graph paper. Begin marking drifts on the plot plan corresponding to the plant shapes above. You may find it helpful to draw a line down from each shape so that you can keep track of which drift stands for which shape. Work from the front to the back.

[3] Make sure the length of each drift matches the length of the shape. The width of the drift will depend on the depth of the garden, the number of plant tiers in your rough sketch, and the size of plant you've decided to use for the shape. You will probably need to adjust the size of the drifts to fill the space. Let some drifts weave around their neighbors to add movement to the design. Leave about a foot of space between drifts so that you can get into the garden and work among the plants.

[4] Measure the size of each drift, counting the number of squares it encompasses. This will tell you the number of plants it will take to fill each drift and whether the plant you've chosen for the space will fit. You might need to adjust the size and shape of a drift to fit the plants in, or you might want to choose a different plant. Locate the center of each plant in the drift. The distance from the center of one plant to the center of the plant beside it should equal the mature width of the plant. Avoid placing the plants in rows within the drifts, because straight lines tend to have a rigid look.

design a container garden

Designing a perennial garden in a container can be a pleasant way to pass an afternoon with summerlong results. Most perennials make good container plants not just for the flowers but for their texture and form. Perennials in containers flourish and fade with the seasons, unlike annuals, which burst with color but need replacing the following year. A container garden of perennials can be as simple as an 8-inch flowerpot planted with a clump of 'Elijah Blue' blue fescue, or as complicated as a three-tier creation of flowers, vines, and grasses.

A single perennial can stand on its own if it has a sculptural form. Hosta, many ornamental grasses, and evergreen perennials such as bergenia fit that description; when you pot them up they look attractive for months.

Some of the most attractive container designs are the most basic. Several maidenhair ferns grown in a red-glazed ceramic pot would add panache to any shady deck.

For more complicated designs, select plants of different heights. A mix of chartreuse-and-green hosta such as 'Guacamole' surrounded by small variegated ivy plants evenly spaced around the pot makes a striking statement for a sheltered shady area. If season-long interest is of no concern, grow a stunning perennial with a short season of interest, such as old-fashioned bleeding heart, and change the display after the bloom has passed.

Also consider growing aggressive perennials such as bee balm, mint (Mentha spp.), ivy (Hedera spp.), and evening primrose in pots on decks or patios. Then you can enjoy their flowers without the maintenance hassle of restraining them in the ground.

CHOOSING CONTAINERS

Pots should be in proportion to the plants they hold. Large containers suit big perennials such as bear's breeches or 'Sum and Substance' hosta. Small pots are good for little plants.

Matching plant and container sizes is not just about looks. It's also a matter of providing enough room for the plant to grow. Growing a large perennial in a too-small container not only stresses the plant but increases the time you must spend watering and maintaining it. A 12-inch-diameter container can hold one 1-gallon perennial or two 4-inch nursery-pots of perennials. An 18-inch pot accommodates one 2-gallon perennial or three plants in 4-inch pots. Although newly planted pots of perennials may look sparse in the beginning, they need the room to expand to their mature size.

Beyond size, think about the container's material and design. The range of materials is larger than ever and includes traditional terra-cotta and plastic pots, glazed ceramic, concrete, plastic-coated steel, and lightweight plastic foam molded to look like classical containers.

Terra-cotta pots have a timeless appeal, and their rusty color makes the perfect complement for green-leaved plants. Keep in mind that terra-cotta is heavy and porous. It dries out quickly after watering, especially on hot, windy days. In a cold climate, it cracks as the soil inside it freezes and thaws.

Rot-resistant redwood, cypress, and cedar work well in informal designs. Styles range from contemporary and traditional to historic reproductions.

Plastic pots are inexpensive and hold moisture longer than terra-cotta. Fiberglass and resin pots are lightweight and combine the benefits of terra-cotta and plastic with the designs of expensive limestone or cast-iron containers. Plastic and fiberglass are well-suited to perennials grown in cold climates.

Beyond that, the only limit to what will work as a container for your perennial garden is your imagination. A tipped wheelbarrow, a leaky rowboat, and old hiking boots or high-top sneakers are possibilities for whimsical garden pots.

ARRANGING PLANTS

Play with your plants while they're still in their nursery pots until you find a layout you like. Keep tall perennials in the back or center of the pot, depending on how you will view the container. Intersperse medium height perennials with ones that trail around the edges. You can also use perennials of different textures and colors such as daisies and coral bells, which have dense, mounding leaves, to create an informal design.

BELOW: For a traditional look, pick fast-drying terra-cotta pots or lightweight plastic pots that resemble classical designs.

CHOOSING

Garden centers understand human nature. They create lovely display gardens featuring beautiful perennials while they are in bloom. By showing the many ways that plants can be used,

PLANTS

display gardens give shoppers good ideas to try at home. And these gardens really work, sending people down the aisles to fill their shopping carts with exciting new plants.

The only negative to this scenario is that plants shouldn't be an impulse purchase when you're planning for long-term results. Not until you know the growing conditions in your garden and the perennials that will survive in those conditions can you make intelligent decisions about what to buy. Although it doesn't hurt to try a few perennials whose survival could be questionable, filling your garden with such plants will guarantee disappointment and delay your success.

The exercises presented in the last chapter, "Design Your Garden," had you make several lists relating to the aesthetic qualities of the perennials. Now you're going to whittle down that list to the most appropriate plants for your garden by considering soil, light, and rainfall. These are the building blocks of plant life. Once you know what conditions your garden offers and which plants will survive in those conditions then you can move on to deciding which perennials to buy to work with your design.

plants for the site

COLD HARDINESS

In most gardens, cold temperatures are the limiting environmental factor to what can be grown. While some plants easily tolerate −20°F, others quickly succumb when temperatures drop to just 10°F. Select your perennials first for their cold hardiness, then for their adaptability to other environmental conditions, and finally for their design role.

Plant-hardiness zones identify the coldest temperatures expected in a region. The map on page 190, which was developed by the United States Department of Agriculture, will help you determine the hardiness zone of your region; then, as you browse the encyclopedia, you'll see that each entry gives the hardiness zone for the plant. Any perennial with a hardiness rating that matches the zone for your region—or that can take colder weather—should do fine in your yard. For example, if you live in Zone 6, you can grow perennials that are hardy in Zones 4 to 6 but not those that are hardy only to Zone 7.

Microclimates put a kink into this statement. These are small areas where the soil and climate differ from surrounding areas. For example, cold air has a tendency to accumulate in low-lying areas. Low spots may be colder than the rest of your yard. In fact, they may be enough colder that the perennials you plant in them need to be a whole zone hardier than those in the rest of your landscape.

Southern exposures tend to be warmer; those facing north are usually colder. Areas near the house tend to be warmer than outlying parts of the yard. You might be able to grow perennials that are not hardy elsewhere on your property in beds next to the house, especially if the wall faces south.

ABOVE: House and garden walls protect perennials from windy, cold weather and may allow you to grow nonhardy plants.

SOIL

Most perennials grow the fastest, are the sturdiest and healthiest, and bloom the brightest in loose, well-drained, weed-free, fertile loam with a pH of about 6.5.

Not every garden site provides such ideal conditions. For example, the arid climate of the Southwest has alkaline soils, whereas in the Northeast the climate is moister and the soils are more acidic. The silty loam of the Mississippi River floodplains has natural fertility and texture that supports good plant growth, but gardens there often experience long periods of drought.

Luckily, you can find perennials that thrive in the variabilities of soil, moisture, and pH of each region. You can also do a lot to improve the soil, especially its tilth, drainage, and weediness. However, you'll have the most luck, and your perennials will be easiest to grow, if you select plants that are adapted to your site conditions. The first step, then, is learning what you've got.

tilth To differentiate one type of soil from another, pick up a handful of soil and feel its texture.

For most perennials, loamy soils are the best. Made up of sand, clay, and organic matter, they are loose, fertile soils that hold water and nutrients, drain well, and are easy to work.

Sandy soils have their good and bad points. On the bad side, sandy soils tend to be dry and infertile, because water and nutrients flow through them rapidly. On the plus side, sandy soils are easy to work, warm quickly in spring (much faster than clay soils), and don't become waterlogged. You can improve sandy soil and increase its capacity to hold water and nutrients without losing any of its good qualities by tilling in compost or other organic matter, such as peat moss, manure, and composted bark.

Clay soils also have their pluses and minuses. Because they are made up of microscopic particles, clay soils are the most fertile of soils and can hold the most moisture. But those small parti-

ABOVE LEFT: On a slope, the soil is warmer and drier at the top and wetter and cooler at the bottom.
ABOVE RIGHT: Use drought-tolerant plants in fast-draining gritty soil, which heats up and dries out quickly in the sun.

cles mean that clay soils have tiny pores, which make it difficult for water and oxygen to penetrate the soil. When wet, clay soil is cold; it's the last to thaw and warm up in spring. It's also sticky and difficult to work. When dry, clay soil is rock hard.

You can improve clay soil by tilling in organic matter. It loosens the soil and opens pores so water drains through.

Soil Types

SANDY SOIL
If it feels gritty and the soil particles are large or appear sandy or gravelly and won't hold together, you have a sandy soil.

CLAY SOIL
If the soil feels smooth, holds tightly together, and is very malleable, it is a clay soil.

LOAMY SOIL
If the soil feels equally smooth and gritty, has large particles as well as small, and holds together but can't be shaped, your soil is loamy.

PERENNIALS FOR
ALKALINE SOIL
- Adam's needle
- Baby's breath
- Delphinium
- Dianthus (photo)
- Moss phlox
- Obedient plant
- Wormwood
- Yellow corydalis

PERENNIALS FOR
ACID SOIL
- Bleeding heart (photo)
- Bugbane
- False Solomon's seal
- Foxglove
- Japanese iris
- Primrose
- Royal fern
- Wood fern

fertility and pH The main source of nutrients for plants is the sand, silt, and clay that make up the soil. Water clinging to soil particles gradually breaks down the minerals and becomes the nutrient-rich solution that nourishes plants.

This natural supply of nutrients also depends on the soil pH. Soil pH is measured on a scale from zero to 14. A pH below 7 is acid; above 7 is alkaline; pH 7 is neutral. Arid places have alkaline soil, whereas moist areas tend to be acidic.

In high pH soils, some nutrients become tied up and unavailable to plants. For example, iron is not available when the pH is above 8.5. Although alkalinity and acidity can be modified by amending the soil with lime or sulfur, the modifications are never permanent. In highly alkaline and acidic soils, it is more practical, less frustrating, and typically less expensive to select perennials that have a strong preference for the soil's existing pH.

moisture and drainage Every yard has unique wet and dry areas. A garden catching overthrow from the neighbor's sprinklers will be wetter than a garden under the eaves of your home, which block rainfall, or next to a brick wall, which wicks away moisture. Water collects in low areas and rolls off high spots. Clay and loamy soils stay wetter longer than do sandy soils.

In addition, moisture patterns—rainfall and snow amounts—vary in each region. The Pacific Northwest has wet winters and dry summers, whereas the Great Plains tends to have dry winters and wet summers. In the Desert Southwest and southern California, plants need to survive long periods of heat and drought, while plants that flourish in heat and humidity do fine in the southeastern United States.

Drainage describes how water and oxygen move through the soil. Water

TIP SOIL TESTS PROVIDE DATA ABOUT THE SOIL'S ABILITY TO NOURISH THE PLANTS GROWING IN IT. THEY MEASURE THE NUTRIENTS IN THE SOIL AND ITS pH, AND THEY PROVIDE RECOMMENDATIONS FOR IMPROVING THE SOIL. SOIL TESTS ARE AVAILABLE FROM YOUR LOCAL COOPERATIVE EXTENSION OFFICE AND THROUGH PRIVATE LABORATORIES. (SEE PAGE 85 FOR INFORMATION ON TAKING A SOIL TEST.)

flows through soil pores, drawing air behind it. For most perennials, the best soil is one that is well-drained. Such soil feels like a moist sponge; the mineral particles, water, and oxygen combine in the right ratio to offer ideal growing conditions for the majority of plants.

Excessively wet and dry soils inhibit the root growth of most perennials. Wet conditions can damage soil structure. In wet soil, plants grow poorly, need staking, die back, wilt, and come under attack from insects and diseases. Even though hardy, perennials growing in poorly drained soil often die over the winter. Several recent research projects have demonstrated that wet soil in winter is a big killer of perennials.

You'll have better luck with your garden if you select perennials that are adapted to the moisture and drainage conditions in your yard. Many perennials have developed ways to conserve moisture.

Test Soil for Drainage

To test your soil for drainage, dig an 18-inch-deep hole, fill it with water, then time how long it takes for the water to drain out.
- If the hole empties in less than 3½ hours, the soil is very well drained.
- If the hole empties in 3½ to 24 hours, the soil is well-drained.
- If the hole empties in 24 to 72 hours, the soil is moderately well-drained.
- If the hole empties in more than three days, the soil is poorly drained.

For example, silvery, gray, or blue-green plants often have hairy leaves and stems. The hairs trap moisture transpiring from the leaf and create a humid zone around the plant. Other plants, such as marsh marigold, thrive in waterlogged soils.

Check on soil moisture and drainage at the same time you examine soil tilth. Soil that feels cool is moist. Dry soil feels warm. Poorly drained soil is soggy and may smell sour or rotten. It is usually sticky and compacts when squeezed.

PERENNIALS FOR DAMP SOIL
- Astilbe
- Bigleaf ligularia (photo)
- Bugbane
- Cardinal flower
- Featherleaf rodgersia
- Japanese iris
- Joe-Pye weed
- Marsh marigold
- Royal fern

PERENNIALS FOR DRY SOIL
- Barrenwort
- Bigroot cranesbill
- Butterfly weed
- False indigo
- Heart-leaf brunnera
- Lilyturf
- Sedum (photo)
- 'Valerie Finnis' artemisia
- Yucca

RIGHT: A full-sun garden is one that receives at least six hours of sunlight a day. The perennials that thrive in such gardens do well without the sheltering shade of trees or buildings.
BELOW: Beautiful shade-loving perennials such as these mixed hostas flourish under a leafy canopy of shrubs and trees.
OPPOSITE PAGE: Some of the loveliest perennial gardens grow in partial shade, which varies between four and six hours of sunlight per day.

LIGHT

Too much or too little sunshine may affect your plant's health. Most plant labels indicate the amount of sun necessary for growth with icons representing full sun, half sun/half shade, and full shade. The encyclopedia in the back of this book also details the light requirements of each plant.

Full sun means that the plant needs at least six hours of sunlight per day. If planted in shade, the plant will stretch toward the light; its stems will elongate and the whole plant will become spindly. Full-sun plants growing in shade will bloom less and, over time, weaken and may eventually die.

Anything less than six hours of sun is considered shade. Partial shade—or half sun/half shade—varies from two to six hours of sunlight per day. Full shade occurs where a site receives two hours or less of sun daily, such as under evergreens, in corners, next to north-facing walls, or beneath densely branched big-leaved trees such as Norway maple.

Part-shade plants often thrive where they get about four hours of sun in the morning, then shade for the rest of the day. They will also thrive in dappled shade, where shadows dance across the garden all day long. But they can't take hot afternoon sun, which is more intense than morning sun. In full sun, full- and part-shade perennials will scorch, fade, dry out, and often die.

Climate plays a role in how much sun and shade a plant can take. Many perennials considered full- or part-shade plants will grow in full sun in areas that have mild—moist and relatively cool—summers. In the South, many of these plants struggle in the heat, even in shade.

Check the "features" list at the top of each entry in the Encyclopedia, starting on page 118, for the plants' light and soil needs. Then pare your lists to the perennials that will thrive in your garden.

PERENNIALS FOR FULL SUN
- Artemisia
- Basket-of-gold
- Blue oat grass
- Butterfly weed
- False sunflower
- Hollyhock
- Mexican feather grass
- Moss phlox
- Purple coneflower
- Russian sage

PERENNIALS FOR PARTIAL SHADE
- Astilbe
- Bleeding heart
- Coral bells
- Goatsbeard
- Hosta
- Japanese anemone
- Marsh marigold
- Masterwort
- Yellow wax bell

PERENNIALS FOR FULL SHADE
- Barrenwort
- Hay-scented fern
- Jacob's ladder
- Lenten rose
- Lily-of-the-valley
- Lilyturf
- Lungwort
- Solomon's seal
- Toad lily
- Yellow corydalis

choose plants for the design

Long after flowers have faded, colorful leaves of purple, yellow, blue-green, and variegated cream-and-green add pizzazz to this shady spot.

Once you have an idea of which perennials will thrive in your garden, then you can begin to focus on getting the maximum design impact from your choices. Most people base their selections on what the flowers look like, however, considering that some perennials bloom for as little as two weeks, a focus on flowers can leave your garden lacking through much of the summer. This is especially true for small gardens, where each plant plays a major role in creating the garden's overall effect.

To prevent your garden from being a flash in the pan, make sure to include a few long-blooming perennials as well as perennials that offer more than one season of interest. Attractive seed heads, fall color, and winter structure are just a few of the traits that create extended interest in a garden. The seed heads, for example, not only look good but also draw hungry birds. Also note flower and foliage fragrance and how the leaves affect the garden plan when the plant is not in flower.

LONG BLOOM SEASON

Although most perennials bloom for only a few weeks each year, a few can flower nonstop for as long as 14 weeks. Perennials with a long bloom season keep the garden colorful for months. If you live in the North, this is a boon, because a cold-climate landscape can be gray, white, and brown for six or more months of the year. During the short growing season, you want color and lots of it. Long-blooming perennials offer that color economically by flowering for months instead of weeks.

Yet you don't have to live in a cold climate to appreciate the versatility that long-bloomers offer. When combined with shorter-blooming perennials, they can provide a dependable base color for the garden while the shorter-bloomers contribute successive waves of harmonizing or accent colors.

Several coreopsis cultivars stand out for their length of bloom. These cultivars often bloom from June to October, particularly when cut back in late summer. 'Creme Brulee' threadleaf coreopsis has a fine texture with narrow bright green leaves and yellow flowers. 'American Dream' pink coreopsis and the hybrids 'Flying Saucers' and 'Tequila Sunrise' have yellow-centered pink flowers from June to October.

One of the longest bloomers is 'Butterfly Blue' pincushion flower, which can bloom from June to the first frost in the northern United States. Some bearded irises and daylilies are bred to rebloom,

bringing a second flush of color to the garden. 'Mardi Gras' sneezeweed is a relatively new cultivar that begins blooming in early June and continues nonstop till mid-August.

Although some perennials naturally bloom for weeks on end, others can be pushed to extend their bloom period. Deadhead the plants before they set seed. Some perennials will put on as good of a show as the first round of blooms; others will bloom sporadically as long as you keep them free of faded flowers.

FOR A SUCCESSION OF COLOR

Continuous flowering counts most where space is limited. To extend your garden's color through the seasons, select perennials with different periods of bloom. Make lists of perennials that bloom in spring, summer, and fall. Decide which ones fit your growing conditions, and cross the others off your lists. Then compare your lists to the requirements of your design.

Choose two or three plants from each list for extended color harmony. Site each

season's flowering plants close enough in the garden that the colors intertwine. When flowers fade, cut back stems unless you want the seed heads to develop.

You can choose one color scheme that lasts through the entire growing season, or different color schemes for spring, summer, and fall. Colors in the flower garden seem to intensify as the season progresses, going from spring pastels to the deep gold, orange, and bronze hues of fall.

Growing a garden that blooms from spring to fall is easy with a bloom chart. Such a chart displays a perennial's season of bloom. The chart on page 80 and 81 shows periods of bloom as well as times when the foliage is outstanding or the seed heads are of particular interest. By consulting a bloom chart, you see which perennials overlap in a period of bloom and which plants bloom successively. By checking the chart and the growth requirements for each plant in the encyclopedia, you can create harmonious color schemes with plants that thrive in your environment.

FOLIAGE

The leaves of most perennials last far longer than their blooms. For that reason, plants with beautiful foliage hold tremendous garden power. They screen unwanted views, soften harsh lines, and create superb visual interest. Good foliage plants stand out for their color, variegation, texture, structure, and, in some instances, all four traits.

Colorful leaves bring visual appeal to the garden. Foliage in every shade of green forms a natural backdrop for most garden flowers. Leaves of chartreuse, gold, and red draw your attention. Bronzy leaves look sophisticated and work especially well with flowers in red, orange, and yellow. Foliage in light gray-blue or variegated green and white can brighten a shady corner. The foliage of variegated hosta and heartleaf brunnera stays lovely long after their short seasons of bloom have passed. Likewise, you could grow 'Desdemona'

PERENNIALS WITH LONG BLOOM SEASON
- 'Becky' Shasta daisy
- 'Goldsturm' black-eyed Susan
- Knautia
- 'Mardi Gras' sneezeweed
- 'Moonbeam' coreopsis
- 'Stella de Oro' daylily
- Pincushion flower (photo)

LEFT: Near a blue-leafed hosta, fine-textured clumps of golden 'Ogon' dwarf sweet flag flank a Japanese maple with deep burgundy leaves, giving season-long structure and color to the garden.

bigleaf ligularia not for its orange daisy clusters but for its grand leaves, which are bronzy green on top and dark maroon underneath.

In the dry days of summer, silver leaves come into their own, especially when they separate swaths of brightly colored flowers. A mass of silver or gray-green leaves softens and blends flowers of discordant hues.

Silvery foliage is so valuable in the garden that the flowers of silver perennials may never enter into the picture. In fact, many people remove the flowers as they form so that nothing detracts from the leaves. If you don't want to go to that much effort, there are non-blooming silver plants. For instance, 'Powis Castle' artemisia forms a lacy 2-foot silvery mound in the perennial border and rarely blooms. If you plan to grow lamb's-ears only for its fuzzy silver leaves and not its spikes of pink flowers, try 'Big Ears', a flowerless cultivar.

Because leaves change through the seasons, foliage plants provide different effects at different times of the year. The spring leaves of some plants bear little resemblance to their late-summer counterparts. For example, a peony spurts up in spring as a cluster of red shoots,

then it ends the growing season as an elegant shrubby clump of medium to dark green leaves. 'Othello' bigleaf ligularia leaves start out the season dark purple but later mature to bronzy green with maroon underneath. Ostrich fern's spring fiddleheads make tiny curled sculptures. In summer, its jumbo fronds, which grow

up to 6 feet tall and 3 feet wide, look like a badminton shuttlecock.

Leaves may also change from summer to fall. Arkansas amsonia has bright green leaves throughout most of the growing season, but in autumn it turns golden yellow. Likewise, bloody cranesbill's green spring and summer foliage becomes a vivid red. Flame grass, which starts the season with red-tinged grayish-green leaves, goes from red-orange to wine-red in cool fall temperatures.

Some evergreen perennials maintain a year-round garden presence. Their foliage persists through winter but may need some trimming to remove damaged leaves in spring. Adam's needle, heart-leaf bergenia, and hellebore are evergreen perennials that bring year-round structure to the garden.

Perennials with Interesting Foliage

BEAUTIFUL FOLIAGE
- 'Chocolate' Joe-Pye weed
- Coral bells
- Golden hakone grass
- Heart-leaf bergenia
- Hosta
- 'Jack Frost' heart-leaf brunnera
- Lungwort
- Maidenhair fern
- 'Matrona' sedum

FALL COLOR
- Arkansas amsonia
- Bigroot cranesbill

EVERGREEN LEAVES
- 'Elijah Blue' blue fescue
- Heart-leaf bergenia
- Lenten rose
- Snowy woodrush

VARIEGATED LEAVES
- 'Frances Williams' hosta
- Hybrid foamy bells
- 'Jack Frost' heart-leaf brunnera
- 'Silver Dragon' creeping lilyturf

YELLOW TO CHARTREUSE LEAVES
- 'Gold Heart' old-fashioned bleeding heart
- 'Sum and Substance' hosta
- 'Sunshine Blue' and 'Worcester Gold' bluebeard

BLUE LEAVES
- Blue oat grass
- 'Elijah Blue' blue fescue
- 'Hadspen' blue hosta

RED, MAROON, AND PURPLE LEAVES
- 'Amethyst Myst' coral bells
- 'Britt Marie Crawford' ligularia
- 'Husker Red' smooth white penstemon

SILVER TO GRAY-GREEN LEAVES
- Artemisia
- Lamb's-ears
- Lavender
- Lavender cotton
- Rose campion
- Russian sage
- Woolly speedwell

BRONZE LEAVES
- 'Amber Waves' coral bells
- 'Bronzita' weeping brown sedge

The beauty and structure of these upright sedums and ornamental grasses persist through most of the winter.

MULTISEASON INTEREST

When you match plants to your plan, choose a few with multiseason interest. Perennials that are interesting in more than one season ensure your landscape is attractive when most plants look dead. They add depth and structure, even under the cover of snow. If you choose plants with fall, winter, and early spring interest, your garden can look good in every season.

Multiseason interest often results from the architecture of the plant. Perennials with a sculptural form, such as bear's breeches, become the focus of the winter garden. They especially stand out when little else is around to distract the eye. Similarly, after lavish flowers and lush leaves have passed, vistas open and grow more conspicuous when the distant views are framed by structural winter plants.

The top growth of most perennials dies back to the roots in autumn. Evergreen perennials typically maintain their form

year-round. For example, Adam's needle keeps its gray-green hue and striking form all winter, thanks to its stiff, fibrous, swordlike leaves. Evergreen Lenten rose has leathery dark green foliage and large flowers from late winter to late spring. Many coneflowers possess stems strong enough to stand upright in winter. Coneflowers have persistent seed heads—sometimes round, sometimes long and tapering. Each seed head adds a winter garden boost—for its interesting shape and for the hungry birds that may perch on the stem to feed.

Fleshy succulents have excellent winter form that stands up to winter storms. October daphne, for example, forms low circular mounds of arching blue-green stems that turn pink in winter. Upright forms such as 'Autumn Joy' and 'Autumn Fire' sedums have flattish rose

to burgundy flower clusters in fall. Rich deep brown seed heads follow, persisting through the winter. The winter seed heads of 'Matrona' sedum are a handsome rusty brown.

Many ornamental grasses also maintain their form throughout the winter until early spring. Backlit by wintry morning sun, the frosted translucence of their leaves seems magical. Even when they collapse under heavy snow and ice, they leave swellings in the landscape that define the garden view.

TIP FOR MAXIMUM WINTER IMPACT IN A BED OR BORDER, CLUSTER PLANTS WITH DIFFERENT STRUCTURES AND TEXTURES. FOR EXAMPLE, MASS GLOBE THISTLE WITH 'CLOUD NINE' SWITCH GRASS OR GREAT CONEFLOWER AND TALL MAIDEN GRASS.

container garden perennials

Many perennials that you grow in the ground will flourish in containers. If you supply the right light, soil, moisture, drainage, and nourishment for healthy growth, nature takes care of the rest.

When choosing container plants, think about the traits that make a successful garden design. Look at plant form, color, and texture. Consider the container and where you plan to place it. Then create a harmonious grouping that takes all these facts into account. When in doubt,

choose a simple design using one to three different perennials that fit the needs of your site and design.

If you plan to combine several perennials in one pot, make sure that they all have similar growth requirements. For example, a pot of sun-loving prickly pear, Adam's needle, and a variegated sedum would be a showy, easy-to-grow pairing.

If you live on a windy site, look for plants with tough leaves and strong stems that can stand up to the wind.

ABOVE: Several cultivars of hosta thrive in terra-cotta and ceramic containers.
OPPOSITE: Multicolored ajuga (*Ajuga reptans*) and hosta fill a windowbox. Golden hakone grass grows in a pot among the other plants in the garden.

Adam's needle, bear's breeches, daylily, and many ornamental grasses do well in windy conditions. In a shady location, try a large planter of tall astilbe, leathery bergenia, and spotted dead nettle.

Hardy perennials grown in pots can last for years, especially with winter protection. In Zone 5 or colder areas, however, potted perennials are vulnerable to freezing temperatures because their roots are growing above ground. Store them in a protected location such as a garage or a cool basement, where the temperature stays around 32°F or a bit warmer. Keep them there until spring, when outdoor temperatures begin to warm.

If a perennial grows too big for its pot, divide it and keep the healthiest pieces for your garden. An elegant grass such as 4- to 6-foot-tall maiden grass needs a large container, whereas 12-inch 'Little Bunny' or 'Little Honey' dwarf fountain grass grown singly suits a small one.

THIS BLOOM CHART WILL HELP YOU choose perennials for your garden. Arranged alphabetically by common name, the chart shows the flowering period of many popular perennials. It also displays peak times for other decorative features such as exceptional foliage, colorful autumn leaves, winter structure, or ornamental seed heads. The pink bars show typical flowering times; green represents other sources of visual interest. By consulting this bloom chart, you can make beds and borders that look good from spring to fall. You'll discover garden workhorses offering season after season of beauty. Moreover, you'll see which perennials have overlapping periods of bloom, enabling you to create lush groupings in your garden.

PLANT NAME	SPRING (E M L)	SUM. (E M L)	FALL (E M L)	WINTER (E M L)
Allegheny foam flower				
Anise hyssop				
Arkansas amsonia				
Artemisia				
Asiatic hybrid lily				
Aster				
Astilbe				
'Autumn Joy' sedum				
Baby's breath				
Balloon flower				
Barrenwort				
Basket-of-gold				
Bearded iris				
Bear's breeches				
Bear's foot hellebore				
Bee balm				
Bethlehem sage				
Big blue lobelia				
Big leaf ligularia				
Bigroot geranium				
Black-eyed Susan				
Blanket flower				
Blue oat grass				
Blue star				
Bluebeard				
Boltonia				
Bush clematis				
Butterfly weed				
Cardinal flower				
Carpathian bellflower				
Catmint				
Checkerbloom				
Cheddar pink				
Chinese astilbe				
Christmas rose				
Chrysanthemum				
Clustered bellflower				
Columbine				
Columbine meadow rue				
Common beard-tongue				
Common sage				

PLANT NAME	SPRING (E M L)	SUM. (E M L)	FALL (E M L)	WINTER (E M L)
Common yarrow				
Compact pincushion flower				
Coneflower				
Coral bells				
Cowslip				
Creeping baby's breath				
Creeping phlox				
Creeping veronica				
Crested iris				
Crimson pincushion				
Crocosmia				
Daylily				
Delphinium				
English primrose				
Evening primrose				
False indigo				
False Solomon's seal				
Feather reed grass				
Fern-leaf yarrow				
Fleabane				
Foamy bells				
Fragrant bugbane				
Frikart's aster				
Garden phlox				
Gas plant				
Gayfeather				
Germander				
Geum				
Giant coneflower				
Globe thistle				
Gloriosa daisy				
Goatsbeard				
Goldenrod				
Goldenstar				
Ground clematis				
Hardy begonia				
Hardy hibiscus				
Heart-leaf bergenia				
Heart-leaf brunnera				
Hollyhock				

E = early   M = mid   L = late

PLANT NAME	SPRING			SUM.			FALL			WINTER		
	E	M	L	E	M	L	E	M	L	E	M	L
Horned violet		█	█									
Hosta			█	█	█							
Hybrid agastaches				█	█							
Hybrid anemone						█	█					
Hybrid astilbe			█									
Hybrid cinquefoil				█	█							
Hybrid foam flower		█	█									
Hybrid lobelia				█	█							
Hybrid mullein				█								
Hybrid speedwell				█								
Hybrid violet		█										
Hybrid yarrow				█	█							
Jacob's ladder			█									
Japanese iris				█								
Joe-Pye weed						█	█					
Labrador violet				█								
Lady's mantle			█	█								
Lamb's-ears			█	█								
Lavender				█	█							
Lavender cotton				█	█							
'Lavender Mist' meadow rue				█								
Lenten rose	█	█	█						█	█	█	█
Lilyturf				█	█	█	█					
Louisiana iris				█								
Lungwort	█	█										
Maiden grass					█	█	█	█				
Maiden pink				█	█							
Maltese cross				█								
Marsh marigold	█	█										
Masterwort				█								
Meadow rue				█								
Meadowsweet				█								
Moss phlox	█	█										
Nepal cinquefoil				█								
Nettle-leaved mullein				█								
Northern sea oats							█	█				
Obedient plant						█						
Old-fashioned bleeding heart			█									
Olympic mullein				█								
Oriental hybrid lily				█	█							
Oriental poppy			█									
Ornamental onion			█	█	█							
Ornamental oregano				█	█							
Ozark sundrops				█	█							
Pacific bleeding heart			█	█								
Pasque flower	█	█										
Patrinia					█							

PLANT NAME	SPRING			SUM.			FALL			WINTER		
	E	M	L	E	M	L	E	M	L	E	M	L
Peach-leaf bellflower				█	█							
Peony			█	█								
Perennial fountain grass	█	█	█	█	█	█	█					
Perennial salvia				█	█							
Pincushion flower				█	█							
Pink coreopsis				█	█	█						
Purple coneflower						█	█	█	█			
Queen-of-the-prairie				█	█							
Reblooming bearded iris			█	█								
Reblooming daylily				█	█							
Rodgersia				█	█							
Rose campion				█	█							
Russian sage			█	█	█	█	█					
Sea holly				█	█							
Shasta daisy			█	█								
Showy evening primrose			█	█	█							
Siberian iris			█									
Siebold primrose			█									
Smooth white penstemon				█	█							
Sneezeweed						█	█	█				
Snowdrop anemone			█	█								
Solitary clematis				█	█	█	█					
Spike speedwell				█	█							
Spotted bellflower				█	█							
Spring cinquefoil			█									
Star astilbe				█	█							
Stokes' aster				█	█							
Sweet violet		█	█									
Switch grass							█	█	█	█	█	█
Thinleaf perennial sunflower							█	█				
Threadleaf coreopsis				█	█	█						
Thrift			█	█								
Thunberg bush clover							█	█				
Toad lily					█	█	█	█				
Torch lily			█	█	█							
Tree mallow				█	█							
Turk's-cap lily				█	█							
Variegated Solomon's seal		█	█									
Wherry's foam flower	█	█	█									
White gaura				█	█	█						
Woodland phlox		█	█									
Woolly speedwell				█	█							
Yellow corydalis				█	█	█						
Yellow foxglove			█	█	█							
Yellow meadow rue				█	█							
Yellow waxbells							█	█				
Yucca				█	█	█	█					

GROWING

PERENNIALS

In this chapter you'll discover the best ways to give your plants what they need. You'll learn how to plant perennials successfully as well as how to water, feed, and mulch them. You'll also learn that just like people, perennials need good nutrition and water to survive and thrive.

Although weeds are part of every gardener's life, you'll make your life easier if you keep them from getting out of hand. With the right tools and weed control products targeted to different types of weeds, you'll see just how easy it is to create a weed-free garden for you and your family to enjoy.

Garden tasks include staking your perennials for the best display. This chapter demonstrates several easy staking methods for different shaped plants. It also offers plant grooming hints to enhance the presentation of your blooms.

Over time, most perennials need dividing to stay vigorous and beautiful, and this chapter shows you how to do the job. To keep all of these tasks in order and to simplify your gardening responsibilities, a list of seasonal chores at the end of the chapter will help keep you on track. By consulting these short simple lists for spring, summer, fall, and winter, remembering what to do and when to do it will be a breeze.

There's no time like now to make a new perennial garden! Watch your dreams take shape as you prepare the soil, make necessary improvements, and lay out the garden before planting. Then it's time to shop. Search online, study mail-order catalogs, and check out local nurseries and garden centers, where you can browse up and down rows of tempting blooms. Garden making is fun and easy when you take it step-by-step.

After removing the sod, rototill the soil to break up the clods. Add the necessary amendments and organic matter, then till again.

PREPARING SOIL IS like cooking a healthy meal. You start with a recipe that takes into account what is nourishing and how much of each ingredient you need. Like people, soils change over time, and requirements for growth and maintenance may vary from year to year. Soil tests help gardeners keep up with these changes and ensure they use the correct recipe.

Soil tests measure soil fertility. Fertility describes how much and what kind of mineral nutrition is available to your plants at the time of the test. Soil tests also measure soil pH, or relative acidity and alkalinity, on a scale from 0 (low/very acid) to 14 (high/very alkaline). Plants may have difficulty absorbing the necessary nutrients from the soil when the pH falls at either extreme. Most garden plants thrive in slightly acid soil with a pH around 6.5.

Soil tests also measure levels of organic matter in the soil. Organic matter, is composed of decomposing plant and animal materials. Adding organic matter can keep nutrients from washing away in sandy soils, and it helps aerate clay soils. Plants tend to be healthier when grown in soils high in organic matter.

Fall is an ideal time to test soil. Because soil-testing laboratories are less bogged down with samples than in spring, you'll receive the results in plenty of time to prepare your soil before the planting season gets under way. Contact your county cooperative extension service or a private testing laboratory for directions on submitting samples.

Lawns, shrub beds, flower borders, and vegetable gardens have varying growth and nutrient requirements, so each area should be tested separately. If putting in several perennial borders, test each of these spaces individually, too, because slopes, low-lying areas, and spots near the foundation could have different soil conditions.

[1] Before digging, you'll need to take several samples from around your garden when testing the soil. First, clear the area where you plan to take the sample. Lift the sod or scrape off any mulch. Also rake up twigs, thatch, leaves, and other debris on the soil surface.

[2] Dig the holes about 8 inches deep. One hole per 100 square feet should be adequate. (For lawns, dig one hole per 1,000 square feet.) From the bottom of each hole, scoop a trowelful of soil and put it in a clean plastic pail. Mix the samples together, then let this mixture dry.

[3] Once the soil is dry, measure 1 to 2 cups of soil and place it in the bag provided by the laboratory. Fill out the paperwork for the lab tests.

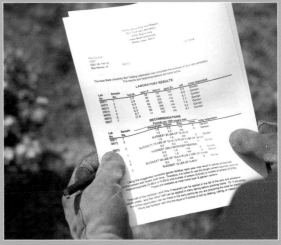

[4] You will receive the test results in the mail. Study the results, and apply fertilizer and other soil amendments at the suggested rate.

MATERIALS NEEDED

- Rake
- Narrow trowel, spade, or soil probe
- Clean plastic pail

technique: improve the soil

ONCE YOU RECEIVE THE RESULTS of your soil test, you're ready to make the improvements necessary for a beautiful perennial garden. The test results will provide recommendations on which amendments your soil requires and the amounts to use. Possible soil amendments include organic matter, which will condition the soil and provide small amounts of nutrients; plant food to ensure the soil holds adequate nutrients to meet your perennials' needs; and lime or sulfur to alter soil pH. Think of it this way: The organic matter feeds and conditions the soil; fertilizers get plants off to a healthy, uniform, and dependable start.

Good organic soil conditioners include compost, leaf mold, and aged manure. You can buy these materials in bulk or make the compost and leaf mold at home. Bagged commercial products are also available, including Miracle-Gro Garden Soil, which contains peat moss, manure, compost, and plant food. Adding organic materials to soil improves the structure of clay and sandy soils. They help to loosen clay so that air and water move more readily through the soil; and they help to improve the water- and nutrient-holding ability of sandy soils. Organic materials are often a good source of micronutrients, which they release over an extended period of time.

When it comes to plant food, you have a choice between organic products, such as blood meal, bonemeal, fish emulsion, and Miracle-Gro Organic Choice Garden Fertilizer, and conventional plant foods. Organic products provide low doses of nutrients over a long period. Conventional plant foods offer low cost and fast results. They come in several formulations including ones that provide immediate feeding and those that feed over an extended period.

Complete plant foods contain all three of the major nutrients: nitrogen, phosphorus, and potassium. Most plant foods are available as a water-soluble powder, a condensed liquid, or solid granules. The granules will be the easiest to use when amending soil before planting the bed. Follow soil test recommendations for the amount to use.

Lime, a natural product derived from limestone, raises soil pH (makes it more alkaline) and increases the soil's calcium and magnesium levels. Sulfur lowers soil pH (makes it more acidic). Soil test recommendations are usually aimed at bringing the pH to the neutral to slightly acid range.

[1] Begin by marking an approximate outline of the garden's boundaries with stakes and string (for straight edges) and rope or garden hose (for curves). Step back and check the shape of the garden and its size and location. This is your first full-scale look at how the garden will appear in its surroundings. If you don't like what you see, making changes is as easy as pulling up and moving the stakes. To ensure that the garden is exactly the size you planned, measure it with the 50-foot tape and make adjustments as necessary. You can also simply adjust the size and shape of the garden until you find a balance that pleases you, then measure it and adjust the number of plants you buy.

MATERIALS NEEDED

- Stakes
- String
- Rope or garden hose
- 50-foot tape measure
- Landscape paint
- Sod lifter, spade, or sod cutter
- Spade, tiller, or garden fork
- Nonselective herbicide, such as Roundup
- Miracle-Gro or Organic Choice Garden Soil or other organic matter, such as compost, well-rotted manure, or leaf mold
- Fertilizer, such as Miracle-Gro Bloom Booster Plant Food
- Rake

[2] Mark the final outline of the bed with landscape paint, then remove the stakes, string, ropes, or hoses.

[3] Remove the sod from within the bed. One way to do this is to cut under the sod with a spade, making short jabs with the spade as a helper pulls up on the sod. Several types of sod lifters are also available, including a power sod cutter.

[4] Break up the soil with a rotary tiller or a spade, then let the garden sit for a week. If any weeds or stray sprigs of grass pop up, pull them or spray them with Roundup. Repeat this process at least two more times, or until weeds and grass cease to be a problem.

[5] Spread a 2- to 4-inch-layer of soil conditioner, such as compost, leaf mold, aged manure, or Miracle-Gro Garden Soil (regular or Organic Choice) over the garden. If your soil test results included a recommendation for organic matter, use the amounts specified.

[6] Top the material with plant food, following soil test recommendations. Till, spade, or fork the amendments into the top 6 inches of garden soil. Do not dig when the soil is wet, because doing so can wreck the soil's structure.

[7] Break up clods and remove large rocks and debris that you unearth during the digging process. Rake the soil surface smooth.

technique: improve drainage

Growing perennials in raised beds improves drainage and allows you to control the soil's composition.

SOIL IS A MIX of solids—minerals, decomposing plants, and live organisms such as worms, fungi, and bacteria—and voids between the solids, which hold water or air. These voids or pores are among the most important of soil components, allowing water and oxygen to move through the soil to nourish roots. The ideal soil is well-drained, with about half the pore space filled with air and the other half with water. In wet situations where water fills nearly all of the pores, roots become oxygen starved, which causes plants to wilt.

TIP SOMETIMES PEOPLE THINK THAT ADDING SAND TO HEAVY CLAY SOIL HELPS TO INCREASE DRAINAGE. WHAT IT REALLY DOES IS MAKE THE SOIL AS HARD AS CONCRETE!

If your soil is soggy and you want to grow plants that prefer drier conditions, build a raised bed. Raising a bed uses gravity to aid drainage.

A raised bed can be framed with wood or other material and filled with topsoil such as Miracle-Gro Garden Soil. Or it can be made by spreading topsoil over the area and raking it into a berm. Make sure the topsoil is enriched with organic matter, which tends to be airy and promotes conditions that create pore space.

Take the drainage test on page 71 to determine how high to raise the bed, then follow these steps to create a berm-style raised bed.

STEP BY STEP

[1] Measure and mark the outline of the bed as described on page 86 and 87. Clear the area of rocks, sticks, or trash, then break up the soil with a rotary tiller or spade and remove visible weeds or grass. Dig down as deep as the bed will be high, about 8 to 12 inches for perennials. (You won't be removing this soil, just breaking it up.)

[2] Determine how much topsoil you will need for your bed. Figure the garden's square footage, then multiply that amount by the height you plan to raise the bed. You should build up the garden an inch for every inch of water remaining in the drainage-test hole one day after flooding the hole (see page 71).

[3] Order topsoil. Topsoil comes in bulk by the truck-load or in bags. For a large garden, ordering in bulk is the most efficient approach. However, you must be sure of your source. Ask that the supplier certify the soil. Before the driver dumps the soil, check it out. Grab a handful, moisten it, and work it in your palm. If the soil is heavy clay, reject the shipment.

[4] Spread a few inches of the topsoil over the garden, then till it into the existing soil. This helps create a transition between the existing soil and the topsoil that ensures there's no abrupt change in drainage patterns.

MATERIALS NEEDED

- 100-foot tape measure or yardstick, depending on bed size
- Landscape paint
- Spade or tiller
- Topsoil
- Rake

[5] Spread the remaining topsoil over the garden, and rake it smooth.

[6] Berm the soil, sloping the edges toward the center. The sides of the bed slant in at a 45-degree angle and the top is flat and smooth.

buying plants

ABOVE: Although local nurseries and garden centers may not have the biggest selection of perennials, the ones they sell generally will thrive in local conditions.

You've researched your conditions and prepared the bed. Now it's time for every gardener's delight: plant shopping. Check out local nurseries, garden centers, and fund-raising plant sales at schools, churches, and plant societies. And worry not. If you can't find exactly what you want near home, your dream perennials are as close as your mailbox.

There are few differences between local and mail-order perennials. Local sources often have lower or similar prices as mail-order ones. Their plants are generally larger and often come with a one-year guarantee if the plant dies. Mail-order sources offer access to a much wider selection.

The best nurseries have trained staff to answer gardening questions and help you find what you need. If you can do without advice and like to browse and experiment with plants, take advantage of big

chain stores, which offer a wide selection of perennials, ornamental grasses, and supplies at low prices. Charity plant sales and divisions from friends are two more ways to expand your garden at little cost.

Most perennials come in 4-inch pots, 1-gallon containers, or inexpensive plugs, which are young plants with a root ball resembling a wine cork or a small wedge. Mostly available through mail-order sources, plugs take longer to reach maturity than 4-inch or 1-gallon plants. Most 4-inch perennials will reach their mature size within two to three years. Occasionally you can find fully mature plants in extra-large pots. These usually cost a lot, but they make sense if your plan calls for slow-growing perennials, such as gas plant or false indigo.

Before buying, calculate the approximate square footage of each plant grouping in the bed. Divide the area by the perennial's mature width. The result will be the number of plants you need to buy for each grouping. You can find the width of many mature perennials in the plant selection guide at the end of this book. Plant width or recommended spacing may also be available on the plant label that the nursery provides.

At the nursery, look for strong stems

ABOVE: Check root balls before buying plants. Look for a fine network of roots evenly dispersed throughout the soil.
ABOVE RIGHT: Avoid potbound plants with tightly packed, encircling root systems.
RIGHT: Open boxes of mail-order perennials immediately after they arrive and plant as soon as possible.

and fresh, healthy foliage. Leave spindly plants on the shelf.

Also look for nonblooming plants. Perennials transplant better before they flower. Choose named cultivars if you need a particular color for your design.

Examine plants carefully, especially those from private gardens and fund-raisers. It's easy to bring insects and diseases home from other people's gardens. Check the soil, stem, and both sides of leaves for insects, larvae, holes, or discoloration. Leaves should be uniformly green, unblemished, and appropriately sized. Small, limp leaves and dried brown leaf edges are signs of improper watering and poor health.

Check plant roots. Roots should form a fine visible network throughout the potting soil. Potbound plants, which have dense roots that circle the pot, do not transplant well.

MAIL-ORDER NURSERIES

Mail-order nurseries sometimes ship perennials bare-root. Bare-root plants should be dormant (not in active growth) when shipped. Look for a symmetrical root system and moist, fibrous white-tipped roots with no signs of damage or disease.

Because you can't inspect mail-order plants before buying them, you might want to limit your first orders until you get a sense of the quality and size of the plants provided by the nursery. Or, ask your gardening friends for their recommendations.

With your plan in hand, lay out the perennials still in their pots and check the design before planting.

THE FIRST STEP in planting perennials is to lay out the bed. This also is an excellent time to check the design.

Determine the location of plant groups by estimating their locations in the bed or by using reference points and measurements from the planting plan.

Arrange the plants, still in their pots, according to your design so that you can preview the plan before planting.

If the bed doesn't look as you had hoped it would, move the plants around. For a bed that lacks visual unity, try repeating a plant group throughout the garden. If the layout looks bland, add three to five perennials with tall spire-like blooms near the front of the garden as an accent. Remember that gardens are not set in stone and that you can change your design at a later date.

[1] To place the plants where you specified in your design, create one or more reference points from which to measure in the garden. Find the center of the garden and mark the spot with a stake. In a large garden, measure a set distance on either side of the stake and mark those points as well. For example, if you have a kidney-shaped bed, make additional reference points at the center of each curved area.

[2] Site each plant group relative to the staked reference point. On the scaled drawing, measure the distance from the reference point to the center of each plant group, then transfer those measurements to the actual garden. Start with drifts near the center of the bed and work out toward the edges. Use chalk, lime, string, or landscaper's paint to outline the shape and location of the various drifts.

[3] Set the potted perennials in marked drifts. Use a ruler or tape measure for accurate spacing between plants. For example, allow 1 square foot of space for a plant that grows 12 inches wide, measuring out 6 inches in all directions. If you're saving money by buying plants as plugs or in small pots, you can plant closer for a fuller effect. Keep in mind, however, that you'll have to weed out some of the plants as they mature. When placing potted perennials in the bed, avoid making straight rows. Offset plants, so that when they grow in, the results will look natural.

MATERIALS NEEDED

- Garden plan
- Tape measure/ruler
- Stakes
- Chalk, lime, or string
- Plants from the nursery

[4] Step back and study the bed to see if you like the design. Adjust the location and arrangement of the plants and the shape of the drifts until the design of the garden pleases you. On a piece of paper, note any areas that need more plants. Write the name of each plant along with an estimate of the additional number needed. Refer to your notes when buying more plants.

technique: planting perennials

WHEN YOU'RE READY TO PLANT. CHOOSE A CLOUDY DAY OR OTHER TIME WHEN THE SUN IS NOT INTENSE, ESPECIALLY WHEN PLANTING BARE-ROOT PERENNIALS. BECAUSE ROOTS CAN DRY OUT QUICKLY ON HOT, SUNNY, AND WINDY AFTERNOONS, PLANTING EARLY IN THE DAY IS USUALLY BEST.

container perennials

[1] Dig a generous hole with a trowel or spade. For 4-inch pots and smaller, use a trowel for digging. For larger pots, use a spade. In old beds where the soil hasn't been worked in a while, make the planting hole one to two times wider than the nursery pot, but no deeper. Dig so that the sides of the hole slope toward the center of the bottom. In well-prepared gardens, dig the hole as wide and as deep as the pot.

[2] Check the depth of the hole by setting the pot in it. The plant crown should be level with the surrounding soil. Planting perennials too deep invites stem- and crown-rot problems; planting too high, so that the perennial's shoulders sit above the surrounding ground, is likely to retard plant growth. You can check the level by laying the handle of your spade, a ruler, or other straight object over the hole. The top of the container soil should be even with the bottom of the handle.

[3] Take the plant out of the pot by flipping it over, keeping one hand stretched over the soil around the plant. Tap the pot with your other hand until the plant is free of the container. For a stubborn pot, rap the rim of the container against the edge of a table, a wheelbarrow, or a chair arm. Or roll the pot back and forth on the ground while firmly pressing on it.

[4] Tease apart any pot-bound roots encircling the root ball. Or make four shallow slices around the root ball with a sharp knife, cutting from the bottom to halfway up the root ball.

[5] Set the plant in the hole, evenly spreading the loosened roots. Recheck the depth of the crown or top of the potting soil, and adjust the depth of the hole as needed.

[6] Backfill the hole halfway, firming the soil with your hands. Then fill the hole with water to settle the soil. When the water has been absorbed, finish backfilling the hole; firm the soil and water again. Use a gentle spray, such as from a water breaker, a fan-spray sprinkler, or a flood bubbler, to avoid splashing the soil out of the hole.

[1] Trim dead or broken roots off of the bare roots, then soak the roots in a pail of water to rehydrate any dry ones. Take care to keep the other roots intact, because the bigger and healthier the root system at planting, the faster a bare-root perennial will take off when growth begins in spring.

[2] After a one-hour soaking, it's time to plant your bare-root perennial. Dig a hole as wide as the spread-out roots and as deep as the roots reach.

[3] At the center of the hole, form a mound of soil. This mound helps to keep the plant at the right depth in the hole, and it helps to anchor the plant while you fill the hole. Form the mound by scraping dirt in the bottom of the hole into a pile high enough that the crown or eyes (buds on the roots) sit just below the soil surface.

MATERIALS NEEDED

- Trowel or transplant spade
- Sharp knife
- Watering can or hose and sprinkler

[4] Set the plant on the mound and evenly spread its roots over the soil. Follow step 6 on the facing page to finish planting your bare-root perennial.

[5] Mulch the entire garden, bare root and container perennials alike. Leave at least an inch of bare ground around each plant. This prevents moisture from accumulating around plant crowns, which can lead to root and crown rot.

technique: planting container gardens

Simple combinations work perfectly in container gardens. This planting includes variegated 'Stairway to Heaven' Jacob's ladder and dark-leafed 'Chocolate' white snakeroot (*Eupatorium rugosum*).

MATERIALS NEEDED

- Ornamental containers
- Miracle-Gro potting mix
- Perennials for planting (4-inch to 2-gallon pots)
- Trowel or small shovel
- Watering can or hose and sprinkler
- Sharp knife

CONTAINER GARDENS are fun to grow and easy to plant. Keep in mind that the container should be large enough to accommodate a full-size perennial, and it needs one or more drainage holes. If the container you like has no drainage, drill holes into the bottom to make it usable.

Remember to choose the right size plants to fit your pot. A 1-gallon perennial or two 4-inch potted perennials should fit nicely into a 1-foot-diameter decorative container. Larger containers accommodate larger or more numerous plants. Thus an ornamental pot 18 inches in diameter could contain a 2-gallon perennial or three perennials in 4-inch pots.

If plants ever outgrow their containers, you can either divide and repot them or move them into the garden.

[1] If your container doesn't have a drainage hole, drill one or more holes in the pot. Use a masonry bit for terra-cotta or pottery containers. A regular bit is fine for plastic and fiberglass pots.

[2] Fill the container three-quarters full with soil specially formulated for containers, such as Miracle-Gro Potting Mix or Miracle-Gro Moisture Control Potting Mix. Set the plants on top of the soil, and recheck your arrangement from every viewpoint of significance. Also make sure that the top of each plant's root ball sits 1 to 3 inches below the rim of the container. If the perennials are level with the container rim, you'll have trouble watering.

[3] Remove the plants from their nursery pots by rapping their rims against the edge of the container. Turn each pot upside down, holding your hand over the nursery soil, and slip off the pot. If the roots are pot-bound and encircling the root ball, gently tease them apart, or slice the root ball shallowly on four sides from top to bottom with a sharp knife.

[4] Set the plants in the container, following the final design in Step 2. If necessary, adjust your design. Double check to make sure the depth of potting soil in the container is at the correct level.

[5] Scoop potting mix around the root balls, gently pushing it in to fill all empty spaces. Cover the root balls themselves with no more than ½ inch of mix. Firm the potting mix. Make sure you still have an inch or two of "head room" for watering. If you fill the container to the brim with potting mix, water will run over the sides instead of soaking into the mix.

[6] Water thoroughly with a slow, gentle spray. Fill the pot to the top, then let the water soak in until it drips from the drainage holes. Gently bounce the pot to eliminate any air pockets in the soil mix.

caring for your garden

Water early in the day so that leaves dry quickly as the day warms, which helps to prevent the diseases that develop on wet foliage. Also, because mornings tend to be calm, winds won't blow the water off target if you water then.

WATERING

Perennials need water to thrive. They use it to carry dissolved minerals—the nutrients for plant health and growth—from the soil to the leaves. As it moves through the plants, water gives plants structure. It exits the plant through tiny pores in the underside of the leaves in a process called transpiration. Transpiration helps cool plants on hot days. And as plants transpire, more water is pulled up into the roots, through the plants, and out the pores. Water transpires more quickly from plant leaves on hot, dry, or windy days, sometimes faster than it can move up from the plant's roots.

When you water a garden, water travels down into the soil, filling tiny pores—or air pockets—between soil particles. In clay soils, water moves slowly, sometimes pooling on the soil surface. In porous sandy soils, gravity pulls water down fast. Typically, the longer you water one spot, the deeper the water moves, filling the soil's air pockets and saturating the soil.

The right amount of water for your perennial garden depends on the plants you grow, the amount of rainfall in your area, and how hot, sunny, and windy the day. Ideally, perennials should receive about an inch of water each week of the growing season. Even drought-tolerant perennials benefit from regular watering, especially while they are becoming established after planting.

A little water each day is not enough for most garden plants. It is better to water your plants deeply and at length once a week. Light watering promotes shallow roots that draw their moisture from the surface soil. Deep watering encourages longer roots and a stronger root system better adapted to times of drought. The wider and deeper a perennial's root system, the more extensive the area from which it pulls moisture and nutrients from the soil.

Watering slowly is also a good idea. Slow watering allows the soil to absorb surface moisture. If you apply water fast, it puddles on the ground before it is absorbed; pooled water can evaporate before it benefits your plants.

Install drip and soaker hoses early in the year before the plants have filled out. Before long, the mature foliage of the perennials will cover most of the hose.

HERE ARE SOME TIPS FOR EFFECTIVE WATERING:

- Group your perennials by their cultural needs. Keep drought-tolerant plants separate from those that need abundant moisture.
- Water seedlings and new transplants frequently until they are established.
- Remember that even drought-tolerant plants need extra water during periods of prolonged drought.
- Add organic matter to the soil to increase its ability to retain water.
- Apply a 3-inch layer of mulch to your flower beds to cool the soil and discourage evaporation from the soil surface. If you use soaker hoses to water the garden, you can set them out, then hide them under a cover of mulch.

There are several ways to water your perennial garden slowly and deeply. One is to use inexpensive soaker hoses. Because they apply water directly to the ground without shooting it into the air, minimal evaporation occurs when watering with these hoses. Wind them through your beds in spring, leaving them in place throughout the growing season. As the plants grow, they'll cover up the hoses, or you can hide the hoses under a blanket of mulch. When you're ready to water, simply connect the soaker to a garden hose and turn on the spigot.

Automatic systems are more costly to install but offer more options, from bubblers to sprinklers to drip systems. In the long run, automatic systems with rain

sensors help save water, time, and effort, and give you the ability to water the garden even when you're out of town.

Hand-watering perennials using a fan nozzle attached to a hose suits certain garden situations. For example, tender seedlings recently transplanted into the garden benefit from gentle hand-watering.

If you decide to use an overhead sprinkler in your perennial garden, set it to deliver about 1 inch of water every four or five days, depending on how well your soil holds moisture. Water early in the morning when winds are calm to ensure the water isn't blown off target or evaporated before it reaches plants and avoid watering at night because moisture on the foliage may promote disease.

ABOVE: Water moves through soil in a sort of bell-shape pattern that is narrow on top and broad at the bottom. Place soaker hoses close enough to your plants that the broad portion reaches their roots.

FEEDING

Just as good nutrition helps people grow strong, it also supports vigorous growth and abundant blooms for plants. Healthy perennials resist pests, diseases, and environmental stresses better than their less sturdy counterparts. In the wild, nature supplies all the nutrient needs of plants, but in gardens where they must always look their best, nature can't always keep up. Instead, it's up to you to meet perennials' nutritional needs. The key nutrients for vibrant growth are nitrogen, phosphorus, and potassium.

Perennials grown for gorgeous leaves require abundant nitrogen, which aids leafy growth. For fabulous flowers and root growth, plants need phosphorus and potassium. Using plant food formulated for flowering plants, such as Miracle-Gro Shake 'n Feed Continuous-Release Bloom Booster, ensures the proper balance of nutrients to encourage maximum bloom.

TIP AFTER APPLYING GRANULAR PLANT FOOD AROUND YOUR PERENNIALS, WATER THE GARDEN THOROUGHLY TO ENCOURAGE THE ABSORPTION OF NUTRIENTS INTO THE SOIL.

The best time to feed perennials is during the period starting when growth begins in early spring and lasting until flower buds develop. For summerlong effects, use a controlled-release fertilizer such as Osmocote Smart Release Plant Food or Miracle-Gro Shake 'n Feed Continuous-Release Plant Food.

A foolproof recipe for feeding perennial transplants consists of scratching in a slow-release plant food at planting, then watering in the transplants with Miracle-Gro Water-Soluble All-Purpose Plant Food. Two weeks later, follow up with another dose of liquid fertilizer. For the rest of the growing season, the slow-release plant food will meet your perennials' nutrient needs.

Water-soluble fertilizers provide immediate effects, but you need to use them more frequently than continuous-release plant foods, typically every 7 to 14 days. Dry water-soluble plant foods are available as pellets or granules and should be applied about once a month. Slow-release plant foods last for months and need just one or two applications during the entire growing season.

No matter which type of plant food you use, read the label carefully to determine the correct amount to apply and how to apply it for optimal results.

ABOVE: Apply liquid or soluble plant food every two weeks for maximum flowering and plant growth.
LEFT: If using a granular plant food, apply it to the soil around the base of your perennials, then scratch it into the soil with a small garden fork or hand rake.
OPPOSITE PAGE: The ergonomic Miracle-Gro LiquaFeed is calibrated to apply plant food at the correct rate. The fertilizer is premixed and comes in handy pint bottles.

Shredded bark mulch and other organic mulches help to smother weeds, increase soil moisture retention, moderate soil temperature, and, after they decompose, improve soil texture.

MULCHING

Once you discover the benefits of mulch, you'll never want to do without it. A layer of organic mulch such as shredded bark, leaf mold, and pine needles helps unify your garden's appearance and makes it look tidy and attractive. Mulch can also decrease garden maintenance.

Mulch increases the soil's ability to retain moisture by protecting the soil surface from wind and sun, both of which increase evaporation. It also moderates soil temperature, thus promoting healthy root systems. Organic mulches improve the soil by breaking down into fertile humus when they decompose. Mulching helps to smother weeds by blocking the light and air that their seeds need to germinate and grow.

The list of popular organic mulches varies by region. Pine needles, leaf mold (crushed dried leaves), cocoa hulls, coffee grounds, shredded bark, bark chips, salt hay, gravel, and homemade or commercial composts are just a few of the organic mulches available. (If you have dogs, be aware that cocoa hulls contain the same toxic chemical as chocolate.)

Look for mulch products bearing Mulch and Soil Council Certification to ensure the product is made from natural materials. Avoid mulches made from reprocessed woods, such as pallets, timbers, or scrap wood salvaged from buildings destroyed by hurricanes and other natural disasters. The wood in these materials could have been treated with CCA (copper chromate arsenate).

Apply mulches that break down into humus within 12 to 18 months (leaves, compost, salt hay, or cocoa hulls) 2 to 3 inches deep. Use only 1 to 2 inches of mulches that break down slowly, such as bark or wood chips. Keep mulch about an inch away from the stems and crown of your perennials.

Renew the mulch layer as it thins and as necessary after spring thaws and rains but before weed seeds germinate. This job is easy to do when you have the right tool. A well-balanced mulch fork can make the difference between a quick job and a sore, tired back.

You can also mulch perennial container gardens with a fine organic mulch such as cocoa hulls or with decorative pebbles or gravel.

Mulches come in many forms. Some of the best and most widely available include cocoa hulls, shredded bark, small or mini bark pieces, pea gravel, and large bark chunks.

MINI BARK

PEA GRAVEL

SHREDDED CEDAR

LARGE BARK

COCOA SHELLS

Staked perennials may look odd in spring, but by early summer when the plants have filled out and matured, the stakes become nearly invisible, hidden by the foliage.

MOST PERENNIALS stand up by themselves. Sometimes, however, plants with large flowers and thin stems need a little help. In fact, the richer and moister your soil, the more you may need to stake the lush growth that these conditions promote.

Staking keeps soft-stemmed or top-heavy perennials upright and strengthens them in wind and rain. When a plant is properly staked, its foliage hides the supports.

Stake perennials early in the season when they are small, so their leaves and stems grow up naturally through the support.

Staking techniques are as abundant as the fertile imagination allows. They range from commercial metal stakes with a dark green coating that blends with the foliage to natural support from twigs and other flowering plants. Indeed, no right or wrong methods for staking perennials exist, so experiment and find ways that work well for you and your garden.

> **TIP** THERE'S NO RIGHT OR WRONG STAKING METHOD FOR PERENNIALS. DO WHAT WORKS BEST FOR YOU AND YOUR PLANT.

STAKING A MULTISTEMMED PERENNIAL

[1] Use stakes that are 8 to 12 inches longer than the mature height of your perennial. Insert three to five stakes—or more for large plants—at equal distances around multistemmed perennials such as peony or chrysanthemum. Position the stakes just inside the outer row of stems to hide them. Push the stakes several inches into the ground.

[2] Attach twine to the first stake about a foot above the ground. Weave the twine around the other stakes until you've encircled the entire clump. Each time you wrap the twine around a stake, loop it twice for stability.

[3] Crisscross the twine across the clump and above the plant, tying to the opposite stake and creating a star pattern. A second star pattern farther up the stakes helps to keep tall perennials from flopping over. You can tie this second tier now, or wait a few weeks to do so.

[4] Make sure that the tops of the stakes are shorter than the plant's mature height. If necessary, clip the stakes to keep them appropriately sized. As the perennial grows, slip loose stems inside the staking framework to keep them erect.

MATERIALS NEEDED

- Green or tan bamboo or metal stakes
- Twine
- Pruners

ABOVE: Protect a tender stem from harm by tying it to a stake with a figure-eight knot that loops once around the plant.
RIGHT: You can buy many types of stakes, including this sturdy single-stem stake, at local nurseries and garden centers.

MORE STAKING METHODS

Homemade and commercial staking systems abound.

pea brush Another staking method you can try with multistemmed perennials is pea brush. These are simply branched twigs set into the soil near a floppy plant for support. Prunings from butterfly bush or any other twiggy shrub will do the job. For best results, arrange the twigs over emerging perennials, which will grow through the twigs as the season progresses. Pea brush works with most clump-forming perennials, including lilies and Shasta daisies.

mesh cages These give sprawling perennials such as baby's breath, asters, or 'The Pearl' yarrow the support they require. Make a chicken wire cylinder a bit narrower than the mature width of the plant. Set it over the perennial early in the season, tying the edges together with twine or threading a stake through the overlapped edges and into the ground. Thread a few more stakes through the wire mesh to hold the cage in place.

grid stakes Sometimes called peony cages, grid stakes are effective commercial staking systems. These usually have three $1\frac{1}{2}$- to 2-foot legs attached to a flat circular grid. Press the legs into the ground over the emerging plant. Stems grow up through the grid; by the time the plant flowers, the grid is hidden. Peonies do especially well with this type of support. The grid holds up the blooms, preventing them from falling over in wind and rain.

single-stakes Perennials such as foxglove, delphinium, and hollyhock that have tall stems topped by heavy flower spikes may need individual stakes to stay standing. Insert a long stake into the ground next to a stem. Bind the stem to the stake in several places with twine, Velcro plant ties, padded wire, raffia, or old nylon stockings.

To tie, make a figure eight with the binding. Fasten twine to the stake, then loop it around the stem. Cross back over the twine and tie the end to the stake. Leave enough slack for the stem to move.

no-stake staking You can also use strong-stemmed plants to hold up floppy neighbors, making staking unnecessary. Lax-stemmed plants, such as white gaura and clematis, weave in and out of sturdy plants nearby, creating pleasant contrasts in shape and texture. Blazing star, salvia, and many grasses are effective supports for weavers.

CLOCKWISE: *Above left*, Staking with pea brush means to support plants with twigs set into the soil. *Above right*, Set a commercial grid over an emerging bushy perennial such as false indigo; as the "bush" grows, it covers the metal stake. *Lower right*, The loose billows of lady's mantle blooms get help in standing up from stronger-stemmed blue-flowered catmint (*Nepeta subsessilis*). *Lower left*, Use a bamboo stake to support a single long stem with a heavy flower head at the top.

ABOVE: Once a perennial such as this hosta has finished flowering, deadhead by cutting off spent flower stalks with pruners. This improves the plant's appearance and keeps it from setting seed.

GROOMING

Just as regular haircuts help people look their best, timely grooming benefits beautiful perennial gardens. Deadheading, pinching, disbudding, and cutting back perennials make gardens look good, and these activities keep plants healthy and free from the pests and diseases that could plague an overgrown garden. To groom perennials, carry pruners on your garden strolls and take these simple steps.

deadhead If you see faded flowers on your perennials, cut them off with pruners or snap them off between thumb and forefinger. Deadheading improves a plant's appearance and keeps it from spreading by seed. Because the plants aren't allowed to go to seed, deadheading may also extend flowering or encourage the plant to produce a second wave of blooms. With perennials that bloom on tall stalks, deadhead by removing the entire flowering stem when nearly all of the flowers have faded. For perennials that have single flowers or that bloom on branched stems, cut off individual flowers as they fade; remove the stems when all blooms are spent.

cut back To encourage fresh foliage and, in some cases, a second flush of

To pinch a perennial, remove the growing tips by squeezing the soft stem tips between your thumb and forefinger. Or cut off the tips.

BELOW: Use pruners to cut back perennials after blooming. Snip old flower stems to the ground or to basal leaves, which are often larger than stem leaves.

BOTTOM: Neaten the appearance of daylilies by snapping off individual faded flowers at their base, using your thumb and forefinger. Take care to not knock off remaining flower buds.

bloom, prune the stems of straggly, fast-growing early bloomers such as catmint, spiderwort, and lungwort to the ground in July. After you have pruned them, these perennials will quickly regrow into handsome compact mounds.

pinch Pinching in late spring promotes a bushy habit. The shorter plants that result may need no staking. Pinching is easy. With shears, pruners, or thumb and forefinger, remove the soft, young growing tips at the end of the stems. If you pinch the entire plant all at once, you'll ensure a fabulous display of flowers. By spreading out the pinching phase, you can lengthen the period of bloom. Be aware that pinching delays flowering. If you are trying to time your garden's peak bloom for a special event, pinching will affect the schedule.

disbud You can manipulate perennials such as peonies and chrysanthemums to create large, show-stopping-size blooms or to increase the number of flowers. For large, high-quality flowers, remove side buds early in the season but leave the bud at the tip of the flowering stem. Pinch off the bud at the end of each flowering stem if you want a lot of blooms and don't care if they are smaller than normal.

This short-handled hoe is a good tool for weeding in tight areas between desirable plants. For best results with this tool, slice the weed below it's crown.

WEED CONTROL

Any plant that you don't want in your garden is a weed. Even the perennials you so lovingly planted can become weeds if they self-sow and spread into spots you didn't plan on them growing in. Weeds make a mess of your design and vie with your flowers for light, water, and nutrients. With the right tools, weeding can be painless.

Mulching and applying preemergence weed controls stop weeds from moving into your garden. A 2-inch layer of organic mulch smothers annual weeds by depriving them of the light and air they need to germinate. Preemergence weed controls such as Miracle-Gro Garden Weed Preventer keep weed

seeds from germinating and seedlings from developing. Apply them in early spring. First, remove any existing weeds, smooth the soil, then apply the control. Spread mulch over the soil, then water to activate the weed control.

If weeds have already germinated, your options for eliminating them are to pull, cultivate, or spray them with a postemergence herbicide such as Roundup. Tackle this job before the weeds set seed, or you may end up with even more weeds the next year.

Many tools are available for weeding. Fishtail weeders and garden forks loosen soil around the roots and pry up the crown of the weed as you pull. Well-sharpened hoes effectively slice off roots.

Short-handled hand tools allow more control of the process than long-handled ones, especially when working in tight corners. When using them, you're less likely to slice off the roots of your perennials, but they are harder on your back. A way to get around this is to use long-handled tools in the open areas between plant drifts, where you can see the hoe's head, then switch to hand tools when weeding right next to the plants. Take out the entire root of the weed; otherwise, it may grow back.

Most available postemergence herbicides will damage your perennials as readily as they kill weeds, so use them carefully. Apply the herbicide on a calm, windless day to prevent drift—microscopic spray droplets that float easily in

the air to damage or kill nearby plants. In close quarters, place a large sheet of cardboard beside or around a particular weed to block the spray from splattering neighboring perennials. If the weed touches the desirable plant, you can paint the weed's foliage with Roundup, Take care to not drip it on other plants.

Perennial weeds such as dandelions or bermudagrass present different challenges. Spray a systemic herbicide such as Roundup on them, taking precautions to protect neighboring plants. Or use a knife weeder to remove taprooted perennials such as dandelions. Insert the steel shaft into the soil, catch the base of the taproot in the v-notch of the weeder, and force the plant up.

ABOVE: Save time on maintenance later in the season by applying weed preventer before weed seeds germinate. Weed preventers work by stopping germination or by keeping seedlings from fully developing. **RIGHT:** This fork weeder works well on plantain and on young dandelions before their taproot grows too long. Slip the tines under the plant's crown and pop the weed out of the ground.

WEEDING WISDOM

Walk in your garden weekly, removing young weeds before they mature. Avoid shaking soil off the roots of pulled weeds, because any seeds that have set can fall on the ground where they will germinate in the warmth and light. Rather than tossing weeds on your compost pile, throw them in the trash, where even if their seeds germinate, the weeds won't spread in your garden. Similarly, avoid leaving pulled weeds in the garden to dry and decay; the plants may reroot, or seeds may germinate. When mulching, avoid using hay and unsterilized manure, both of which may contain viable weed seeds.

Plants in containers usually need more frequent watering than those in the ground. The amount of water depends upon the weather, the size and material of the pot, and the location of the container.

CARING FOR CONTAINER PERENNIAL GARDENS

Growing a container garden is similar to growing a garden in the ground. Wherever they live, perennials need water, nutrition, grooming, and light. Potted perennials, however, will need plant food and water more frequently. Because their roots are confined, they have no options for exploring and tapping into distant pockets of nutrients and water, like garden plants do.

watering Watering is critical to success in growing perennials in container gardens. Check the soil frequently to prevent water stress. Even a little stress can reduce the quality of the plants, leading to scorched leaves and reduced bloom.

The frequency of watering and the amount of water needed varies with the plant, the climate, and the size and material of your pot. The larger the plant, the hotter and windier the climate, and the smaller the pot, the more often you will need to water. Terra-cotta and unglazed pottery wicks water from the soil, so you need to pay attention to plants growing in those types of containers. Grouping containers together will help reduce heating and increase humidity levels around plants, in turn reducing the need for water and making watering more efficient.

Fill the space between the soil surface and the pot lip with water. Use a breaker-style nozzle to create a soft shower, which is easy on tender stems and keeps the water from "digging" holes in the soil. Stop when you see water running out of the drainage holes. Allow water to drain fully. If you've put a saucer underneath the pot, promptly empty it. Standing water rots root tips and provides a breeding ground for mosquitoes.

Avoid overwatering. Too much water in the soil mix suffocates plant roots. Feel deep into the soil to make sure that it is really dry.

feeding The more you water container gardens, the more nutrients are washed from the soil. And because plants are limited to whatever nutrients are in the pots, container-garden perennials are at risk of not getting enough nutrients. For healthy plants and optimal blooms, feed twice as often with half as much plant food as you would use for perennials that are growing in the ground.

During the first year of the container garden, regular feeding is less critical if the plants are growing in a potting soil that is premixed with continuous-release fertilizer granules. The granules supply nutrients for three months or more. But for best results, supplement the granules with Miracle-Gro All-Purpose Plant Food, using it at the labeled rate every 7 to 14 days.

In following years, you will need to pay much more attention to feeding. Replace the original dose of plant food that came in the potting soil with continuous-release plant food, such as Osmocote or Miracle-Gro Bloom Booster. Carefully scratch the granules into the soil surface, following label directions.

grooming Deadheading and staking are just as important to perennials that are growing in containers as those in the garden. Install stakes early in the season before plants begin to grow. With scissors or pruners, cut off spent flowers before the plants set seed, or simply pinch the stems below the flower. Maintain the form of the plant by trimming back stems that look too long for the overall form of the plant. With clean pruners, cut the stem just above a bud or a leaf. Also, turn containers at least once a week so that all sides of the plants receive adequate sunlight and develop at a similar rate.

overwintering Keeping perennial container gardens alive over the winter in cold climates can be a challenge. Cut back the plants as they stop growing. Water the container, then mulch to hold in the moisture. Moist potting mix is far more insulating than dry mix.

If the perennial is not hardy in your region, store it in a protected area, such as a cool basement or an unheated garage. Make sure the space isn't so warm that the plant continues growing, yet not so cold that temperatures drop below the plant's tolerance.

Hardy perennials can be left outside, but you will need to insulate their roots. A tidy way to do this is to wrap the container with several layers of bubble wrap, covering its sides and top. Next wrap a weatherproof tarp around the container, then top it off with burlap, which will make the insulation less obtrusive.

ABOVE: Regularly prune and turn the pots of perennials in a container garden to ensure that plants look attractive.
LEFT: In cold climates, you can overwinter hardy potted perennials by storing them in a shed or near a warm outdoor wall. Or, insulate the plants with bubble wrap, a weatherproof tarp and burlap.
BELOW: In spring, remove the insulation and gradually expose plants to outside temperatures. Placing potted perennials near a wall until all danger of frost has passed, will help to protect them from late freezes.

STRONG, HEALTHY perennials resist pests and diseases better than weak or exhausted ones, and perennials are strongest and healthiest when they have adequate room to grow. When your perennials grow too large for their spot in the garden, or when the vigor of the clump declines, it's time to divide them. Dividing means to dig up the plant, cut out and discard the oldest portions of the roots and crown, and slice the rest of the plant into smaller pieces. When you are through, you'll have plenty of "new" perennials that you can use to expand your garden or share with your friends and neighbors.

The time to divide perennials is fall for spring- and early-summer bloomers. Divide late-summer and fall bloomers in spring. This timing gives the roots plenty of time to become reestablished before the plants bloom again.

Make sure that your tools are clean before dividing the plants, to avoid transferring diseases.

TIP IF YOU'RE NOT SURE WHEN TO DIVIDE YOUR PERENNIALS, CHECK THE NUMBER OF BLOOMS. IF FLOWERS ARE FEWER THAN IN PREVIOUS YEARS, IT'S TIME TO DIG AND DIVIDE THEM.

STEP BY STEP

[1] Dig around the entire outer edge of the plant with a spade. Slice under the plant to free it from the ground. Keeping a sharp edge on the spade will ease cutting through woody roots.

[2] Lift the whole plant from the ground. If necessary, rinse off the roots so you can see what you're doing. This will make it easier to see the oldest and woodiest sections that show no new growth. Often, these are the inner portions of the clump. Cut away and discard these sections.

[3] With two garden forks, divide the remaining portions into smaller pieces. This technique works best with perennials that have multiple crowns, such as Shasta daisies, daylilies, bee balm, and coneflower. Each crown is essentially an individual plant with leaves and roots. Insert the forks into the clump back-to-back, then pry the handles apart to separate the plants.

[4] You can also cut the clumps with a sharp spade or knife, which works especially well for perennials with woody roots or thick rhizomes. Make sure that each chunk contains living roots and fresh eyes, buds, or young leaves.

MATERIALS NEEDED

- Spade
- Garden forks or sharp knife
- Hose and water
- Compost

[5] Replant the divisions. Mix compost, leaf mold, or Miracle-Grow Garden Soil into the planting area to replenish the soil.

seasonal chores

Since organic mulches like shredded bark break down into humus over time, you will need to refresh your mulch every two to three years, preferably in the spring.

Babying perennials soothes the spirit, while good gardening practices invigorate your plants. Moreover, regular grooming and maintenance ultimately save time, effort, and money; by being around the plants, you'll discover problems early enough to fix them.

SPRING

- Clean up beds: Remove debris. Cut back herbaceous perennials left in place over winter. Take boughs and other winter mulches off plants.
- Tidy up winter-damaged foliage of evergreen perennials such as heart-leaf bergenia, Lenten rose, and coral bells.
- Prune winter-killed stems from woody perennials, such as salvia, lavender,

and Russian sage. Wait until plants begin growing so that you can tell which parts of the plant are dead and which are alive.
- Pull any weeds that have popped up. Apply weed preventer before weed seeds begin to germinate.
- Feed emerging perennials.
- Stake plants while they are small.
- Plant new perennials. Make sure to get bare-root perennials in the ground while they're still dormant.
- Divide fall-blooming perennials.
- Lightly rake to freshen mulched areas. Where organic mulch has washed away or broken down, renew it before new weeds emerge.
- Edge the beds.

SUMMER

- Pull weeds regularly to prevent them from becoming established.
- Keep the beds edged.
- Make sure your perennials have plenty to drink, especially during a drought.
- Cut back early-blooming perennials to encourage fullness, fresh leaves, and sometimes a second flush of flowers.
- Pinch later-blooming perennials to control height and avoid staking.
- Deadhead faded flowers.
- Continue feeding container plants until late summer.
- Divide bearded iris and daylilies that have finished flowering.
- Pay attention to your color scheme as it unfolds in the garden.

- Dig new beds and borders, except in very hot climates.
- Pick Japanese beetles off your hollyhocks by hand.
- During periods of extreme heat and drought, check your container plantings twice a day to see if they need water, paying special attention to pots in sunny, windy sites.
- Fill holes in beds with garden mums and other fall-blooming perennials.
- Cut flowers and foliage for indoor arrangements.
- Start collecting seeds from rare or favorite perennials to share with your friends. Dry ripe seeds in brown paper bags and store them in clearly labeled envelopes.

FALL

- In cool climates, plant perennials until mid October. In warm climates, plant until the ground freezes.
- Cut back herbaceous perennials to about 10 inches. Compost clean trimmings, but discard sick or insect-infested material to avoid spreading problems throughout your garden.
- Mulch beds.
- Leave woody, evergreen, and strong-stemmed perennials with handsome seed heads, such as mullein, sedum, purple coneflower, and ornamental grasses, until spring. They add beauty to the winter landscape.
- Divide spring- and early-summer-blooming perennials.

WINTER

- Place protective mulches such as conifer boughs over marginally hardy perennials after the soil freezes to prevent them from being heaved from the ground as soil thaws and refreezes .
- Walk through the garden every few weeks, pressing down frost-heaved perennials where necessary.
- Skim gardening catalogs, checking out new plants or old favorites in new colors.
- Think about last summer's garden. What did you like? What can you improve? Jot down the answers to jog your mind next summer.
- Plan next year's garden.
- Order seeds and plants from catalogs.

TIP CLEAN TROWELS, BYPASS PRUNERS, AND OTHER GARDENING TOOLS AFTER EACH USE TO PREVENT THE SPREAD OF FUNGAL DISEASE AND TO KEEP THEM FROM RUSTING.

Perennials can make your garden a delightful place to work, play, and entertain. In previous chapters, you've seen how planning ahead helps make your dream garden a reality, saving you time and money in the process. Finding healthy plants and planting them right moves you further down the garden path. Maintaining your garden keeps it vigorous and protects it against the pests and diseases that sometimes visit your land.

ENCYCLOPEDIA

Now it's time to look at specific plants and select the ones that are best for your garden. To help you decide, look at the key facts about the plant at the top of each entry, including the primary decorative characteristics described under "features," such as flowers, foliage, fragrance, and form. Cold hardiness comes next, because perennials should be hardy enough to survive the lowest average winter temperature for your climate. The flowering period for many perennials is short—about two to three weeks each year. Perennials spend most of the growing season without blooms, so look at the plant's approximate size both in and out of bloom for an idea of how it will look in consecutive stages of growth. Different plants need varying amounts of light and grow in diverse soils; that information also appears at the top of the entry, with the key facts.

If a plant's key points meet your needs, then read the discussion that follows to learn more about the plant—its attributes, its landscape uses, and how to care for it in your garden. At the end of the entry are recommended species and cultivars. Although these recommendations are not comprehensive, they include both old and new varieties with distinctive ornamental characteristics.

When possible, the recommended cultivars are those that resist pests and diseases. Buying pest- and disease-resistant perennials increases your garden's viability and decreases the amount of time it takes to maintain your plants. Because no two gardens and no two climates are exactly alike, the recommendations include a range of perennials that thrive in different areas of the United States and Canada. Some standard perennials on the list are easy to locate at nurseries and garden centers; unusual selections are available by mail order.

common name index

The entries in the encyclopedia are alphabetized by their scientific, or latin, names. If you know a plant only by its common name, this cross-reference chart will help you find it in the book.

FOR THIS PLANT	LOOK UNDER	PAGE
Adam's needle	Yucca	177
Anise hyssop	Agastache	123
Arkansas amsonia	Amsonia	125
Aster	Aster	128
Autumn joy	Sedum	171
Avens	Geum	145
Baby's breath	Gypsophila	146
Balloon flower	Platycodon	165
Barrenwort	Epimedium	141
Basket-of-gold	Aurinia	130
Bearded iris	Iris	152
Beard-tongue	Penstemon	163
Bear's breeches	Acanthus	122
Bee balm	Monarda	159
Bee delphinium	Delphinium	138
Bellflower	Campanula	133
Bethlehem sage	Pulmonaria	167
Big blue lobelia	Lobelia	158
Bigleaf ligularia	Ligularia	157
Bishop's hat	Epimedium	141
Black cohosh	Cimicifuga	135
Black-eyed Susan	Rudbeckia	169
Blanket flower	Gaillardia	144
Blazing star	Liatris	156
Bleeding heart	Dicentra	139
Bloody cranesbill	Geranium	145
Blue false indigo	Baptisia	130
Bluebeard	Caryopteris	134
Blue fescue	Grasses, Festuca	180
Blue lilyturf	Liriope	158
Blue mist spirea	Caryopteris	134
Blue oat grass	Grasses, Helictotrichon	180
Bluestar	Amsonia	125
Bugbane	Cimicifuga	135
Bugloss	Brunnera	132
Bush clover	Lespedeza	155
Butterfly weed	Asclepias	128
Butterfly milkweed	Asclepias	128
Canadian columbine	Aquilegia	126
Cardinal flower	Lobelia	158
Carpathian bellflower	Campanula	133
Catmint	Nepeta	160
Checkerbloom	Sidalcea	171
Cheddar pink	Dianthus	138
Christmas fern	Ferns, Polystichum	178
Christmas rose	Helleborus	147
Chrysanthemum	Chrysanthemum	134
Cinnamon fern	Osmunda	178
Cinquefoil	Potentilla	166
Cohosh	Cimicifuga	135
Columbine	Aquilegia	126

FOR THIS PLANT	LOOK UNDER	PAGE
Columbine meadow rue	Thalictrum	174
Coneflower (yellow)	Rudbeckia	169
Coneflower (purple)	Echinacea	140
Coral bells	Heuchera	149
Cowslip	Primula	167
Cranesbill	Geranium	145
Creeping lilyturf	Liriope	158
Creeping phlox	Phlox	164
Crimson pincushion	Knautia	153
Daisy	Leucanthemum	156
Daylily	Hemerocallis	148
Dittany	Dictamnus	139
English daisy	Leucanthemum	156
English primrose	Primula	167
Evening primrose	Oenothera	160
Fairy candles	Cimicifuga	135
False indigo	Baptisia	130
False blue indigo	Baptisia	130
False Solomon's seal	Smilacina	172
False spirea	Astilbe	129
Featherleaf rodgersia	Rodgersia	168
Feather reed grass	Grasses, Calamagrostis	180
Fernleaf yarrow	Achillea	122
Ferns		178
Fingerleaf rodgersia	Rodgersia	168
Fleabane	Erigeron	142
Foam flower	Tiarella	175
Foamy bells	×Heucherella	150
Fountain grass	Grasses, Pennisetum	180
Foxglove	Digitalis	140
Fragrant bugbane	Cimicifuga	135
Garden phlox	Phlox	164
Gas plant	Dictamnus	139
Gayfeather	Liatris	156
Germander	Teucrium	174
Globe thistle	Echinops	141
Gloriosa daisy	Rudbeckia	169
Goatsbeard	Aruncus	127
Goldenrod	Solidago	172
Goldenstar	Chrysogonum	135
Grasses		180
Hakone grass	Grasses, Hakonechloa	180
Hardy begonia	Begonia	131
Hardy geranium	Geranium	145
Hardy hibiscus	Hibiscus	150
Harebell	Campanula	133
Hay-scented fern	Ferns, Dennstaedtia	178
Heart-leaf bergenia	Bergenia	131
Heart-leaf brunnera	Brunnera	132
Helen's flower	Helenium	146
Hellebore	Helleborus	147
Hollyhock	Alcea	123
Hosta	Hosta	151
Hyssop	Agastache	123
Jacob's ladder	Polemonium	165
Japanese anemone	Anemone	125
Japanese forest grass	Grasses, Hakonechloa	180
Japanese painted fern	Ferns, Athyrium	178

FOR THIS PLANT	LOOK UNDER	PAGE
Joe-Pye weed	Eupatorium	143
Kansas gayfeather	Liatris	156
Lady fern	Ferns, Athyrium	178
Lady's mantle	Alchemilla	124
Lamb's-ears	Stachys	173
Lavender	Lavandula	154
Lavender cotton	Santolina	170
Lavender mist	Thalictrum	174
Lenten rose	Helleborus	147
Lily	Lilium	157
Lilyturf	Liriope	158
Live forever	Sedum	171
Lungwort	Pulmonaria	167
Maiden grass	Grasses, Miscanthus	180
Maidenhair fern	Ferns, Adiantum	178
Male fern	Ferns, Dryopteris	178
Mallow	Lavatera	155
Maltese cross	Lychnis	159
Many-flowered sunflower	Helianthus	147
Marsh marigold	Caltha	133
Masterwort	Astrantia	129
Meadow rue	Thalictrum	174
Meadowsweet	Filipendula	143
Mexican feather grass	Grasses, Stipa	180
Missouri primrose	Oenothera	160
Mondo grass	Grasses, Ophiopogon	180
Monkey grass	Grasses, Ophiopogon	180
Montbretia	Crocosmia	137
Moss phlox	Phlox	164
Mugwort	Artemisia	127
Mullein	Verbascum	176
Mum	Chrysanthemum	134
New England aster	Aster	128
Obedient plant	Physostegia	164
Orange coneflower	Rudbeckia	169
Oriental poppy	Papaver	162
Ornamental onion	Allium	124
Ornamental oregano	Origanum	161
Ostrich fern	Ferns, Matteuccia	178
Oswego tea	Monarda	159
Ozark sundrop	Oenothera	160
Pacific bleeding heart	Dicentra	139
Pasque flower	Pulsatilla	168
Patrinia	Patrinia	162
Peach-leaf bellflower	Campanula	133
Peony	Paeonia	161
Perennial salvia	Salvia	169
Perennial sunflower	Helianthus	147
Pigsqueak	Bergenia	131
Pincushion flower	Scabiosa	170
Pinks	Dianthus	130
Plantain lily	Hosta	151
Primrose	Primula	167
Purple coneflower	Echinacea	140
Queen-of-the-prairie	Filipendula	143
Ragged robin	Lychnis	159
Red hot poker	Kniphofia	154
Rocky Mountain columbine	Aquilegia	126

FOR THIS PLANT	LOOK UNDER	PAGE
Roger's flower	Rodgersia	168
Rose campion	Lychnis	159
Royal fern	Ferns, Osmunda	178
Russian sage	Perovskia	163
Sage	Salvia	169
Scabious	Scabiosa	171
Sea holly	Eryngium	142
Sea pink or sea thrift	Armeria	126
Sedges	Grasses, Carex	180
Sensitive fern	Ferns, Onoclea	178
Shasta daisy	Leucanthemum	156
Shield ferns	Ferns, Polystichum	178
Siberian iris	Iris	152
Silver mound	Artemisia	127
Smooth white penstemon	Penstemon	163
Snakeroot	Cimicifuga	135
Sneezeweed	Helenium	146
Sneezewort	Achillea	122
Snowdrop anemone	Anemone	125
Snowy woodrush	Grasses, Luzula	180
Solitary clematis	Clematis	136
Solomon's plume	Smilacina	172
Solomon's seal	Polygonatum	166
Spike gayfeather	Liatris	156
Spike speedwell	Veronica	176
Spiny bear's breeches	Acanthus	122
Star of Persia	Allium	124
Stoke's aster	Stokesia	173
Stonecrop	Sedum	171
Sundrops	Oenothera	160
Sunflower	Helianthus	147
Sweet flag	Grasses, Acorus	180
Switch grass	Grasses, Panicum	180
Threadleaf coreopsis	Coreopsis	136
Thrift	Armeria	126
Thunberg bush clover	Lespedeza	155
Tickseed	Coreopsis	136
Toad lily	Tricyrtis	175
Torch lily	Kniphofia	154
Tree mallow	Lavatera	155
Turk's-cap lily	Lilium	157
Variegated solomon's seal	Polygonatum	166
Violet	Viola	176
Wall germander	Teucrium	174
Waxbells	Kirengeshoma	153
Whirling butterflies	Gaura	144
White boltonia	Boltonia	132
White gaura	Gaura	144
White snakeroot	Eupatorium	143
Wild blue indigo	Baptisia	130
Willow amsonia	Amsonia	125
Wood fern	Ferns, Dryopteris	178
Wormwood	Artemisia	127
Yarrow	Achillea	122
Yellow corydalis	Corydalis	137
Yellow foxglove	Digitalis	140
Yellow waxbells	Kirengeshoma	153
Zebra grass	Grasses, Miscanthus	180

SPINY BEAR'S BREECHES *(Acanthus spinosus)*

Features: Dramatic texture and height. Long-lasting white flowers with showy purple hoods on stiff, erect spikes from late spring to midsummer.
Hardiness: Zones 5 to 10
In-bloom size: 3- to 4-foot by 2- to 3-foot upright spire
Out-of-bloom size: 2-foot-tall mound
Light: Full sun to partial shade; light shade in hot areas
Site: Well-drained, loose, average to fertile soil

DESCRIPTION AND USES: Grow this plant for its architectural form both in and out of bloom, when its mound of long, coarse, thistlelike leaves gives structure to the perennial border. On its own, spiny bear's breeches makes a fine specimen plant. It has a strong form both in a container and in the ground. Use fresh or dried spikes in flower arrangements. Native to the Mediterranean region, spiny bear's breeches combines well with silver mound artemisia, porcupine grass, and golden-edged creeping thyme.

CARE: Spiny bear's breeches prefers average to fertile soil and regular moisture, but it will tolerate poor, dry soil once it is established. Soil must be well-drained; wet feet can kill the plants. In loose soil, spiny bear's breeches forms large colonies. Plants spread by roots; even small root pieces left in the ground after moving the plant can grow into new plants.

Cut back bear's breeches when spent flower spikes deteriorate, usually some weeks after blooming. Fresh basal leaves will emerge, although the plant will not bloom again. If most of the foliage looks good, remove individual scraggly leaves. In the North, mulch to protect roots in winter. Let the foliage, which is evergreen in warm climates, remain on the plant through the winter. Cut off tattered leaves in spring. Powdery mildew, snails, and slugs may affect this plant.

RECOMMENDATIONS:
■ **Balkan bear's breeches** *(A. hungaricus)* grows 2 to 4 feet tall by 2 to 3 feet wide. Reddish-purple hoods top its pale pink flowers, which rise on 3-foot spikes. Zones 6 to 9.
■ **Common bear's breeches** *(A. mollis)* grows 5 feet tall by 3 feet wide. It produces large, glossy leaves and purplish flower stems with mauve-hooded white flowers. Zones 6 to 10. **Golden bear's breeches** ('Hollard's Gold'): gleaming chartreuse leaves.

YARROW *(Achillea spp.)*

'Moonshine' hybrid yarrow

Features: Red, white, pink, or yellow flowers from late spring to midsummer. Ferny green or silver leaves.
Hardiness: Zones 3 to 8
In-bloom size: 16- to 40-inch by 24- to 36-inch upright to mounded
Out-of-bloom size: 12- to 24-inch-tall mound
Light: Full sun
Site: Well-drained average soil and average moisture

DESCRIPTION AND USES: This drought-tolerant perennial favorite is a butterfly-attracting garden staple. Yarrow's fast growth rate makes it an excellent choice to mass in beds and borders. The flower heads and ferny gray-green leaves contrast well with daylilies, beard- tongue, perennial salvia, and Shasta daisies. Use cut flowers in fresh and dried arrangements.

CARE: Plant yarrow in spring or fall. Although drought-tolerant, yarrow performs best in well-drained soil with regular watering during dry spells. Prompt deadheading promotes rebloom; cut flowering stems at their base.

Some yarrows, including sneezewort and tall forms of fern-leaf and common yarrow, flop over in humid air, rich soil, and shade. Such plants may benefit from staking or cutting back early in the season. If leaves look tatty after blooms fade, cut the plant to the ground to promote new basal foliage. Cutting back also encourages compact growth and discourages self-sowing. Yarrow is mostly pest-free and resistant to rabbits and deer. Wait till early spring to cut back dead foliage to take advantage of the plant's winter interest.

RECOMMENDATIONS:
■ **Fern-leaf yarrow** *(A. filipendulina)* grows 3 to 5 feet by 2 to s3 feet. It has tight, flat clusters of yellow flowers from mid- to late summer and finely cut, pale green leaves. Zones 3 to 8.
■ **Common yarrow** *(A. millefolium)* is a low-growing species with white, or pink, or red flowers. Zones 3 to 9.
■ **'Angel's Breath' sneezewort** *(A. ptarmica)* features long, slender foliage, that looks much different from other yarrows. It grows 18 inches by 12 inches wide and has small, white double flowers, which are good for cutting. Zones 2 to 9.
■ **Hybrid yarrows 'Coronation Gold':** 36 inches by 18 inches; flat yellow flowers good for drying; gray foliage. Zones 3 to 9. **'Moonshine':** 24 inches by 18 to 24 inches; lemon yellow blooms; ferny gray-green leaves. Zones 3 to 7.

ANISE HYSSOP *(Agastache foeniculum)*

Features: Fragrant foliage and spiky purple flowers from midsummer to fall. Draws bees, butterflies, and hummingbirds. Licorice-scented edible foliage.
Hardiness: Zones 5 to 10
In- and out-of-bloom size: 36-inch by 30-inch upright oval
Light: Full sun to partial shade
Site: Well-drained average garden soil

DESCRIPTION AND USES: Anise hyssop's long-blooming, nectar-rich purple flower spikes appeal to insects, butterflies, and hummingbirds. Its medium-textured grayish-green leaves have a minty anise scent, taste like licorice, and make a pleasant addition to tea. An upright American prairie plant, anise hyssop suits the middle or back of the border, giving excellent support to showier perennials. Plants tend to have sparse foliage at their base, and shorter perennials in front will help to hide the bare feet, as does growing anise hyssop in a mass. Use anise hyssop in containers and fresh flower arrangements, or dry the blooms for later use.

CARE: This easy-care perennial needs no staking when planted in well-drained, average to poor soils. In rich, wet soils or when given too much fertilizer, it will grow lanky and flop over. Plants prefer average amounts of water but will tolerate drought, heat, and humidity once they are established. Anise hyssop has no serious pests or diseases and is rabbit- and deer-resistant. Anise hyssop may need winter protection in cold parts of Zone 5. Plants will self-sow; unless you plan to grow a field of anise hyssop, keep an eye out for seedlings.

RECOMMENDATIONS:
■ **White Korean hyssop** (*A. rugosa* 'Alabaster') grows 3 feet tall by 2 feet wide and has white flower spikes and coarse-textured leaves. Zones 5 to 8.
■ **Giant hyssop** (*A. barberi*) have reddish-purple blooms arranged loosely on the spike. Zones 6 to 9. **'Firebird':** 3 feet by 2 feet; raspberry-red flowers. **'Tutti Frutti':** 4 to 6 feet by 2 feet; lavender-pink flower spikes with sweet-fruit-scented leaves.
■ **Hybrid agastaches** hardy only to Zone 6. **'Apricot Sunrise':** 3 feet by 2 feet; spikes of light orange flowers; gray-green leaves. **'Blue Fortune':** 3 to 4 feet by 2 feet; blue-purple flowers from July to September.

HOLLYHOCK *(Alcea rosea)*

Features: Dramatic height. Informal, old-fashioned appearance. Bright pink, red, maroon, purple, yellow, or white spikes in early to midsummer. A cottage garden favorite.
Hardiness: Zones 3 to 8
In-bloom size: 4- to 8-foot by 2-foot upright spire
Out-of-bloom size: 3- to 3½-foot-tall mound
Light: Full sun
Site: Fertile, well-drained soil

DESCRIPTION AND USES: Valued for its size and color, this short-lived perennial has lofty floral wands that look stunning at the back of a border, growing against a brick, adobe, or clapboard wall, or silhouetted against a dark yew hedge. Hollyhock blooms open from the bottom to the top of the spike throughout the summer, attracting butterflies and hummingbirds. Plants are fast-growing and upright with large, coarsely lobed leaves. Short varieties make good container plants. Grow hollyhocks in cottage gardens with roses, white daisies, and clematis.

CARE: Hollyhocks thrive in rich, well-drained soil with plenty of moisture. Japanese beetles, leaf miners, and hollyhock rust are problems, though new varieties may resist the latter. Stake tall varieties. Deadhead after flowering for a tidier look unless you want seeds to ripen and self-sow. Toward summer's end, cut tall flowering stems back to fresh leaves.

RECOMMENDATIONS:
'Chater's Double Hybrids': double blooms in pink, red, maroon, salmon, violet, white, and yellow. **'Crème de Cassis':** 5 to 6 feet by 2 feet; 2- to 4-inch, heavily veined, white-rimmed dark raspberry flowers; double, semidouble, and single flowers all on the same stalk; more brightly colored in warm regions; reliably perennial. **'Nigra':** 5- to 6-foot spikes; deep maroon single blooms. **'Queeny Purple':** 2 to 3 feet by 1 to 1½ feet; stands erect without staking; 3- to 4-inch purple double blooms; long bloom season. **'Old Barnyard Mix':** 5 to 6 feet by 2 feet; 3- to 5-inch yellow-centered single flowers in bright, pastel, and deep jewel colors and bicolors, including yellows, oranges, and rosy and brick reds; rust-resistant.

LADY'S MANTLE (Alchemilla mollis)

ORNAMENTAL ONIONS (Allium spp.)

German garlic

Features: Elegant mounds of pleated light gray-green leaves. Clusters of tiny vivid chartreuse flowers from late spring to midsummer. Outstanding edging or ground cover plant.
Hardiness: Zones 4 to 7
In- and out-of-bloom size: 1½-feet by 2-feet, ground-hugging
Light: Partial shade
Site: Moist, well-drained soil

DESCRIPTION AND USES: This plant's mounded foliage is ideal for softening the edge of a path or creating a lush ground cover in a lightly shaded spot under a tree. The velvety leaves are pleated when they open, then fan into a scalloped to rounded shape. Slightly cupped, the foliage often holds early morning dewdrops. Clusters of greenish-yellow flowers appear on arching stems in early summer. The bright chartreuse hue combines well with both pastel and primary colors in borders and bouquets. The blooms are charming dried and are long-lasting in fresh bouquets.

CARE: This easy-to-grow perennial flourishes in moist, well-drained soils and partial shade. In cool climates, lady's mantle also thrives in full sun. If you grow lady's mantle as a ground cover, let some of the plants go to seed so they will spread. If your design calls for a single clump or a small group, remove the faded flowers to prevent self-sowing. In spring before new growth emerges, remove last year's dead leaves. Spring is also the time to divide lady's mantle, though it rarely requires it. As summer progresses, you can renew any shabby plants by cutting back the leaves. Plant lady's mantle 12 to 18 inches apart for a lush mass. A tough plant, lady's mantle is pest- and disease-free.

RECOMMENDATIONS:
'Thriller': 18 inches, more erect than the species; larger leaves.
■ **Alpine lady's mantle** (Alchemilla alpina) grows just 5 to 6 inches tall. It has small white-edged gray-green leaves deeply divided into six lobes. The chartreuse flowers are in 6-inch-wide clusters. Plants self-sow. They are good in rock gardens. Zones 3 to 7.

Features: Attractive flat or rounded grassy leaves with a light onion or garlicky taste and scent. Edible flowers attract butterflies. Use in the front or mid border.
Hardiness: Zones 3 to 9
In-bloom size: 15- to 20-inch by 12- to 24-inch arching
Out-of-bloom size: 12-inch arching
Light: Full sun to partial shade
Site: Well-drained soil

DESCRIPTION AND USES: Valued for their edible leaves and fragrant flowers, ornamental onions grow from a bulb to form thick clumps of green leaves, which may be arching, upright, or swirled on the ground. They look attractive at the front and in the middle of perennial beds and borders and in rock, herb, and vegetable gardens. Round-topped clusters of starry white, purple, or pink flowers cap bare, upright stems held above the leaves. With many species, the leaves die back soon after the plants bloom, but the dried flowers persist and add both texture and color to the garden.

CARE: Ornamental onions prefer average, well-drained soil in full sun or partial shade. Fast-growing and easy to cultivate, they multiply by self-sowing and by forming new plants along their tuberous roots. Plant ornamental onions in spring. Divide clumps every two to three years by digging up and separating the bulbs in spring.

RECOMMENDATIONS:
■ **German garlic** (A. senescens 'Glaucum') grows 12 inches tall by 6 inches wide. With its bluish-gray-green leaves swirling around a central point, German garlic is a textural wonder at the front edge of the garden. Small, round lilac to mauve blooms rise a few inches above the foliage in mid- to late summer. Zones 4 to 8.
■ **Star of Persia allium** (A. christophii) grows 24 inches tall by 8 to 10 inches wide. It has broad, strappy leaves that often die back before the flowers are fully open. Starry silvery-purple flowers appear in late spring to early summer and grow in open spheres 8 to 10 inches in diameter. Faded blooms dry to an attractive beige and continue to give structure to the garden. Zones 4 to 8.
■ **Garlic chives** (A. tuberosum) grows 8 to 9 inches tall and 6 inches wide. It has persistent foliage and showy white blooms with a scent like that of violets in late summer. This species can be invasive, so deadhead the flowers before they set seed.

ARKANSAS AMSONIA *(Amsonia hubrectii)*

Features: Clusters of star-shape pale blue flowers in late spring; bright yellow fall color; fine texture.
Hardiness: Zones 5 to 9
In- and out-of-bloom size: 3-foot by 3-foot upright
Light: Full sun to partial shade
Site: Moist, well-drained soil of average fertility

DESCRIPTION AND USES: This shrubby plant is noted for its fine landscape texture and four seasons of garden interest. The leaves are linear and medium green until fall, when they turn brilliant yellow. Clusters of starry light blue flowers appear at the stem tips in late spring, followed quickly by abundant seedpods. The plant's attractive form persists in the landscape until beaten down by heavy winter snows. Arkansas amsonia adds dimension and depth to the perennial garden. Mass it under honeylocust or young birch trees, where it can thrive in the dappled shade. Use it in prairie gardens and meadows, where it will rapidly spread by seed.

CARE: Arkansas amsonia requires little care. Plant it in full sun to partial shade. It prefers moist, well-drained soil of average fertility but tolerates wetter and drier soils. In the right conditions, amsonia self-seeds aggressively. Deadhead after blooming if you don't want it to spread. If soil is very fertile or the plant is in shade, you may want to cut it back to 6 inches after blooming to encourage more compact growth.

RECOMMENDATIONS:
■ **Blue star** *(Amsonia tabernaemontana)* is a carefree native plant that resembles Arkansas amsonia except for its wider, darker green leaves, slightly coarser landscape texture, and lack of brilliant fall color. Zones 3 to 9.

HYBRID ANEMONE *(Anemone ×hybrida)*

Features: Slightly cupped, open pink to white flowers in late summer and fall.
Hardiness: Zones 5 to 8
In-bloom size: 3- to 5-foot by 2-foot airy mound
Out-of-bloom size: 1- to 1½-foot-tall mound
Light: Partial shade to full sun in the North
Site: Moist, fertile, well-drained soil high in organic matter

DESCRIPTION AND USES: Hybrid anemones are worth growing for their pastel blooms from late summer until midfall. The graceful single or semidouble flowers come in white and shades of pink with a ring of golden stamens at the center. They grow on tall, sparse stems that give the plant a see-through quality. Flowers are excellent cut, and you can use the seed heads in flower arrangements. Leaves are lobed and look like maple. Because of the plant's ultimate height and slowness to send up shoots in spring, it's best to grow it in the middle of the border. Some are vigorous spreaders and, once established, will quickly form a large mass.

CARE: Grow hybrid anemones in moist, fertile, well-drained soil with plenty of organic matter. Plant them in spring. Partial shade is best, especially in warm climates, but they grow well in full sun in colder areas. After a heavy fall frost, cut them back and mulch with pine boughs in cool climates. Divide plants to control their spread.

RECOMMENDATIONS:
'Honorine Jobert': 36 inches tall; abundant 2-inch white single blooms for six weeks or more in late summer to fall. **'Queen Charlotte':** 3 to 5 feet; 3-inch pink semidouble flowers with bright golden stamens. **'Party Dress':** 20 inches by 36 inches; 3½-inch pink double blooms; shiny green leaves.
■ **Japanese anemone** *(A. hupehensis)* is similar to hybrid anemones, having rosy-mauve flowers and blooming a week or two earlier. Zones 5 to 8. **'September Charm':** 24 inches; pink single flowers.
■ **Snowdrop anemone** *(A. sylvestris)* is a spring-blooming, spreading perennial with fragrant white single flowers and yellow stamens. Plants grow 6 inches by 12 inches. The attractive leaves have five deeply cut lobes. Zones 4 to 8.

COLUMBINE (Aquilegia vulgaris)

Hybrid columbine | Rocky Mountain columbine

Features: Flowers in shades of pink, blue, white, red, and yellow attract hummingbirds. Excellent border plant and woodland ground cover.
Hardiness: Zones 3 to 9
In-bloom size: 2- to 3-foot by 1- to 1½-foot rounded clump
Out-of-bloom size: 1-foot rounded clump
Light: Partial shade to full sun
Site: Rich, moist, well-drained soil

DESCRIPTION AND USES: Perfect for perennial, cottage, and woodland gardens, these old-fashioned plants come in many new colors and forms. Columbine has nodding blooms with curved spurs at the back. They resemble frilly caps. The flowers grow on erect stems above mounds of attractive, lobed grayish-green leaves. Cut flowers look charming in spring arrangements.

CARE: Columbine prospers in sun to partial shade in moist, well-drained soil high in organic matter. It has a short life span but self-sows readily. Break off dried seedpods and shake the seeds where you'd like new plants to grow. To avoid unwanted self-sowing and to lengthen the season of bloom, deadhead the plant before it goes to seed. Remove any leaves with narrow, tan leaf miner tracks and discard them in the trash. Renew the plant by cutting it to the ground after flowering.

RECOMMENDATIONS:
■ **Rocky Mountain columbine** (A. caerulea) is a short, 1- to 2-foot-tall columbine with long-spurred blue-and-white blooms. Zones 3 to 8.
■ **Canadian columbine** (A. canadensis) is a tall North American native reaching 36 inches by 12 inches has ferny foliage. The droopy flowers with upright spurs are red on the outside and light yellow on the inside. Zones 3 to 8. **'Little Lanterns':** 8 to 10 inches by 8 to 12 inches; red-and-yellow flowers.
■ **Hybrid columbines** (A. ×hybrida): large, upright flowers in a wide range of colors on tall stems. Zones 3 to 9. **McKana Hybrids:** 24 to 36 inches tall; flowers in white, yellow, red, pink, blue, and lavender. **'Nora Barlow':** 36 inches tall; shaggy double flowers in dark rosy pink and white. **'Lime Frost':** 14 to 18 inches tall; variegated yellow-and-green-splotched leaves.

THRIFT (Armeria maritima)

Features: Buttons of pink, white, or rosy purple on upright stems from mid- to late spring. Evergreen tufts of grassy leaves. Good for naturalizing.
Hardiness: Zones 4 to 8
In-bloom size: 8- to 12-inch-tall by 8- to 12-inch-wide rounded tufts
Out-of-bloom size: 3-inch by 8- to 12-inch grassy tufts
Light: Full sun
Site: Well-drained sandy soil

DESCRIPTION AND USES: Thrift's diminutive, ball-shaped, deep pink to white flower clusters sit on straight bare stems and are good for cutting. They open in mid- to late spring and occasionally throughout the summer. The dense grassy mounds of foliage are evergreen and look attractive year-round in warm climates. Use thrift as an edging; in rock gardens, troughs, and containers; tucked in stone walls; and at the front of perennial borders. Thrift spreads by seed in poor, dry, sandy soils. In small spaces, it makes an effective seaside ground cover that tolerates both wind and ocean spray.

CARE: Plant thrift in neutral to slightly alkaline sandy soil in full sun. It needs excellent drainage year-round. Deadheading promotes reblooming in fall, especially in the North. Few pests bother this plant, but it can rot in the center in humid climates or moist soils. Cultivars may be less hardy; a mulch of pine boughs helps protect them. Plants are drought-tolerant and deer-resistant.

RECOMMENDATIONS:
■ **Pyrenees thrift** (A. juniperifolia) is a dwarf, growing 2 to 4 inches tall. The short-stemmed, pale lilac flowers are tiny, too, just ³/₈ inch across. Zones 4 to 8. **'Bevan's Variety':** deep pink flowers.
■ **Hybrid thrifts 'Nifty Thrifty':** pink flowers; yellow-edged evergreen leaves. **'Victor Reiter':** 2 to 6 inches; light pink flowers in spring; evergreen leaves. **'Rubrifolia'** (ruby sea thrift): 4 inches by 6 inches; magenta flowers in spring; leaves open wine red in spring and turn green in summer.

SILVER MOUND ARTEMISIA
(Artemisia schmidtiana 'Nana')

Silver mound | 'Powis Castle'

GOATSBEARD *(Aruncus dioicus)*

Features: Silvery mounds of soft, fine-textured leaves. Drought-tolerant and deer-resistant.
Hardiness: Zones 3 to 7
In- and out-of-bloom size: 12-inch by 24-inch rounded mound
Light: Full sun
Site: Poor to average sandy soil

DESCRIPTION AND USES: Silver mound's pale silky leaves bring light and contrast to rock and perennial gardens. Its low cushiony form and silvery foliage create easy transitions between colors in the perennial border. Silver mound looks stunning with 'Blue Clips' Carpathian bellflower, 'Purple Rain' salvia, 'Walker's Low' catmint, and 'Royal Candles' speedwell. The silver leaves also harmonize with ornamental grasses such as 'Sapphire' blue oat grass and burgundy-leaved 'Rubrum' fountain grass, a tender perennial.

CARE: Grow silver mound in poor to average sandy soils in full sun. It is drought-tolerant and needs excellent drainage and air circulation. Wet winters may cause it to rot. Keep silver mound compact by cutting it back and removing flower buds before they bloom. (The flowers are insignificant.) If silver mound becomes floppy or opens up in the center, shear it back to promote new growth.

RECOMMENDATIONS:
■ **Western mugwort** (*A. ludoviciana*) is 2 to 3 feet tall with aromatic silver leaves. Zones 4 to 9. **'Silver King'** and **'Silver Queen':** 3 feet and 2½ feet, respectively; aggressive silver-leaved spreaders; give them plenty of room to expand. **'Valerie Finnis':** 18 inches by 18 to 24 inches; moderate spreader with silvery white leaves; good in rock gardens and raised borders. Zones 3 to 8.
■ **Beach wormwood** (*A. stelleriana*) has tiny yellow flowers and furry leaves. It grows to 2 feet tall. Zones 4 to 8. **'Silver Brocade':** 8 inches by 12 inches; woolly white leaves, ideal for softening the edge of containers and low stone retaining walls.
■ **Hybrid artemisias 'Huntington':** 18 inches to 4 feet; aromatic, filigreed silvery leaves; Zones 5 to 7. **'Powis Castle':** 2 to 3 feet by 2 to 3 feet; mounded lacy silver leaves; good in warm climates. Zones 6 to 8.

Features: Open plumes of creamy flowers in early summer. Effective shrubby specimen or background plant.
Hardiness: Zones 3 to 7
In-bloom size: 4- to 6-foot by 4-foot upright, airy column
Out-of-bloom size: 1- to 2-foot mound
Light: Shade
Site: Moist, well-drained soil

DESCRIPTION AND USES: This grand shade dweller has ferny deep green leaves and long creamy white flower plumes that bloom in early summer. Grown by a shady brook or in a moist woodland garden, goatsbeard, with its bold shrubby form, makes an attractive specimen or a fine companion for ostrich fern and big-leaved hostas. The seed heads provide winter interest.

CARE: Goatsbeard thrives with plenty of moisture in partial shade. It grows successfully in sun in cool-summer climates and if it receives shade in the heat of the day. If grown where the roots are moist and where temperatures are relatively cool, goatsbeard will be trouble-free. Sometimes the plant self-sows. Pull unwanted seedlings; once established, goatsbeard has sturdy roots that are hard to dig.

RECOMMENDATIONS:
'Kneiffii': 3-foot plant with 1½-foot creamy plumes and finely cut leaves.
■ **Dwarf goatsbeard** (*A. aethusifolius*) grows just 8 to 12 inches tall by up to 18 inches wide. It has small, tight ivory blooms. The lacy foliage and mounded form are perfect for edging a path and in the front of a shade border.

BUTTERFLY WEED (Asclepias tuberosa)

Features: Brilliant orange flowers in summer followed by large seedpods. Attracts monarch butterflies. Drought-tolerant prairie native.
Hardiness: Zones 4 to 9
In- and out-of-bloom size: 2-foot by 2-foot upright oblong
Light: Full sun
Site: Light, lean, well-drained soil

DESCRIPTION AND USES: Valued for its fiery orange blooms, this butterfly magnet belongs in wildlife gardens, mixed borders, and meadow and prairie gardens, where it harmonizes with red, yellow, and other hot hues. Many kinds of butterflies sip its nectar, and monarch caterpillars devour its lance-shaped leaves, although the damage doesn't harm the plant.

Butterfly weed, a type of milkweed, is generally healthy and easy to grow. It emerges late each spring, so label its garden location lest you forget where you planted it. The flowers appear in large clusters; the seed heads look good in dried arrangements. Milkweeds exude a white sap when stems are cut.

CARE: Grow butterfly weed in full sun and light, lean, well-drained soil. The plant self-sows, so deadhead before seeds form if you don't want it to spread. Deadheading also produces a second flush of bloom. Butterfly weed's long taproot makes it difficult to transplant and divide. It needs excellent drainage to thrive.

RECOMMENDATIONS:
'Gay Butterflies': 2 to 3 feet; yellow, orange, and red flowers.
■ **Swamp milkweed** (*A. incarnata*) is native to moist sites. It produces fragrant pink flower clusters on 4- to 5-foot stems from summer through fall. **'Ice Ballet':** 40 inches; white flowers.

ASTERS (Aster spp.)

New England aster

Features: Pink, blue, white, purple, or lavender daisies. Fall-blooming varieties add color late in the gardening season. Attracts butterflies.
Hardiness: Zones 4 to 9
In- and out-of-bloom size: Size and shape vary greatly among species from dwarf to giant and upright to rounded
Light: Full sun
Site: Well-drained soil

DESCRIPTION AND USES: Asters are staples of the perennial garden. Treasured for their bright-hued daisies in autumn, asters actually bloom from June to October, depending on the cultivar. Many popular species are mildew-resistant and come in a wide range of sizes and colors. Grow asters in meadow and prairie gardens, in perennial beds and borders, and in containers with ornamental grasses.

CARE: Although white wood aster thrives in sun and partial shade, most other asters need full sun. In the South, where they may be short lived, asters benefit from some shade. To avoid powdery mildew, wilt, and other diseases, plant asters in well-drained soil where they will have good air circulation. To control self-sowing, cut plants back after they bloom and before they set seed. Dividing plants every couple of years also helps control spreading. Cutting back asters by half in late spring results in bushier plants that are less likely to need staking, although tall varieties may need some support.

RECOMMENDATIONS:
■ **'Wood's Pink' bushy aster** (*A. dumosus*): grows 18 inches tall and has pink single flowers from August through October, it is mildew-resistant. Zones 4 to 8.
■ **'Monch' Frikart's aster** (*A. frikartii*): is 2 feet tall and has lavender-blue semidouble blooms from June to September. Zones 5 to 8.
■ **'Blue Bird' smooth aster** (*A. laevis*): is 3 to 5 feet tall with yellow-centered violet-blue flowers in cone-shaped clusters in September and October, it is mildew-resistant. Zones 3 to 8.
■ **'Lady in Black' calico aster** (*A. lateriflorus*): grows to 3 feet, it has small white flowers in September and October and tiny blackish-purple leaves on a mounded, shrubby plant. Zones 5 to 7.
■ **'Purple Dome' New England aster** (*A. novae-angliae*): reaches 18 inches tall and has bright purple flowers in September and October. Zones 4 to 8.

ASTILBE (Astilbe spp.)

Features: Showy, feathery pink, red, white, or lavender plumes in summer. Attractive ferny leaves. Elegant woodland garden flower.
Hardiness: Zones 4 to 8
In-bloom size: 10- to 40-inch by 18- to 36-inch airy, upright clump
Out-of-bloom size: 6- to 30-inch-tall mound
Light: Partial to full shade
Site: Moist, well-drained soil

DESCRIPTION AND USES: Astilbe brings a graceful note to shady landscapes. Mass it for a ground cover or plant it grouped in perennial beds and borders—along with blue-leaved hosta and Japanese painted fern—or next to a pond or stream. The arching plumes rise above the foliage and look good in fresh or dried arrangements. Astilbes bloom in early, middle, or late summer, depending on the type.

CARE: Astilbe needs consistently moist, well-drained soil in partial to full shade. Although the plant has few diseases, leaves may dry out and turn brown in times of drought. Astilbe spreads by seed or division. To use it as a ground cover, avoid deadheading so it can self-sow. Divide every few years.

RECOMMENDATIONS:
■ Chinese astilbe (*Astilbe chinensis*) and its cultivars tend to be more drought-tolerant than other astilbes. Zones 4 to 8. **'Pumila':** 10 by 12 inches in bloom, foliage 6 inches; lavender-pink plumes; dark bronzy-green leaves; excellent ground cover or edging plant. **'Superba':** nearly 4 feet tall; magenta flowers; shiny dark green leaves. **'Visions in Pink':** 1½ to 2 feet tall; fluffy pale pink blooms; bluish-green leaves.
■ 'Sprite' star astilbe (*Astilbe simplicifolia*) grows 12 to 18 inches tall. It has shell pink plumes in mid- to late summer, followed by reddish-brown seed heads. Zones 4 to 8.
■ Hybrid astilbes **'Deutschland':** 24 to 30 inches; ivory plumes in late spring and early summer; dark green leaves. **'Rheinland':** up to 30 inches tall and wide; clear pink flowers. **'Fanal':** 24 inches by 18 to 24 inches; dark red flowers in midsummer; red-bronze leaves.

MASTERWO

Features: Showy pincushion flowers in pink, rose, red, purple, and white from late spring to midsummer. Delightful in shady cottage gardens. Excels in moist cool climates.
Hardiness: Zones 5 to 7
In- and out-of-bloom size: 30- by 18-inch rounded clump
Light: Partial shade
Site: Moist soil rich in organic matter

DESCRIPTION AND USES: Masterwort's flowers have high, cushioned centers ringed with pointed bracts, giving them old-fashioned appeal. Flowers occur in upright clusters on strong stems. Plants grow well in heavy clay soil and are ideal for shady stream banks and moist garden spots. They tolerate full sun where moisture is plentiful. Attractive fresh or dried.

CARE: Masterwort grows best in moist soil rich in organic matter. Plants self-sow but do not come true from seed. To avoid unwanted seedlings and to prolong bloom, deadhead after the first flush of flowers. Although masterwort grows in average soil, it does best with plenty of moisture. Division is rarely necessary.

RECOMMENDATIONS:
'Alba': 2 feet; white flowers. **'Claret':** deep red flowers; blackish 22-inch stems; basal mound of palm-shape leaves. **'Ruby Cloud':** 1½ to 3 feet; long-blooming, deep purplish-pink flowers, excellent for cutting. **'Ruby Wedding':** 2 to 2½ feet; dark ruby red flowers all summer.

BASKET-OF-GOLD (Aurinia saxatilis)

Features: Abundance of tiny gold blooms in spring. Low, bushy mat with hairy gray-green leaves. Let billow over rocks and walls.
Hardiness: Zones 3 to 7
In- and out-of-bloom size: 9- to 12-inch by 12- to 18-inch rounded mound
Light: Full sun
Site: Very well-drained soil

DESCRIPTION AND USES: Neon yellow flowers look dazzling in rock gardens, tucked in the crevices of dry-stone walls, or softening the edges of gravel paths. After flowering, semi-evergreen grayish-green leaves form a low mat. Basket-of-gold looks good with spring bulbs and other colorful, low-spreading plants such as 'Snowflake' moss phlox and 'Blue Panda' blue corydalis.

CARE: Grow this short-lived perennial in full sun and soil that is very well drained. Plants thrive in poor, dry soil. They need no fertilizer and require watering only in times of drought. Plant in masses about 8 to 12 inches apart, and cut back after flowering. Divide in fall if necessary. Heat and humidity defeat this plant, which is often grown as an annual in the South.

RECOMMENDATIONS:
'Compacta': 8 to 10 inches. 'Sulphurea': 6 to 8 inches; lemon-yellow blooms; gray-green foliage. 'Citrina': also 6 to 8 inches; lemon-yellow blooms; gray-green foliage.

BLUE FALSE INDIGO (Baptisia australis)

Features: Long spikes of violet-blue blooms in late spring. Drought-tolerant and deer-resistant. Shrubby native wildflower attracts butterflies.
Hardiness: Zones 3 to 8
In- and out-of-bloom size: 3- to 4-foot by 3-foot broad oval
Light: Full sun
Site: Lean, well-drained to dry soil

DESCRIPTION AND USES: This perennials' lupine-blue spires appear from late spring to early summer, followed by handsome nodding black seedpods. The pods, used as rattles by pioneer children, make a clattering noise when shaken. Attractive blue-green leaves resemble those of clover. Blooms and seedpods are valued for flower arrangements. Use false indigo for screening, at the back of perennial borders as a backdrop for showy shorter flowers, in containers, and in prairie and meadow gardens.

CARE: Although false indigo takes a while to establish, it's worth the wait. This easy-care, long-lived perennial resists pests and diseases and is drought-tolerant. It grows best in lean soil in a sunny, well-drained spot. After flowering, false indigo may need staking, especially if you let the seedpods remain on the plant. Otherwise, cut back the plant by one-third to promote sturdier, more compact growth. A deep taproot makes false indigo difficult to transplant and divide.

RECOMMENDATIONS:
■ Lesser wild indigo (B. a. minor) looks similar to the species but is smaller, growing up to 2 feet tall and wide. Its violet-blue flowers appear in early to midsummer. Zones 3 to 8.
■ White wild indigo (B. alba) has purplish new growth and long-lasting white flowers on a 2- to 3-foot plant. Zones 5 to 8.
■ Hybrid false indigo 'Purple Smoke': 48 to 52 inches; open spikes of smoky purple flowers on charcoal stems in late spring and early summer; gray-green foliage. Zones 4 to 9. 'Carolina Moonlight': 40 to 50 inches; spires of pale yellow flowers; blue-green leaves. Zones 4 to 9.

HARDY BEGONIA *(Begonia grandis)*

Features: Striking heart-shape leaves are green on top and red underneath. Droopy sprays of red buds mature to pink flower clusters from summer to fall.
Hardiness: Zones 6 to 9
In- and out-of-bloom size: 15- to 24-inch by 18-inch spreading clump
Light: Partial to full shade
Site: Moist, fertile, well-drained soil

DESCRIPTION AND USES: Hardy begonia adds elegance and color to shady garden areas. Its big leaves are heart-shape at the base, olive green above, and red-flushed below, with red veins and stems. Red-stemmed pink flowers are held in loose sprays. The plant has a mounded, spreading habit. Hardy begonia naturalizes by means of tiny bulbs that form where leaf stems attach to the main stems. The little bulbs fall to the earth in autumn and sow themselves in the soil. Grow this perennial in woodland gardens and shady borders, or as a ground cover in partial shade. It blends well with low ferns, hosta, and Siberian bugloss.

CARE: Hardy begonia comes up late in spring. It prefers moist, fertile, well-drained soils high in organic matter. Deadhead faded blooms to extend flowering. Cut to the ground in late fall, and apply a generous layer of mulch for winter protection.

RECOMMENDATIONS:
'Alba': 18 to 24 inches; nodding clusters of pink-tinged white flowers; stems and leaves greener than the species. **'Heron's Pirouette':** 15 inches; deep pink flower clusters larger than the species; extra-large leaves. **'Wildwood Premier':** 18 to 24 inches; drooping pinkish-white blooms in late summer and early fall; red-flushed leaves.

HEART-LEAF BERGENIA *(Bergenia cordifolia)*

Features: Foot-long leathery evergreen leaves tinged purple in cold weather. Fragrant deep pink flower clusters on tall, thick red stalks in spring.
Hardiness: Zones 4 to 8
In-bloom size: 20- by 30-inch-tall mound of cabbage-shape leaves
Out-of-bloom size: 12-inch-tall mound
Light: Sun to partial shade
Site: Moist soil of average fertility high in organic matter

DESCRIPTION AND USES: Bergenia's thick, shiny evergreen leaves are deer-resistant and take on a bronzy tint in fall. The foliage is so leathery that it squeaks when you rub it between your fingers, giving it the nickname pigsqueak. In spring, this low-maintenance mounded perennial produces clusters of pink-cupped flowers held above the leaves on fat stalks. Bergenia spreads slowly and makes an outstanding impenetrable ground cover when mass planted in partial shade. It looks good in rock gardens and at the front of the perennial border growing with ferns, cranesbill, Bethlehem sage, and lady's mantle. Bergenia holds its shape even under a blanket of snow.

CARE: Bergenia is easy to grow in sun or partial shade and moist soil of average fertility but high in organic matter. In early spring, cut off leaves showing winter damage, and remove flower stalks once flowers fade. Because it's evergreen, leave it stand in fall.

RECOMMENDATIONS:
'Bressingham Ruby': 12 to 16 inches; dark rose-pink flowers; burgundy fall color. **'Bressingham White':** 12 to 16 inches; flowers open pink and turn white. **'Magic Giant':** 12 to 18 inches; rosy blooms on red stems; huge purplish leaves turn bronzy purple in winter. **'Ruby Elf':** 6 inches tall; reddish-lavender blooms in spring; ruby red winter color. **'Winterglut':** 12 to 18 inches; red flowers in spring; dark green leaves with rich red fall color.

BOLTONIA *(Boltonia asteroides latisquama)*

Features: White daisies in late summer and early fall attract butterflies. Use at the back of a moist, sunny border.
Hardiness: Zones 4 to 8
In-bloom size: 5-foot by 2- to 4-foot upright
Out-of-bloom size: 1- to 2-foot mound
Light: Full sun to partial shade
Site: Moist, well-drained soil of average fertility

DESCRIPTION AND USES: Boltonia looks like a giant bushy aster; let it naturalize in informal cottage gardens and moist wildflower meadows. It produces abundant 1-inch-diameter yellow-centered, white daisies, which grow in open clusters on sturdy branched stems and offer late-season interest in the perennial garden. The flowers attract butterflies and are good for cutting. Narrow grayish-green leaves are not showy. Boltonia pairs well with blue star, Joe-Pye weed, 'Silver Feather' maiden grass, and 'Cloud Nine' switch grass.

CARE: Boltonia is a low-maintenance, mildew-resistant perennial that grows best in full sun to partial shade in moist, well-drained soils of average fertility. It needs no staking unless grown in exposed windy sites, partial shade, or extremely fertile soils. Cut back boltonia to 1 foot in late spring to encourage branching. In favorable conditions, boltonia's root system expands fast, and the plant can become enormous. Control this growth by dividing plants every three to four years.

RECOMMENDATIONS:
'Pink Beauty': 5 feet; pink flowers, silvery-blue leaves, and a more relaxed habit than the species. **'Snowbank':** 3 to 4 feet; white flowers.

HEART-LEAF BRUNNERA *(Brunnera macrophylla)*

'Jack Frost'   Heart-leaf brunnera

Features: Bold heart-shape leaves up to 8 inches long. Airy clusters of tiny blue flowers in spring. Excellent woodland ground cover.
Hardiness: Zones 3 to 8
In-bloom size: 18-inch by 24-inch coarse, round mound
Out-of-bloom size: 12-inch rounded mound
Light: Partial shade
Site: Consistently moist soil high in organic matter

DESCRIPTION AND USES: This clump-forming perennial with fuzzy heart-shaped basal leaves looks spectacular planted along a woodland path or massed in dappled shade under a grove of birches. In spring, tall, airy clusters of blue flowers resembling forget-me-nots rise above the mounded leaves. Ferns, primroses, Jack-in-the-pulpit, and pink bleeding heart make fine companions. Variegated cultivars lighten dark corners of a shade garden, particularly when planted in a mass.

CARE: Brunnera prefers partial shade but can grow in full sun or in cool-summer climates in consistently moist soil high in organic matter. In hot climates, brunnera's foliage may scorch; remove the damaged leaves, especially on variegated varieties. After blooming, cut off flower stems at the base to tidy up the plant and prevent self-sowing, or leave seedlings if you're using the plant as a ground cover. Deadhead variegated cultivars before seeds form; seedlings do not resemble the parent plant. Divide every ten years.

RECOMMENDATIONS:
'Hadspen Cream': 10 to 12 inches by 15 to 18 inches; dark green leaves with creamy white edges. **'Jack Frost':** 12 to 18 inches; 3- to 5-inch-wide silver leaves with narrow green edges and decorative veins; dramatic close up and at a distance. Zones 3 to 7.

MARSH MARIGOLD (Caltha palustris)

Features: Yellow flowers in spring; shiny kidney-shape deep green leaves. Outstanding choice for streams, bogs, and pond edges.
Hardiness: Zones 5 to 7
In- and out-of-bloom size: 12- to 15-inch by 15-inch rounded clump
Light: Full sun to partial shade
Site: Consistently moist to wet soil

DESCRIPTION AND USES: This wetland plant's handsome rounded leaves, up to 4 inches wide, are harbingers of spring. They emerge early in the growing season, followed in midspring by cheery 1- to 2-inch-diameter buttercup blooms held above the foliage. The loose, leafy clumps persist for a while but then go dormant, so you may want to grow marsh marigold with plants such as royal fern and blue flag iris, for later-season interest. Marsh marigold is a lovely addition to a water garden, stream bank, or moist perennial garden.

CARE: Marsh marigolds like full sun to partial shade and consistently moist to wet soils. They can grow in water up to 4 inches deep. Plant them 18 inches apart in moist soil or submerge the crowns in water that is a few inches deep. If clumps grow too crowded, divide plants while they are dormant in summer.

RECOMMENDATIONS:
'Plena': 2-inch double yellow flowers. The variety *alba:* Bright white single blooms; deep green leaves.

PEACH-LEAF BELLFLOWER (Campanula persicifolia)

Peach-leaf bellflower | Clustered bellflower

Features: Bell-shaped blooms in early to midsummer. Cottage garden classic. Good cut flower.
Hardiness: Zones 3 to 8
In-bloom size: 2- to 3-foot by 1½- to 2-foot upright spire
Out-of-bloom size: 12-inch mound
Light: Full sun to partial shade
Site: Neutral to slightly alkaline well-drained soil of average fertility

DESCRIPTION AND USES: In June and July, elongated, spiky clusters of bell-shaped violet, blue-violet, or white flowers up to 1½ inches wide rise from a rosette of narrow evergreen leaves. Grow peach-leaf bellflower in masses in the middle of the garden, along with foxglove, garden phlox, and red valerian, or at the front of the border, where its wiry stems can grow through other plants. Its tendency to self-sow suits cottage and informal gardens. The tall, wiry flower stems make lovely, long-lasting cut flowers.

CARE: Peach-leaf bellflower is easy to grow in full sun to partial shade and neutral to slightly alkaline well-drained soil of average fertility. Extend flowering by deadheading spent blooms. Plants may need staking. Divide every four years or when clumps start to deteriorate. For bouquets, cut just before flower buds open. Although short-lived, it self-sows if you leave a few unpruned flowers to set seed.

RECOMMENDATIONS:
'Chettle Charm': 2½ to 3 feet; creamy white blooms edged in lavender-blue. 'La Belle': 2 feet; double sky-blue blooms. 'Telham Beauty': 30 inches; large lavender-blue bells.
■ Carpathian bellflower (*C. carpatica*) is good in rock gardens and for edging. It forms a dense, spreading clump of 1-inch flowers. Zones 3 to 7. 'Blue Clips' and 'White Clips': blue and white flowers, respectively.
■ Clustered bellflower (*C. glomerata*) has violet or white blooms on 20-inch plants in early summer. Zones 3 to 8. 'Superba': 2½ feet; deep purple flowers; heat-resistant.
■ Spotted bellflower (*C. punctata*) sends up 1- to 2-foot-tall spires of tubular white blooms marked inside with pink or purple from mid- to late summer. Zones 5 to 7. 'Cherry Bells': 1½ to 2 feet by 2 feet; long, pendulous cherry-pink bells in spring and summer; mound of light green leaves up to 20 inches tall when not in bloom.

BLUEBEARD (Caryopteris ×clandonensis)

Features: Fluffy blue flower clusters in August and September. Scented gray-green leaves. Attracts butterflies.
Hardiness: Zones 5 to 9
In- and out-of-bloom size: 3-foot by 3-foot mounded shrub
Light: Sun
Site: Dry, well-drained soil of average fertility

DESCRIPTION AND USES: This deciduous flowering shrub belongs in sunny borders. Its frothy blue flower clusters and low, mounded shape pair well with ornamental grasses and late-blooming perennials such as 'Low Down' perennial sunflower, 'Butterpat' Helen's flower, or 'Happy Returns' daylily. Bluebeard produces fine-textured, aromatic, lance-shape leaves ranging from gray-green to variegated and chartreuse, depending on the cultivar. This airy shrub works well in midborder as a backdrop for other plants. You can also use it massed for more impact.

CARE: Bluebeard is a woody shrub, but it is treated as a perennial because only its roots are hardy in Zone 5. Grow it in full sun and dry, well-drained soil of average fertility. Cut it back in early spring; it flowers on new wood. Thin out some shoots on dense plants to improve air circulation.

RECOMMENDATIONS:
'Arthur Simmonds': particularly cold hardy. 'Dark Knight': dark blue flowers; prefers average to dry soils. 'First Choice': dark purple blooms earlier than other cultivars. 'Petite Bleu': 2 feet tall and wide. 'Summer Sorbet': variegated dark grayish-green leaves with chartreuse edges. 'Sunshine Blue' and 'Worcester Gold': yellow leaves.

CHRYSANTHEMUM (Chrysanthemum spp.)

Features: Lavish flowers in red, pink, yellow, orange, violet, green, or white in late summer and fall; attracts butterflies.
Hardiness: Zones 5 to 9
Size: 12- to 36-inch by 12- to 36-inch mound
Light: Full sun; partial shade in the South
Site: Average to fertile, well-drained soil

DESCRIPTION AND USES: Mums liven up the garden when most plants have finished blooming. Mums can look like globes or daisies, and their petals can be flat, hooked, fringed, or rolled like quills. Mums enhance fall beds and borders and pair well with 'Autumn Joy' sedum, boltonia, fall-flowering asters, and ornamental grasses. They look striking in containers, whether grown alone or with ornamental grasses and trailing greens.

CARE: To help mums survive the winter, plant them in spring for maximum root development; water regularly. Pinching back mums in late spring and early summer (around Memorial Day and July 4) delays blooming and creates tighter, bushier plants with more blooms. If you prefer looser, bigger, earlier-blooming plants, stake mums in late spring so that they don't fall over. Fertilize plants for lush flowering until you see budded blooms. Once they are in bloom, deadhead old flowers to make way for the new. After plants have finished blooming, trim them back to 6 inches and mulch for winter protection. In spring, divide large clumps, removing any dead material. Because shorter days trigger flowering, select the right mum for your climate. Early bloomers suit areas with early frosts; mid to late bloomers are better for the South. In mild climates, planting early-, mid-, and late-season bloomers prolongs flower interest. Hose off spider mites when necessary.

RECOMMENDATIONS:
'Cambodian Queen': dark pink single blooms with a yellow center in fall. Zones 3 to 7. 'Clara Curtis': 2-foot mound of 3-inch fragrant yellow-centered pink daisies in August and September. Zones 5 to 9. 'Gypsy Wine': dwarf with early-blooming scented wine-red pompoms. 'Hillside Pink Sheffield': light salmon-pink daisies in September and October. Zones 4 to 9. 'Marilyn': abundant white double flowers from September to frost.

GOLDENSTAR (Chrysogonum virginianum)

Features: Star-shape yellow blooms in late spring and summer. Low edging or ground cover.
Hardiness: Zones 5 to 9
In- and out-of-bloom size: 3- to 4-inch by 12-inch mat
Light: Sun to partial shade
Site: Well-drained soil of average fertility

DESCRIPTION AND USES: Long-blooming goldenstar has five-petaled vivid yellow blooms. The hairy-stalked flowers face upward in contrast to the fuzzy bright green leaves. Stems form a thick mat and spread quickly but not aggressively. The foliage of this Eastern United States native is herbaceous in cool climates and evergreen in warm climates.

CARE: Low-maintenance goldenstar performs best in moist soils of average fertility but high in organic matter. It thrives in sun to partial shade and needs good drainage.

RECOMMENDATIONS:
'**Allen Bush**': 10- to 12-inch tall ground cover with small yellow flowers. '**Pierre**': 6-inch-tall clump; bigger flowers than the species. '**Australe**': 8-inch-tall ground cover; golden blooms from April to June and in September and October; dark glossy green leaves.

'ATROPURPUREA' FRAGRANT BUGBANE (Cimicifuga ramosa)

Features: Scented bottlebrush white blooms in late summer to fall. Deep bronzy-purple serrated leaves and stems.
Hardiness: Zones 4 to 8
In-bloom size: 4- to 6-foot by 24- to 36-inch spire
Out-of-bloom size: 3½-foot mound
Light: Sun to shade
Site: Well-drained, fertile soil

DESCRIPTION AND USES: Bugbane's purple-leaved cultivars look handsome through the entire growing season because of their striking foliage, which ranges from greenish purple to dark bronzy purple. Twelve-inch creamy white flower spikes on branched stems rise high above the mass of dark divided leaves. 'Atropurpurea' is a splendid accent for the shade garden, whether grown alone or in groups. It looks elegant massed at the back of the border and in woodland gardens with ferns and hardy begonias.

CARE: Bugbane performs best in moist, well-drained, loamy soils high in organic matter. It prefers shade or partial shade in warm climates; it can tolerate full sun in the North as long as the soil stays consistently moist. Divide plants in spring.

RECOMMENDATIONS:
'**Brunette**' fragrant bugbane: pinkish-white blooms on 3- to 4-foot stems and dark bronzy-purple leaves.
■ Kamchatka bugbane (*C. simplex*) has arching flower stems. Zones 3 to 7. '**White Pearl**': a loose, shrubby perennial with abundant dense white bloom spikes held high above the pale green leaves. '**Hillside Black Beauty**': 12-inch-long creamy white fragrant flower spikes on 5-foot stems; deep coppery-purple leaves.
■ Black snakeroot (*C. racemosa*) is a bushy perennial native to Eastern North America with fragrant white bottlebrush flowers in mid- to late summer. Zones 3 to 8.

SOLITARY CLEMATIS *(Clematis integrifolia)*

Bush clematis

Features: Bell-shape blue-violet blooms from late spring to late summer. Ideal for weaving through nearby plants.
Hardiness: Zones 3 to 7
In- and out-of-bloom size: 2- to 3-foot by 2- to 3-foot mound
Light: Full sun to partial shade
Site: Moist, fertile, well-drained soil

DESCRIPTION AND USES: Solitary clematis makes a bushy, sprawling little mound that looks charming when its woody but flexible stems lace among those of nearby plants. Small blue-violet bells nod among green leaves for much of the growing season. Airy seed heads, which persist into fall, resemble puffs of curling silken threads. Plant this clematis with spring-blooming shrubs. The shrubs will support the scrambling clematis, and the clematis will bring spring-to-fall visual interest to the shrubs. Or grow it among early-blooming, strong-stemmed perennials such as blue star or false indigo. Massed on its own, it creates a bushy deciduous ground cover.

CARE: This low-maintenance plant grows best in full sun and moist, fertile, well-drained soil. If you want this nonclimbing clematis to appear taller, use pea stakes for a natural look. Mulch the root area to shade and cool the soil. Cut the plant back to a pair of buds about 6 inches from the ground before it starts leafing out in spring.

RECOMMENDATIONS:
■ **'China Purple' bush clematis** *(C. heracleifolia)* grows 30 inches by 36 inches and has flaring deep blue-violet bells in summer, followed by silky seed heads. Its large dark green leaves and upright stems make this plant look shrubby and coarse-textured. Some people call this fragrant tube clematis. Zones 3 to 8.
■ **Purple-leaved ground clematis** *(C. recta* 'Purpurea') has small but lavish clusters of fragrant, starry white flowers in late spring and summer, followed by silver seed heads. New growth opens purple and turns green as it matures. Plants are 2 to 4 feet by 2 to 3 feet. Grow this sprawler staked and upright, or let it run through shrubs and other perennials. Zones 3 to 7.

COREOPSIS *(Coreopsis spp.)*

'Moonbeam'

'Tequila Sunrise'

Features: Yellow daisies from spring to summer. Outstanding in borders, butterfly gardens, and native-plant gardens. Drought-tolerant.
Hardiness: Zones 4 to 9
Size: 6- to 36-inch by 12- to 36-inch mounds to loose columns
Light: Full sun
Site: Moist, well-drained soil

DESCRIPTION AND USES: Valued in beds and borders for long-blooming yellow daisies that attract butterflies, coreopsis bears golden yellow, pale lemon, pink, or bicolor flowers. Leaves range from medium to fine in texture. Grow it in containers, sunny borders, or wildflower gardens with companions such as Arkansas amsonia and switch grass.

CARE: This perennial needs full sun and moist, well-drained soil; it tolerates heat and drought. Deadheading faded flowers prolongs blooming. Cutting it back after the first flush of flowers encourages rebloom. A second cutting in late summer helps stop self-sowing and flopping. Coreopsis sprawls in rich, wet soil and needs support. Tall cultivars also require staking. Divide plants in spring every three years.

RECOMMENDATIONS:
■ **'Early Sunrise' coreopsis** *(C. grandiflora)* is a short-lived 18- inch perennial with showy 2-inch orangy-gold semidouble to double flowers all summer. Zones 4 to 9. **'Sunray' coreopsis:** 16 to 18 inches; brilliant golden double and semidouble flowers.
■ **'Goldfink' lanceleaf coreopsis** *(C. lanceolata)* is a 10-inch dwarf with golden blooms. Zones 3 to 8. **'Tequila Sunrise' lanceleaf coreopsis:** red-centered, yellow-orange flowers and olive-green leaves with creamy yellow edges.
■ **'Limerock Ruby' pink coreopsis** *(C. rosea)* grows 1 foot by 2 feet tall with rose-red flowers and threadlike leaves. Zones 7 to 9. **'Sweet Dreams' pink coreopsis:** 18 inches tall with 1-inch raspberry-centered white daisies. Zones 6 to 8.
■ **Threadleaf coreopsis** *(C. verticillata)* is fast-growing and long-flowering with a mounded, spreading form and fine-textured leaves. It grows 2 to 3 feet tall. Zones 4 to 9. **'Moonbeam':** small pale yellow daisies. **'Creme Brulee':** 3-foot-wide clump; deeper yellow and sturdier stems than 'Moonbeam'. **'Zagreb':** 8 to 10 inches; yellow flowers.

YELLOW CORYDALIS *(Corydalis lutea)*

Features: Tubular, spurred yellow flowers; ferny leaves. Good in dry-stone walls and rock gardens. Self-sows in cool, dry climates.
Hardiness: Zones 4 to 8
Size: 16-inch by 12- to 18-inch mound
Light: Part to full shade
Site: Moist, well-drained soil

DESCRIPTION AND USES: With its bright yellow blooms and attractive leaves—green on top and frosty gray-green below—yellow corydalis looks charming at the front of a border or as a ground cover in lightly wooded areas, where it can naturalize by self-seeding. It's well-suited for tucking into shady rock crevices and rock gardens. Heat, humidity, and waterlogged soil can kill off this generally healthy plant.

CARE: Grow corydalis in moist, sharply drained, neutral to slightly alkaline soil. Cutting it back after flowering keeps it from self-sowing. Renew the plant after flowering by cutting it back to its basal leaves.

RECOMMENDATIONS:
■ **'Blue Panda' blue corydalis** (*C. flexuosa*) bears lightly fragrant blue blooms in late spring and early summer. The color is more intense in cool climates. Plants go dormant later in summer. Zones 5 to 8. **'China Blue' blue corydalis:** fragrant grayish-blue flowers.
■ **Hybrid corydalis 'Blackberry Wine':** 10 to 18 inches; clustered ³/₄-inch purple blooms from late spring to midsummer; bluish-green leaves.

'LUCIFER' CROCOSMIA *(Crocosmia hybrids)*

Features: Fire-red bloom spikes in mid- to late summer, followed by attractive seed heads. Swordlike basal leaves. Good for cutting and hot-hued borders.
Hardiness: Zones 5 to 11
In- and out-of-bloom size: 36-inch by 18- to 24-inch clump
Light: Full sun
Site: Rich, moist, well-drained soil

DESCRIPTION AND USES: This clump-forming plant has rows of 2-inch brilliant red flowers on the top side of sturdy, arched spikes. Erect, sword-shape bright green leaves, complement the blooms. Planted in groups or masses, Lucifer crocosmia is a perfect midsize choice for tropical gardens and hot borders. Good partners include ornamental grasses and orange-, yellow-, and white-flowered perennials. A stunning cut flower.

CARE: Crocosmia grows from corms, which are hard, scaly, enlarged underground stems. Dependably winter-hardy to Zone 7, crocosmia also grows in Zones 5 and 6 if the corms are dug and stored each fall. In cool climates, keeping crocosmia in the ground through winter is possible if you plant it in a sheltered spot and keep it mulched. Crocosmia tolerates heat and humidity but prefers full sun and rich, moist, well-drained soils. If spider mites bother your plants, use a garden hose to wash them away. Remove damaged leaves; when necessary, renew by cutting to the ground.

RECOMMENDATIONS:
■ **Hybrid crocosmias 'Emily McKenzie':** 15 inches; bright orange flowers with a deep red-ringed throat. **'George Davison':** 16-inch dwarf; yellow blooms and grassy leaves.

DELPHINIUM (*Delphinium* spp.)

Features: Handsome spikes of blue, white, pink, purple, and bicolor blooms in early to midsummer.
Hardiness: Zones 3 to 7
In-bloom size: 1- to 7-foot spire
Out-of-bloom size: 2- to 3-foot mound
Light: Full sun
Site: Rich, moist, well-drained, slightly alkaline soil high in organic matter

DESCRIPTION AND USES: Delphinium produces lush conical flower spikes composed of small single or double flowers in blue, pink, white, and purple. Florets may have white centers, called bees, for a bicolor effect. Plant tall cultivars at the back of sunny cottage borders, where they tower over other plants. Shorter varieties belong in mid border; dwarf plants are charming at the front of the border and in rock gardens.

CARE: Delphiniums like cool-summer climates. If soil is acidic, apply lime to raise pH. Deadhead delphinium to a fresh shoot when flowers fade. After all flowering finishes, cut spikes back to the basal leaf mounds; new flower spikes may appear later in the season. Cut bloom stalks to the ground after all flowering ceases. Stake medium to tall delphiniums early in the season; fertilize in spring and summer.

RECOMMENDATIONS:
■ 'Bellamosum' belladonna delphinium (*D. ×belladonna*) has dark blue flower spikes on 36- by 24-inch branched stems. Zones 3 to 7.
■ 'Blue Dwarf' Chinese delphinium (*D. grandiflorum*) produces 10-inch spikes of gentian blue blooms all summer. Zones 3 to 7. **'Blue Butterfly':** 14-inch deep blue spikes.
■ Hybrid delphiniums **'Round Table Hybrids':** 5 to 6 feet; spikes of light blue, deep blue, lavender, violet, white, purple, and bicolor flowers. **'Summer Nights':** 18 inches; blue blooms spring through summer. Plant 18 inches apart. Heat-tolerant. **'Connecticut Yankee' series:** more heat-tolerant than most delphiniums. Spikes of single flowers in mixed hues.

PINKS (*Dianthus* spp.)

Features: Pink, white, rose, red, or bicolor blooms with a spicy clove scent. Dense, spreading mat of narrow grayish or bluish-green leaves.
Hardiness: Zones 3 to 10
In- and out-of-bloom size: 4- to 18-inch by 15-inch mound
Light: Full sun; afternoon shade in the South
Site: Well-drained, fertile, neutral to slightly alkaline soil

DESCRIPTION AND USES: Pinks bear profuse, often spicily fragrant 1- to 2-inch blooms in late spring to summer. The flowers attract butterflies; they are double, like carnations, or single, which draw hummingbirds. Petals may be shaggy, serrated, or fringed at the tips, and may have contrasting rims or eyes. After blooming, the foliage forms a dense, often evergreen mat of needlelike grayish to bluish-green leaves. Pinks look good at the front of a border, in rock gardens, and massed along paths, where you can smell their sweet, clove scent when you walk by.

CARE: Amending beds with lime, sand, and compost when needed creates the light, neutral to slightly alkaline soil in which pinks like to grow. Crowding promotes pests and diseases, so divide every two to three years. Apply low-nitrogen fertilizer in spring. Avoid using overhead sprinklers or putting bark mulch around pinks. Instead, mulch with pine boughs for winter protection. Deadheading extends bloom, and cutting plants back after flowering keeps them compact.

RECOMMENDATIONS:
■ 'Zing Rose' maiden pink (*D. deltoides*) has single rose-red blooms topping its 8-inch by 12-inch mats of dark green leaves. Zones 5 to 8.
■ 'Bath's Pink' cheddar pink (*D. gratianopolitanus*) has fragrant light pink blooms with dark eyes in spring to summer and grassy light blue-green leaves. Grows 10 inches by 12 inches; tolerates heat, drought, and humidity. Zones 4 to 9. **'Firewatch' cheddar pink:** 6 inches by 12 inches; fringed, fragrant magenta blooms. Zones 5 to 9. **'Tiny Rubies' cheddar pink:** 4 inches by 12 inches; fragrant deep pink flowers with serrated edges. Zones 5 to 8.
■ Hybrid pinks **'Loveliness':** 12 inches by 24 inches; fringed, sweet-scented bicolor single blooms in white, pink, and rose. **'Betty Morton':** 5 to 8 inches; rosy pink single flowers with a dark fuchsia eye in late spring. Zones 5 to 8.

'LUXURIANT' PACIFIC BLEEDING HEART
(Dicentra formosa)

GAS PLANT (Dictamnus albus)

Features: Heart-shape cerise flowers hang on curved stems in late spring and sporadically through the growing season. Spreading mounds of ferny green leaves.
Hardiness: Zones 3 to 8
In-bloom size: 12- to 15-inch by 18-inch mound
Out-of-bloom size: 10- to 12-inch mound
Light: Partial to full shade
Site: Rich, moist, well-drained, humusy soil

DESCRIPTION AND USES: Elongated clusters of deep reddish-pink flowers nod gracefully on arched branching stems over feathery green leaves. Flowers are shaped like 1-inch hearts hooked on either side of the base. Pacific bleeding heart is native to the West Coast. It spreads quickly by roots and seeds to form a lovely ground cover in shady areas and woodland gardens.

CARE: If you plant Pacific bleeding heart in a shady border with other perennials, you may have to dig or pull out seedlings to control the spread. Deadheading before seeds form prevents self-sowing and keeps the garden looking neat. If necessary, cut back tattered foliage as the season progresses. Fungal diseases may affect leaves.

RECOMMENDATIONS:
'Bacchanal': dark brick red flowers; grayish leaves. 'Adrian Bloom': ruby red flowers; blue-green leaves. 'Aurora': small soft-white blooms; ferny blue-green leaves.
■ **Old-fashioned bleeding heart** (D. spectabilis) has rows of heart-shaped bright pink flowers hanging on long, arching stems held high above the divided medium-green leaves. It self-sows and grows in full shade to sun, as long as it has adequate moisture. Especially in sun, old-fashioned bleeding heart goes dormant by midsummer but returns the following spring. Zones 2 to 8. 'Alba': pure white flowers and long-lasting bluish-green leaves. 'Gold Heart': pink flowers and brilliant chartreuse leaves, which scorch in the sun.
■ **Hybrid bleeding hearts** 'King of Hearts': abundant wide, deep pink flowers; disease-free.

Features: Big, open spikes of white to pinkish flowers striped with darker veins in late spring. Attractive mound of thick, shiny, aromatic leaves.
Hardiness: Zones 3 to 8
In-bloom size: 24- to 36-inch by 24- to 36-inch spire
Out-of-bloom size: 16- to 24-inch by 24- to 36-inch mound
Light: Full sun to partial shade
Site: Moist, somewhat rich, well-drained soil with a neutral to slightly alkaline pH

DESCRIPTION AND USES: Gas plant is worth growing for its tough, handsome, glossy, feather-shaped leaflets on stalks that sometimes grow more than a foot long; leaflets smell lemony when rubbed. Gardeners also grow it for its appealing, albeit short-blooming, white to pink bloom spikes of 1-inch lightly scented flowers. Each flower has five petals unevenly spaced around a group of long, prominent stamens. Gas plant's flower spikes add a welcome vertical note to the perennial border in late spring when it blooms and in fall after the starry seedpods have ripened. It looks attractive silhouetted against dark shrubs and planted with coral bells, lady's mantle, or 'Happy Returns' daylily.

CARE: Slow-growing gas plant takes its name from the combustible oil produced by the seeds and flowers. The oil may irritate skin, so wear gloves when working with this plant, which is mostly healthy and free from pests and diseases. Gas plant takes years to become established. Because stems are strong and woody at the base, it probably does not need staking. Avoid dividing or moving it unless you must.

RECOMMENDATIONS:
'Albiflorus': white flowers. 'Purpureus': purplish-pink flowers with dark stems and veins.

YELLOW FOXGLOVE *(Digitalis grandiflora)*

Yellow foxglove

Common foxglove

Features: Spectacular spikes of nodding light yellow bells marked with brown on the inside in early to midsummer.
Hardiness: Zones 3 to 8
In-bloom size: 2- to 4-foot by 1½- to 2-foot spire
Out-of-bloom size: 1-foot by 1½- to 2-foot mound
Light: Partial shade, but tolerates sun to shade in moist, well-drained soil high in organic matter
Site: Average garden soil

DESCRIPTION AND USES: Yellow foxglove brightens woodland landscapes with spikes of pale yellow flowers on hairy stems and lance-shape green leaves up to 10 inches long. It makes an impressive vertical garden accent and looks lovely in shady borders planted with lady's mantle, large-leaved hosta, or Bethlehem sage. It also looks charming planted among shrubs and trees. Yellow foxglove is a perennial that may self-sow in good conditions.

CARE: Although yellow foxglove grows well in average garden conditions, it prefers partial shade and moist, well-drained soil high in organic matter. In warm climates, it requires some afternoon shade. Yellow foxglove often blooms again if you cut off faded flower spikes before they set seed. Once the plant has rebloomed, remove the flower stalks to prevent self-seeding. Divide the clump when the plant is not in bloom.

RECOMMENDATIONS:
'Carillon': 10-inch dwarf with yellow flowers through the summer. **'Temple Bells':** extra-large yellow blooms.
■ **Strawberry foxglove** (*D. ×mertonensis*) bears strawberry-colored bloom spikes up to 3 feet tall; shiny dark green leaves up to 1 foot long. Divide every two to three years. Zones 3 to 8.
■ **Common foxglove** (*D. purpurea*) is a short-lived, self-sowing perennial or biennial that grows up to 6 feet tall. Its tall spikes create excitement in sunny to partly shaded borders and cottage gardens. Plants are often paired with clematis and old-fashioned shrub roses. Zones 4 to 8. **'Alba':** white flowers. **Excelsior Hybrids:** spikes of horizontal flowers in pink, white, purple, and yellow. **Foxy Hybrids:** 2 to 3 feet; pink, cherry, cream, and white flowers with maroon markings. **'Silver Fox':** creamy bells flushed lavender-pink outside and spotted inside; silvery leaves.

PURPLE CONEFLOWER *(Echinacea purpurea)*

Features: Large pinkish-purple daisies with rust-colored cone-shape centers in mid- to late summer. Attracts butterflies.
Hardiness: Zones 3 to 9
In-bloom size: 2- to 3-foot by 1½-foot upright
Out-of-bloom size: 1- to 2-foot by 1½-foot clump
Light: Full sun
Site: Average, neutral to slightly alkaline, well-drained soil

DESCRIPTION AND USES: Valued for its large, sturdy daisies, purple coneflower is a classic of the summer border. New cultivars are available in white, cream, yellow, orange, purple, and burgundy. Excellent for cutting. The flowers attract bees and butterflies; birds eat the seeds when they mature. Purple coneflower looks grand with lamb's-ears, globe thistle, Russian sage, and white gaura.

CARE: Low-maintenance purple coneflower needs well-drained soil; it tolerates heat, humidity, drought, wind, and some shade. It has no pests, but staking may be necessary in rich soil. Clumps expand by creating small new plants around the base. You can transplant these offsets when you divide the clump in spring or fall every five years. This prairie native self-sows, but cultivars may not come true from seed. Deadheading prevents self-sowing and keeps the plant looking good. Saving some late blooms will give winter interest to the garden, feed the birds, and encourage more plants through self-sowing.

RECOMMENDATIONS:
'Magnus': nondroopy rosy petals and a brownish-red cone; 2- to 3-foot stems. **'Orange Meadowbrite':** droopy bright orange petals and a dark cone. **'Kim's Mophead':** dwarf with white flowers and a green cone on 12- to 15-inch stems. **'Razmatazz':** large central ball of short, bright pink petals surrounded by longer, arching pink petals; fragrant blooms 3 to 4 inches wide. **'Ruby Giant':** 7-inch blooms with purple-red petals. **'Sunrise':** fragrant yellow flowers that soften in color as they age. **'Vintage Wine':** horizontal burgundy rays with a dark cone.
■ **'Rocky Top' hybrids** (*E. tennesseensis*) have light pink petals around a blackish cone. Zones 6 to 8.

'VEITCH'S BLUE' GLOBE THISTLE
(Echinops ritro)

Features: Attention-grabbing deep blue globes; deep-cut spiny leaves.
Hardiness: Zones 4 to 9
In-bloom size: 36- to 40-inch by 18- to 24-inch upright
Out-of-bloom size: 15-inch by 18- to 24-inch mound
Light: Full sun
Site: Somewhat fertile, well-drained soil that is neutral to slightly alkaline in pH

DESCRIPTION AND USES: Intense blue spheres cap this tough perennial, which produces coarse grayish-green leaves with hairy white undersides. Erect, branched flower stems emerge from up to 8-inch-long basal foliage. Copious 1- to 2-inch flower heads attract bees and butterflies. Flowers start out dark blue but take on a lighter tint as summer progresses. Deeply cut, thistly foliage has sharp spines. Globe thistle tolerates heat, drought, and infertile soils. Use it in fresh and dried flower arrangements. In the garden, it looks stunning with purple coneflower, coreopsis, and Russian sage and suits well-drained, cottage gardens, roadside beds, seaside plantings, and sunny borders.

CARE: Globe thistle is easy to grow. Stake it in fertile soil, where it may flop. Without grooming, plants can look rangy by summer's end. Keep them tidy by deadheading, which also prevents self-sowing. Plants may flower again if pruned to basal leaves after blooming. Pests and diseases rarely trouble globe thistle. If necessary, divide globe thistle in spring by separating offsets.

RECOMMENDATIONS:
■ 'Blue Globe' globe thistle (E. bannaticus) has deep blue flower heads up to 2½ inches wide. Zones 3 to 8. **'Taplow Blue' globe thistle:** silvery-blue globes.
■ 'Arctic Glow' globe thistle (E. sphaerocephalus) produces 2-inch white balls on reddish stems. Zones 5 to 8.

RED BARRENWORT (Epimedium ×rubrum)

Features: Petite ruby blooms and red-tinged heart-shape leaflets in spring; red to copper fall foliage.
Hardiness: Zones 4 to 8
In-bloom size: 12-inch by 12- to 18-inch mound
Out-of-bloom size: 10- to 12-inch by 18-inch mound
Light: Partial to full shade
Site: Moist, well-drained to dry soils

DESCRIPTION AND USES: Red barrenwort spreads quickly, forming a graceful ground cover, which persists through winter in warm climates. It thrives in dry shade, growing well in shady rock gardens and under shrubs and dense-canopied trees with shallow, greedy roots. For the reddest spring leaves, plant barrenwort under deciduous trees, where it will receive plenty of sunshine before the trees leaf out. Barrenwort's spurred ¾-inch red-and-yellow flowers appear in spring and look like a bishop's hat.

CARE: Barrenwort requires little care. It flourishes in fertile, well-drained soil high in organic matter but spreads well in dry shade. Maintain consistent moisture for the first season in the garden. Remove tattered foliage early in the growing season to tidy up the plant and to make its delicate spring flowers easier to see.

RECOMMENDATIONS:
■ Longspur barrenwort (E. grandiflorum) makes 12-inch-tall spreading clumps of light pink blooms up to 1¾ inches wide. Zones 5 to 8.
■ 'Fröhnleiten' (E. ×perralchicum) is an attractive, vigorous 4- to 18-inch-tall evergreen ground cover with nodding yellow blooms on straight stems above the leaves. Zones 5 to 8.
■ Featherleaf barrenwort (E. pinnatum colchicum) produces yellow flowers on 12-inch stems that top an 8-inch clump of dark evergreen foliage. Zones 5 to 8.
■ 'Sulphureum' bicolor barrenwort (E. ×versicolor) has yellow flowers with coppery new leaves and is a spreading evergreen that grows to 8 to 12 inches by up to 36 inches. **'Versicolor' bicolor barrenwort:** small pale purplish-pink blooms with a yellow center. Zones 5 to 8.
■ 'Niveum' young's barrenwort (E. ×youngianum) grows 6 to 8 inches tall with red-flushed leaves in spring and fall and tiny bright white flowers in late spring. Zones 5 to 8.

FLEABANE *(Erigeron speciosus)*

Features: Showy pink, white, yellow, or purple daisies with a central yellow disk from midsummer to fall.
Hardiness: Zones 4 to 9
In-bloom size: 18- to 30-inch by 12- to 24-inch upright
Out-of-bloom size: 2- to 12-inch by 24-inch low rosette
Light: Full sun
Site: Sandy, well-drained soil

DESCRIPTION AND USES: Fleabane has pastel blooms up to 2½ inches wide and lance-shaped leaves. Cultivars have a yellow center surrounded by narrow petals in colors ranging from pink and purple to yellow and white. Fleabane flowers resemble asters but bloom earlier in the season. Short fleabanes look charming massed in rock gardens and paired with dwarf blue fescue. They also work at the front of borders and the edges of beds. Taller varieties look good grouped in mid border with northern sea oats and 'Moonbeam' coreopsis.

CARE: This low-maintenance perennial is free from pests and diseases. It likes moist, well-drained soil of average fertility but adapts well to leaner sites. Short alpine fleabanes need quick-draining soil. Stake tall fleabane varieties. Pruning fleabane to 6 inches after blooming renews the leaves and makes the plant more compact. Divide every three years in spring to maintain vigor.

RECOMMENDATIONS:
■ Beach fleabane *(E. glaucus)* has pale mauve flowers with yellow flowers from late spring to midsummer. A California native, the 12-inch-tall by 18-inch-wide plants can be found growing on sand dunes. Zones 5 to 8. **'Albus':** 8 inches; big white blooms. **'Sea Breeze':** 24 to 36 inches; large pink daisies with a fat yellow center.
■ Hybrid fleabane **'Azure Fairy':** lavender-blue semidouble blooms. **'Darkest of All':** 24 inches; rich blue-violet flowers. **'Prosperity':** 18 inches; lavender-blue blooms. **'Rose Jewel':** 15 to 18 inches; lilac-rose flowers.

FLAT SEA HOLLY *(Eryngium planum)*

Features: Unusual egg-shape steel blue flower clusters with spiny blue petal-like bracts and stems.
Hardiness: Zones 5 to 9
In-bloom size: 30-inch by 18-inch upright
Out-of-bloom size: 8-inch evergreen mound
Light: Full sun
Site: Well-drained, sandy soil high in organic matter

DESCRIPTION AND USES: Choose sea holly for its striking blue blooms, prickly texture, drought tolerance, and resistance to deer, insects, and diseases. The flowers occur in egg-shape clusters skirted with spiky bluish bracts at the base. The sturdy, branched blue flower stems rise from low rosettes of toothy evergreen leaves. The leaves resemble the deeply cut, spiny leaves of thistles. Sea holly grows in clumps and spreads by seed. Its flowers bloom over a long period in July and August. Sea holly is excellent in fresh and dried flower arrangements, it does well in seaside gardens.

CARE: Sea holly grows erect in lean, sandy, well-drained soil. It falls over in rich soils and needs staking in those conditions. Sea holly's taproot makes it difficult to transplant. Plants are pest- and disease-free. Cut down flowering stems after blooming to prevent excessive self-seeding. For lower maintenance, grow a sterile cultivar such as 'Sapphire Blue', which does not self-sow.

RECOMMENDATIONS:
'Fluela': 36 inches; metallic blue flowers on a loose, bushy plant; green basal leaves. **'Hellas':** 32 inches; metallic blue blooms on branched blue stems; blue-green leaves. **'Silverstone':** 30 to 36 inches; white flowers.
■ 'Miss Willmott's Ghost' giant sea holly *(E. giganteum)* grows 36 inches by 12 inches and is a short-lived perennial or biennial with dramatic gray-green to steel-blue cylindrical flower heads surrounded by silvery bracts. Zones 4 to 7.
■ Moroccan sea holly *(E. varifolium)* sports spectacular variegated dark green leaves with white veins and silver-blue stems topped with gray flower heads. It grows 15 inches tall. Zones 5 to 8.
■ Hybrid sea holly **'Sapphire Blue':** 24 to 30 inches by 18 to 24 inches; steel blue stems, leaves, and egg-shape flower clusters; deeply divided basal leaves; sterile nonspreading hybrid.

'GATEWAY' JOE-PYE WEED
(Eupatorium maculatum)

Features: Jumbo, domed mauve flowers on tall burgundy-streaked stems. Attracts butterflies.
Hardiness: Zones 3 to 7
In-bloom size: 5- to 6-foot by 3- to 4-foot upright
Out-of-bloom size: 5-foot by 3- to 4-foot clump
Light: Full sun to partial shade
Site: Moist, well-drained, fertile soil

DESCRIPTION AND USES: This striking plant is ideal for the back of large late-summer borders, wildflower gardens, and moist meadow gardens, and for cutting. It has 10- to 12-inch rosy flower clusters atop 5- to 6-foot burgundy-mottled stems covered with leaves up to 1 foot long. The plant forms a coarse-textured informal clump that holds its own in the largest perennial garden, especially when massed. Good companions include 'Silberfeder' maiden grass, 'Cloud Nine' switch grass, and 'Herbstsonne' and great rudbeckia to bring nonstop goldfinches and butterflies to your garden in late summer and fall.

CARE: Joe-Pye weed prefers moist soils. Its stems are sturdy and usually need no staking. Limit its height by pinching back stems in early summer. To deter mildew, thin stems for improved air circulation. Divide in spring.

RECOMMENDATIONS:
'Atropurpureum': 6 feet; burgundy blooms; red-tinged leaves. 'Bartered Bride': white flowers; 4 to 6 feet tall.
■ 'Chocolate' white snakeroot (E. rugosum) has erect dark purple stems and deep bronzy-purple leaves that turn greener as the season progresses. In autumn, creamy white flower clusters cover this gorgeous cultivar. Plants grow 3 to 5 feet by 2 to 3 feet. Zones 3 to 7.

'VENUSTA' QUEEN-OF-THE-PRAIRIE
(Filipendula rubra)

Features: Towering wetlands native. Fluffy fragrant plumes of cherry pink flowers in summer. Attractive seed heads.
Hardiness: Zones 3 to 9
In-bloom size: 4- to 6-foot by 3- to 4-foot broadly upright
Out-of-bloom size: 4-foot by 4-foot clump
Light: Full sun to partial shade
Site: Moist, somewhat fertile, well-drained to boggy soil

DESCRIPTION AND USES: 'Venusta' queen-of-the-prairie resembles a giant astilbe, forming a tall, spreading clump in moist, fertile soil. Feathery 6-inch-wide cerise flower clusters rise above deeply cut, three-lobed green leaves on branched red stems. The flowers turn paler as summer progresses. Plant queen-of-the-prairie in moist meadows, wildflower gardens, woodland gardens, wet gardens, and at the back of the perennial border; or grow it by a pond with white astilbe and royal fern.

CARE: Queen-of-the-prairie forms wide clumps in consistently moist to boggy soils high in organic matter. It may need support in bloom but otherwise requires little grooming. The seed heads are appealing. If powdery mildew gives the leaves an unsightly cast, cut down the plants so new leaves will form.

RECOMMENDATIONS:
'Venusta Alba': white flowers.
■ Dwarf Siberian meadowsweet (F. palmata 'Nana') grows 8 to 10 inches tall and has pink plumes and five-lobed leaves. Zones 3 to 7.
■ Meadowsweet (F. ulmaria) produces 10-inch-wide white flower plumes in summer. Plants grow 3 to 4 feet by 3 feet. Zones 3 to 7. 'Aurea': white plumes; gold leaves, which are brighter yellow in shade. 'Flore Pleno': creamy white flowers. 'Variegata': white plumes; yellow and yellow-green leaves.

BLANKET FLOWER (*Gaillardia aristata*)

Features: Red, orange, yellow, bicolor, and tricolor daisies from early summer to fall. Hot-border favorite. Grayish-green leaves.
Hardiness: Zones 3 to 8
In- and out-of-bloom size: 30-inch by 24-inch rounded mound
Light: Full sun
Site: Sandy, well-drained soil high in organic matter

DESCRIPTION AND USES: This cheery perennial brings warmth and bright blooms to the perennial garden. Blanket flower's cheery red, orange, yellow, and multicolor flowers, 3 to 5 inches wide, attract butterflies. Blooms are good for cutting, adding vivid hues to arrangements. Fast-growing blanket flower forms an expanding clump, thanks to its horizontal spreading roots. It tolerates heat, drought, and poor soils. Suitable companions include 'Stella de Oro' daylily, white gaura, and 'Little Honey' fountain grass, which makes a low, cushioned support for the plant.

CARE: This short-lived perennial grows best in well-drained soil of average fertility, but it tolerates poor soil. It blooms from early summer to fall. Deadheading promotes a tidy appearance; retain some seed heads to encourage self-sowing, although cultivars do not typically come true from seed. Divide every two or three years in spring. Blanket flower is healthy and vigorous except in soggy conditions. Cover with boughs for protection from deep, wet snows.

RECOMMENDATIONS:
'Baby Cole': 6 to 8 inches by 15 to 18 inches; 3-inch yellow-tipped red daisies with a wine-red central disk. **'Bijou':** 8 to 10 inches; dwarf version of the popular 'Goblin'; yellow-edged red flowers. **'Fanfare':** 12 to 15 inches by 15 to 18 inches; yellow, orange, or burgundy flowers with rolled petals; dense, mounding form. Zones 5 to 8. **'Goblin':** (also sold as 'Kobold'); 12 inches; deep red blooms with a yellow border from July to frost. **'Torchlight':** 30 inches tall, yellow-edged maroon rays.

WHITE GAURA (*Gaura lindheimeri*)

'Siskiyou Pink'

Features: Star-shape pink or white blooms on airy stems in late spring to early fall.
Hardiness: Zones 5 to 9
In-bloom size: 5-foot by 3-foot branched upright wand
Out-of-bloom size: 1- to 3-foot clump
Light: Full sun
Site: Moderately fertile, well-drained soil

DESCRIPTION AND USES: White gaura looks good in the front and middle of the perennial border, where its see-through, leaning stems can intertwine with other plants in and out of bloom. The species bears wiry wands of pink buds that open to white flowers. Use it alone in a container or mass-plant it in a bed or border. It makes a good companion for Siberian iris and 'Purple Rain' salvia and is appropriate for wildflower and prairie gardens. White gaura tolerates heat, partial shade, drought, and high humidity.

CARE: Good drainage is necessary for this low-maintenance plant. It likes moderately fertile to fertile soils, although plants are more likely to flop over in rich soil. You won't need to deadhead white gaura; faded flowers fall from the stems without help. White gaura is short-lived, but the species may self-sow nearby. To keep plants compact, cut back the stems in early summer.

RECOMMENDATIONS:
'Corrie's Gold': variegated gold-spotted green leaves. **'Passionate Pink':** neon pink flowers; narrow maroon leaves. **'Siskiyou Pink':** 2 feet; reddish-pink flowers; reddish-green leaves. **'So White':** 15 to 18 inches; white flowers. **'The Giant':** 5 feet; 2-inch white flowers. **'Sunny Butterflies':** 24 inches; pink flowers; white-edged grayish-green foliage. **'Whirling Butterflies':** 24 to 30 inches; sterile cultivar with lavish white blooms and red stems.

BIGROOT CRANESBILL
(Geranium macrorrhizum)

Features: Weed-smothering, deer-resistant ground cover. Magenta flowers in late spring or early summer. Aromatic light green leaves with yellow to red fall color.
Hardiness: Zones 3 to 7
In-bloom size: 15- to 20-inch by 36-inch mounds topped with branched clusters
Out-of-bloom size: 12- to 15-inch spreading mound
Light: Full sun to shade
Site: Moist, moderately fertile, well-drained soil

DESCRIPTION AND USES: Bigroot cranesbill makes a dense, adaptable weed-smothering ground cover for well-drained sites. In cool climates, it does just as well on a sunny dry-stone retaining wall as under a tree in dry shade. The scented, sticky light green leaves develop attractive red and yellow fall color. Flowers are bright magenta. Geranium is a good facer plant for hiding the base of leggy shrubs.

CARE: In warm climates, bigroot cranesbill grows best in dappled shade or in morning sun and afternoon shade. In heavy shade, it makes fewer flowers and its habit may be more open. Although many cranesbill species need cutting back after bloom to keep leaves fresh and growth compact, bigroot cranesbill looks good all season. Foliage persists into winter in warm climates. In early spring, trim back dead foliage. New leaves fill in quickly, creating a solid light green mass.

RECOMMENDATIONS:
'Ingwersen's Variety': 14 inches by 42 inches; 1-inch pale pink blooms; red to orange fall color. Zones 5 to 8. **'Lohenfelden':** 8 inches by 20 inches; 1-inch pale pink flowers; long blooming; red fall color. **'Minor':** 9 inches by 36 inches; 1-inch long-blooming magenta flowers; red to yellow fall color.
■ **'Biokovo'** (*G. ×cantabrigiense*) is 9 inches by 24 inches with pinkish-white blooms in early summer and orange to red fall color. Zones 5 to 8.
■ **'Elsbeth' bloody cranesbill** (*G. sanguineum*) grows 1½ feet by 3 feet with deep pink flowers. Drought-tolerant. Zones 4 to 8.
■ **Hybrid geraniums 'Brookside':** 2 feet by 3 feet; blue blooms with white eye; red fall color. **'Jolly Bee':** 2 feet by 3 feet; blue blooms up to 3 inches wide with a white eye. Zones 5 to 7. **'Rozanne':** 20 inches by 24 inches; 2½-inch violet-blue saucers, marbled dark green leaves; mahogany fall color; Zones 5 to 8.

GEUM *(Geum hybrids)*

'Mrs. Bradshaw' Chilean avens   'Leonard's Variety'

Features: Dazzling hot-hued blooms in red, orange, or yellow from late spring through summer. Handsome foliage.
Hardiness: Zones 5 to 7
In-bloom size: 10- to 24-inch by 12- to 24-inch loose mounds
Out-of-bloom size: 10- to 12-inch tight mound
Light: Full sun; requires afternoon shade in warm climates
Site: Fertile, well-drained soil

DESCRIPTION AND USES: Grown for its rose-shaped flowers in electric hues, geum is a hit at the front of the perennial border, especially when massed for impact. Its long-blooming flowers on wiry stems are good for cutting and for bringing life to the garden when they blow in the wind. They rise above a compact basal rosette of hairy leaves that have zigzag or scalloped edges. Geum, which attracts butterflies, looks good in and out of bloom. Good partners include violet-blue 'May Night' salvia and yellow 'Goldquelle' cutleaf coneflower.

CARE: Geum needs continuously moist but well-drained soil during the growing season, so give it plenty of water. In winter, however, soggy soils will kill the plant. Feed it in spring, and deadhead to extend blooming. Geum survives better in cool climates, so make sure you shade it from harsh afternoon sun if you live in the South. Provide geum with the necessary growing conditions to keep it vigorous. It may be short-lived. Plants rarely need division.

RECOMMENDATIONS:
■ **'Lady Stratheden' Chilean avens** (*G. chiloense*) bears buttery yellow semidouble blooms in loose clusters. It grows 15 to 24 inches tall by 24 inches. **'Mrs. Bradshaw' Chilean avens:** 12 to 24 inches by 24 inches; scarlet semidouble flowers.
■ **Beris geum** (*G. coccineum* 'Borisii') has orangy-red single blooms all summer and grows 10 to 18 inches tall. **'Werner Arends':** 18 inches; long blooming with clear orangy-red semidouble flowers.
■ **Water avens** (*G. rivale*) thrives in cool, wet situations. Plants grow 8 to 12 inches tall and bloom in late spring to midsummer. Zones 3 to 8. **'Leonard's Variety'** has coppery-pink blooms in mid- to late summer.

BABY'S BREATH (Gypsophila paniculata)

Features: Clouds of tiny flowers in summer; delicate frosted green leaves.
Hardiness: Zones 3 to 8
In- and out-of-bloom size: 18- to 36-inch by 36-inch open mound
Light: Full sun
Site: Well-drained alkaline soil

DESCRIPTION AND USES: Baby's breath makes the perfect backdrop for showy garden flowers. In bouquets, its airy, loose flower clusters—fresh or dried—make the perfect foil for red roses. Plant baby's breath with foxgloves and roses for a garden with romantic appeal. Use it as a filler or a background in perennial borders and containers.

CARE: Baby's breath is easy to grow in full sun and light, well-drained alkaline soil. If your soil is acidic, add lime. Baby's breath needs average moisture and fertility. Deadhead plants to promote more blooms. Taking off spent bloom stems to the base may stimulate another flush of flowers in fall. Do not divide. Stake tall types with grow-through supports.

RECOMMENDATIONS:
'Bristol Fairy': 2 to 3 feet; white double flowers. **'Flamingo':** 3 to 4 feet; pink double blooms. **'Pink Fairy':** 18 inches; pink double flowers that bloom into fall.
■ **Creeping baby's breath** (*G. repens*) grows just 8 inches by 12 to 20 inches and has bluish-green leaves. It produces white, pink, or purplish flowers. Plants are charming at the front of the border, in rock gardens, or at the edge of a path.

SNEEZEWEED (Helenium autumnale)

Features: Daisies in rich autumnal reds and yellows in late summer to fall.
Hardiness: Zones 3 to 8
In- and out-of-bloom size: 3- to 5-foot by 3-foot upright clump
Light: Full sun
Site: Moist to wet average soil

DESCRIPTION AND USES: Gardeners value this plant for its late-summer to fall daisies in autumnal shades of yellow, orange, and red on strong, branching stems. Each flower has a brown or yellow central dome surrounded by drooping, wedge-shaped petals of red, orange, yellow, copper, or bronze. Sneezeweed suits the middle to back of the perennial border, where it glows when grouped with maiden grass, tall asters, and other late-blooming perennials. Sneezeweed's informal character and love of moisture make it good for moist meadow gardens and wildflower gardens. Its 2-inch blooms attract butterflies, and the seed heads are interesting over the winter.

CARE: Grow sneezeweed in moist to wet soils in full sun. Don't let the soil dry out. Stake it when small, or cut back in late spring or early summer to make plants more compact. Deadhead for more flowers. Divide in spring or fall. Give sneezeweed good air circulation to help prevent powdery mildew and leaf spot. If these are present, cut down the plant after flowering and discard the stems in the trash. Feed lightly in spring and after flowering with a balanced fertilizer.

RECOMMENDATIONS:
'Butterpat': 4 feet; golden petals with a yellow center. **'Indian Summer':** 40 inches; yellow center surrounded by coppery red rays. **'Mardi Gras':** 3 feet; summer bloomer; yellow rays marked with orangy-red around a dark brown cone. **'Moerheim Beauty':** 2 to 3 feet; rust-red blooms aging to orange and gold. **'Wyndley':** 2½ feet; coppery-brown petals.

THINLEAF PERENNIAL SUNFLOWER
(Helianthus decapetalus)

Features: Sunny yellow daisies in late summer to fall; towering size.
Hardiness: Zones 3 to 9
In-bloom size: 6-foot by 3- to 4-foot upright
Out-of-bloom size: 5-foot column
Light: Full sun
Site: Moist, rich soil

DESCRIPTION AND USES: This low-maintenance sunflower features long-lasting blooms that make excellent cut flowers. The gleaming golden 2- to 3-inch daisies with a bronze center attract butterflies, and the seed heads draw birds. Tall and coarse, the plant makes a handsome specimen at the back of border with tall ornamental grasses and sneezeweed. Plant shorter, mounded perennials, such as massed chrysanthemums, in front of perennial sunflower to mask its tall stems. This plant is ideal for wildflower gardens and mixed borders.

CARE: Perennial sunflower likes moist, well-drained, fertile, alkaline soils but tolerates heavy clay soil and a wide range of pH. Although it thrives in full sun, it also does well in partial shade, especially in the South. For best results, apply a slow-release fertilizer at planting, and water during times of drought. Divide perennial sunflower in spring every few years to help prevent disease and improve air circulation. To control height, pinch the plant repeatedly from midspring to early summer. Deadhead to extend flowering. Support with tall stakes or grow-through supports.

RECOMMENDATIONS:
'Capenoch Star': 5 feet; light yellow flowers. **'Plenus':** 5 to 6 feet; yellow double pompom blooms. **'Soleil d'Or':** 4 to 5 feet; 3½-inch yellow pompoms on branched stems all summer. **'Lemon Queen':** 5 feet; single light yellow blooms. **'Low Down':** 12 inches, lavish flowering dwarf.

LENTEN ROSE *(Helleborus orientalis)*

Features: Year-round garden interest. White, green, red, purple, or yellow flowers in late winter or early spring. Striking seedpods. Leathery evergreen leaves.
Hardiness: Zones 4 to 9
In-bloom size: 18- to 24-inch by 24- to 30-inch clumps
Out-of-bloom size: 18- to 24-inch loose mounds
Light: Partial to full shade
Site: Rich, humusy, well-drained soil

DESCRIPTION AND USES: This sturdy, deer-resistant shade lover stands out for long-lasting 2½-inch flowers, unusual seedpods, and bold umbrella-shape dark green leaves that complement more delicate plants. The single or double flowers are cupped and nodding. They bloom in late winter or early spring and last for months. Colors range from green, white, and yellow to pink, purple, maroon, and red. Some may be spotted or washed with another hue. The clustered seedpods look sculptural. Grow in woodlands or shady borders. Mass for a ground cover under the canopy of trees. In the North, Lenten rose tolerates more sunlight.

CARE: Cultivate in protected sites with average to continuously moist soil high in organic matter. It is pH adaptable. Water deeply until established. Cut back damaged leaves in spring. Division is unnecessary. Lenten rose self-sows, but seedlings, though attractive, may not resemble the parent plant.

RECOMMENDATIONS:
■ **Bear's foot hellebore** (*H. foetidus*) grows 32 inches by 18 inches with hanging green bells rimmed in purple. Its leaves reek when crushed. Zone 5.
■ **Christmas rose** (*H. niger*) has pinkish-white blooms with greenish centers and grows 12 inches by 18 inches.
■ **Hybrid hellebores** **'Sunshine Hybrids':** 12 inches; blooms of pink, rose, white, creamy yellow, and mint green splotched with red at the base. **'Lady Hybrids':** 15 inches; dark red to pale pink and white with deep red spots. **'Royal Heritage':** 18 to 24 inches; flowers from white to blackish purple.

DAYLILY (Hemerocallis hybrids)

'Sunset'

'Lenox'

Features: More than 30,000 varieties in every color but pure white and blue from late spring to frost. Handsome strappy leaves.

Hardiness: Zones 3 to 10

In-bloom size: 6- to 72-inch by 12- to 36-inch clumps with upright flower stalks

Out-of-bloom size: 12- to 24-inch clump

Light: Full sun to partial shade

Site: Moist, fertile, well-drained soil

DESCRIPTION AND USES: Valued for their striking appearance and adaptability, daylilies are perpetual garden favorites. Each flower lives for a day, giving the plant its name. Colors range from hot red, orange, and yellow to cool pink, purple, and bicolor. Blooms form deep or shallow trumpets that resemble spiders, stars, circles, and triangles. Doubles contain extra petal-like structures in the middle for a frilly look. Peak bloom is midsummer, but that varies according to the cultivars; some cultivars bloom throughout the season. Others bloom in early, mid-, or late summer. For summerlong bloom, combine cultivars from each bloom group. Evergreen daylilies thrive in the South. Daylilies and daffodils combine well; daylily's straplike to grassy leaves emerge in time to mask the dying spring bulb foliage. Most daylilies form clumps, but some spread vigorously like a ground cover. Daylilies look wonderful with ornamental grasses, salvia, and nettle-leaved mullein.

CARE: Daylilies prefer well-drained, humus-rich soil of average moisture and fertility, but they will grow just about anywhere. These garden heroes adapt to heat, drought, shade, salt, wind, flooding, and foot traffic. They also survive competition from tree roots. Daylilies are so tough that you can plant them or divide them at any time during the growing season. Feed them moderately but regularly. Break off individual faded blooms at the base; remove the entire flowering stalk once it has finished flowering. Divide every three to five years when you start seeing fewer flowers. Snails, slugs, deer, rabbits, and woodchucks eat daylilies. Daylily rust and leaf streak may infect these plants. Planting them where all their cultural preferences are met helps control the diseases.

RECOMMENDATIONS:
'Bitsy': 17 to 28 inches; 2-inch lemon yellow flowers from spring to fall, grassy leaves; vigorous. 'Black-Eyed Stella': 12 to 22 inches; 3½-inch gold flowers with a dark mahogany eye from late spring to fall. 'Happy Returns': 18 inches; 3-inch-deep lemon yellow flowers from May to September. 'Stella de Oro': 12 inches; sturdy plants with gold flowers from June to September. 'El Desperado': 28 inches; 4½-inch mustard yellow flowers with a burgundy-purple eye, frilly red edge, and green throat. 'Hyperion': 36 inches; fragrant 5-inch lemon yellow flowers in June and July. 'Lady Lucille': 22 to 30 inches; 5- to 6-inch orange flowers; shiny leaves; pest- and disease-resistant; late bloomer—from summer into fall; excellent visibility from afar, especially when massed. 'Lullaby Baby': 24 inches; 4-inch ruffled, fragrant creamy pink flowers with a green throat; early to midseason rebloomer. 'Red Volunteer': 29 to 33 inches; 7-inch velvety red blooms for six to eight weeks starting in midseason; rust-resistant. 'Plum Perfect': 11 to 28 inches; 3½-inch purple blooms with darker purple eye, gold throat, deep purple veins, white midribs, and ruffled edges; long blooming, vigorous, semi-evergreen; good for light shade.

CORAL BELLS (*Heuchera* hybrids)

Coral bells

'Amethyst Myst'

'Palace Purple'

Features: Evergreen to semi-evergreen lobed green, purple, bronze, silver, or chartreuse rounded leaves. Dainty white, pink, or red flower spikes in summer.
Hardiness: Zones 3 to 8
In-bloom size: 12- to 24-inch by 12- to 24-inch airy spires
Out-of-bloom size: 7- to 10-inch mound
Light: Full sun to partial shade
Site: Moist, well-drained soil rich in organic matter

DESCRIPTION AND USES: Grow coral bells for spectacular foliage that provides months of interesting color and texture long after the flowers fade. Delicate, tubular red, pink, or white flowers on slender stalks appear mostly in summer. The loose flower spikes attract bees, hummingbirds, and butterflies and make long-lasting cut flowers. Leaves are mostly rounded and lobed; some are ruffled and frilled. They vary in hue from lime, silver, and pinky beige to wine red, blackish maroon, and chocolate brown. Colorful veins often etch contrasting patterns on coral bells' upper surface. Silvery veils cover the leaf surface of some varieties; others have contrasting edges or undersides. Coral bells suit cottage and woodland gardens. Use them to edge beds and paths, or mass-plant under trees as a ground cover, in containers, and at the front of perennial and mixed borders. Good partners include hosta, Japanese painted fern, and astilbe.

CARE: These low-maintenance perennials like moist, well-drained, somewhat acidic soils high in organic matter. Give them full sun in cool climates, partial shade in warm ones. Deadhead to extend blooming, and remove flower spikes at the base when they finish blooming. If you don't find the flowers attractive, cut the stalks to the ground before they bloom. Cut back dead leaves in spring. If any leaves are damaged during the growing season, remove them at any time and new foliage will emerge from the base. Coral bells can compete with tree roots if top-dressed with 1 to 2 inches of compost every fall. Prevent frost heaving and winter damage by mulching with evergreen boughs. Root weevils sometimes cause problems. Divide plants every few years to stimulate more flowering.

RECOMMENDATIONS:

■ Small-flowered coral bells (*H. micrantha*) grows 12 to 24 inches tall and have sparse, yellowish white flowers. **'Palace Purple':** chartreuse flowers on 18-inch stems in late summer and big bronzy-purple leaves. **'Bressingham Bronze':** 8- to 12-inch mounds of coppery-brown leaves with pointed lobes.

■ Coral bells (*H. sanguinea*) have green leaves and colorful pink, red, or white flowers. Plants grow 12 to 18 inches tall by 12 inches wide.

■ Hybrid coral bells **'Amber Waves':** 12-inch flower stems bear light rosy blooms; 8-inch mound of ruffled amber-gold leaves. **'Amethyst Myst':** 9-inch mound of plum-purple leaves fogged with silver. **'Chocolate Ruffles':** purplish flowers on 30-inch stems; 10-inch mound of ruffled leaves that are chocolate on top and burgundy on the bottom. **'Ebony & Ivory':** ivory flowers on 22-inch stems; 10-inch mound of ruffled very dark purple leaves. **'Lime Rickey':** white flowers on 17-inch stems; 8-inch mound of frosted ruffled chartreuse leaves in spring turning lime green. **'Petite Pearl Fairy':** pink flowers on 8-inch stems; 3- to 4-inch mound of bronzy-purple leaves. **'Saturn':** 15 to 18 inches; dark veins over pewter with reddish-edged leaves.

FOAMY BELLS (×Heucherella spp.)

Features: Abundant white, pink, or cream flower spikes in mid- to late spring. Neat evergreen leaves.
Hardiness: Zones 4 to 8
In-bloom size: 10- to 18-inch mounds with loose spikes above
Out-of-bloom size: 5- to 9-inch mound
Light: Full sun to partial shade
Site: Rich, moist, well-drained soil

DESCRIPTION AND USES: Grown for abundant foamy flower spikes and handsome tight mounds of leaves, this perennial occurred by crossing coral bells and foam flower. The resulting hybrid does not reproduce, thus its energy is available for making lavish wands of delicate pink, white, or tawny flowers. The evergreen leaves appear in neat mounds that sometimes change color as the season progresses. Foliage varies from marbled greens to purple, bronze, chartreuse, and yellow. Some cultivars have silver overlays or colorful decorative veining on the leaves. Foamy bells looks terrific at the front of the perennial border. Use it for edging, or group it for a leafy accent between shrubs. Cut flowers are long lasting. Use it in containers alone or with other plants. It harmonizes with catmint, cranesbill, and hosta.

CARE: Pest- and disease-resistant foamy bells is easy to cultivate in rich, moist, well-drained soil high in organic matter. Partial shade is ideal, but foamy bells can adapt to full shade. Green-and-purple-leaved cultivars also do well in full sun, but yellow or pale-leaved plants may burn. To preserve soil moisture, mulch around plants, but don't cover the growing point. Deadheading promotes more flowers. Divide foamy bells in spring or fall every few years, discarding the center and replanting the vigorous edges.

RECOMMENDATIONS:
■ **'Bridget Bloom' white foamy bells** (H. alba) has 14-inch-long light pink flower spikes in late spring to midsummer and marbled green foliage.
■ **Hybrid foamy bells 'Quicksilver':** 18-inch white spikes, pinkish buds, dark stems; low mounded leaves changing from red to green to dark bronze over the season, bronze veins, silver cast. **'Kimono':** 18-inch tawny spikes, 9-inch leafy mound. Spring leaves green, silver, and purple; metallic rose in winter. Needs part shade. **'Sunspot':** 16-inch pink spikes, yellow leaves splotched scarlet. Needs part shade.

HARDY HIBISCUS (Hibiscus moscheutos)

Features: Bright, bold, tropical-looking pink, red, and white blooms in mid- to late summer.
Hardiness: Zones 5 to 9
In- and out-of-bloom size: 3- to 6-foot by 3- to 4-foot upright oval
Light: Full sun
Site: Rich, continuously moist soil with abundant organic matter

DESCRIPTION AND USES: Perfect for borders with a tropical look, hardy hibiscus produces 8- to 12-inch flowers that attract butterflies and the admiration of garden visitors. Hardy hibiscus starts flowering when many perennials are winding down. It makes a stunning garden specimen or a striking late-summer informal hedge. For outdoor drama, grow it with plume poppy and ostrich or royal fern.

CARE: Moisture is a must for this water lover. Plant it in moist to soggy soils with plentiful organic matter. Fertilize regularly during the growing season. Best flowering and plant health is in full sun with adequate air circulation, but hardy hibiscus also grows in partial shade. Pick off Japanese beetles by hand, and keep plants watered in dry spells. Also, note their garden location, because they emerge late in spring. The strong stems need no staking. Cut back in late fall to about 6 inches.

RECOMMENDATIONS:
'Disco Belle Hybrids': 20 to 30 inches tall; 9-inch-wide pink, rose-red, and white blooms. **'Kopper King':** 3 to 4 feet; 12-inch-wide white flowers with a red eye in August and September; ruddy copper leaves with rust-hued underside. **'Lady Baltimore':** 4 to 6 feet tall; 6- to 8-inch-wide ruffled pink flowers with a dark red eye; deeply cut leaves. **'Lord Baltimore':** 4 feet tall; 10-inch-wide bright red flowers.

HOSTA (*Hosta* spp.)

'Frances Williams'   'Patriot'

'Golden Tiara'

Features: Striking mounded foliage in blue, gold, green, or variegated mixes with cream, white, yellow, or chartreuse. White to lavender flowers in summer.
Hardiness: Zones 3 to 8
In-bloom size: 4- to 48-inch by 2- to 48-inch mound with spikes rising above
Out-of-bloom size: 2- to 40-inch mound
Light: Partial shade
Site: Moist, rich, well-drained soil

DESCRIPTION AND USES: Grown more for its bold leaves than for flowers, hosta is a star of the shade garden. The leaves come in a wide range of colors, including brilliant gold, gray-blue, light to dark green, and variegated with cream, yellow, or white, and are medium to coarse in texture with surfaces that may be puckered to wavy or smooth. In summer, one-sided stalks of white to lavender, occasionally fragrant flowers open above the foliage. Use hosta as an accent, massed as a ground cover, in rock gardens, woodland gardens, shady perennial borders, and Japanese gardens. Combine it with Bethlehem sage, goatsbeard, woodland phlox, heart-leaf brunnera, or 'Green Sheen' pachysandra. Hosta stands out in containers, whether used alone or in mixed plantings. The long, stiff flower stalks make excellent cut flowers.

CARE: Hostas require full shade in hot climates. In cool climates, they do better with some morning sun. Because hosta's leaves are its main attraction, some gardeners cut off the flower stems before they mature. Before planting, improve the soil with compost or well-rotted manure. Use a continuous-release product at spring planting, or apply soluble fertilizer starting three weeks after setting them in the ground. Stop fertilizing hosta about six to eight weeks before the first fall frost. Prune back the plant after foliage dies in fall. Most hostas are long-lived. Divide crowded plants in spring or fall when necessary. Lift root clumps and divide them with a sharp spade. Replant sections with healthy roots and top shoots, then apply water and mulch. Discard divisions lacking vigorous roots and shoots. Snails and slugs are frequent hosta pests.

'Blue Mammoth'   'June'

RECOMMENDATIONS:
'Blue Mammoth': 45 by 70 inches; puckered light blue leaves; good screening or focal point; slug-resistant. **'Fire and Ice':** 8 to 10 inches by 12 to 15 inches; bright white leaves with green edges; compact size. **'Frances Williams':** 32 to 36 inches by 36 to 42 inches, round corrugated blue-green leaves with gold borders. **'Guacamole':** 28 to 32 inches by 42 to 48 inches; big leaves with a bright golden center and green edge; intensely fragrant white to light lavender blooms in August. **'Hadspen Blue':** 18 inches by 48 inches; heart-shape, thick gray-blue leaves; slug-resistant. **'Krossa Regal':** 30 inches by 48 inches; vase-shape habit with oval frosty blue leaves. **'Orphan Annie':** 2 inches by 4 to 6 inches; wide creamy leaf margins around a green center. **'Sum and Substance':** 30 inches by 24 inches; huge, thick, rounded chartreuse leaves; sun-tolerant.

SIBERIAN IRIS (Iris sibirica)

Siberian iris

Bearded iris

Crested iris

Features: Purple, blue, white, pink, burgundy, yellow, and bicolor flowers in early summer. Verdant grassy leaves.
Hardiness: Zones 3 to 9
In-bloom size: 24- to 48-inch by 24-inch upright
Out-of-bloom size: 18- to 40-inch upright clump
Light: Full sun to partial shade
Site: Moist, moderately fertile, well-drained soil

DESCRIPTION AND USES: Elegant and tough, Siberian iris is perfect for perennial borders and pond side plantings. This fast-growing, trouble-free perennial produces blooms above the leaves in early summer. The 3- to 5-inch flowers have three upright or horizontal petals and three beardless falls, or lower petals. Although the flowers are not long lasting, the narrow, grassy foliage forms lush green clumps that stay attractive all season. Grow long-lived Siberian iris in front of ornamental grasses with cranesbill, coral bells, and lady's mantle.

CARE: Although Siberian iris prefers moist, fertile, well-drained, slightly acid soils, it adapts to many other conditions. Plant it in early spring or late summer, spaced about 2 feet apart. Keep the roots just belowground. Water regularly until established, after which the plant will tolerate drought. Division keeps Siberian iris blooming and vigorous. Divide every three to four years in spring or late summer. Divide more frequently in fertile soils to manage its spread. The first year after division, flowering may be reduced, especially when replanting small segments.

RECOMMENDATIONS:
'Butter and Sugar': 27 inches; upright white petals, yellow falls.
'Caesar's Brother': 36 inches; deep violet. 'Coronation Anthem': 32 inches; dark blue falls with a white splotch and lighter blue upright petals. 'Lavender Bounty': 36 inches; pale lavender upright petals, darker lavender falls.
■ **Bearded iris** (Iris hybrids) grows 8 to 36 inches by 12 to 24 inches. It produces upright fans of broad, sword-shape leaves from rhizomes (fat horizontal roots) on the soil surface. Flowers may be fragrant and range in size from 1 to 8 inches. Plant rhizomes an inch deep so their tops are above ground. Add bonemeal to the soil when planting. Remove bloom stalks after flowering and any brown leaves. Divide every three to four years, keeping only healthy rhizomes with roots and top shoots. Bearded iris is susceptible to iris borer, iris weevil, slugs, snails, rhizome rot, and crown rot. Discard affected parts in the trash. 'Beverly Sills': 35 inches; pink. 'Harvest of Memories': 38 inches; deep yellow rebloomer. 'Hello Darkness': 37 inches; black. 'World Premier': 37 inches; white upright petals, rich blue falls.
■ **Crested iris** (I. cristata) bears fragrant yellow-crested lilac-blue flowers on 2- to 3-inch stems. Leaves grow 4 to 6 inches tall. This southeastern United States native makes a dense ground cover in dry shade and pairs nicely with barrenwort and bleeding heart. 'Alba': yellow-crested white flowers; less vigorous than the species. Zones 3 to 8.
■ **Japanese iris** (I. ensata) has showy horizontal blue, purple, pink, or white blooms in late spring or summer. It grows 5 feet by 3 feet with tall, swordlike leaves. It thrives in full sun to partial shade and rich, moist to boggy, acid soil. Zones 4 to 9. 'Caprician Butterfly': 32 inches; 8-inch white double flowers with violet veins. 'Variegata': 30 inches; purple flowers with variegated green-and-white leaves.
■ **Louisiana iris** (I. fulva) grows 18 to 60 inches tall and spreads fast in boggy soils. Its beardless flowers attract hummingbirds and butterflies and come in copper, blue, purple, yellow, pink, and white. This iris tolerates heat and thrives in the South. Zones 4 to 9.

YELLOW WAXBELLS
(Kirengeshoma palmata)

Features: Subtle beauty; graceful, bent clusters of waxy yellow flowers in late summer to early fall. Bushy, broad, foliage shaped like maple leaves.
Hardiness: Zones 5 to 9
In-bloom size: 36- to 48-inch by 24- to 36-inch upright
Out-of-bloom size: 24- to 36-inch upright clump
Light: Partial shade to shade
Site: Moist, well-drained, acid soil

DESCRIPTION AND USES: Yellow waxbells is a woodland perennial grown as much for its foliage as for its flowers. Purplish stems contrast with 4- to 8-inch lobed clear green leaves, resembling those of Japanese maple. Large, waxy yellow buds occur in arched, branching clusters at the ends of stems and where upper leaves attach to the stem. When open, the pointed flower petals overlap to form long, narrow bells. Yellow waxbells is perfect for naturalizing in woodland gardens, near shrubs and small trees, or at the edge of a shady pond with Japanese iris and 'Bowles' golden sedge.

CARE: Relatively carefree when grown in partial to full shade and continuously moist, well-drained, acid soils with abundant organic matter. Protect it from harsh afternoon sun and strong winds. Yellow waxbells takes a few years to reach full size. It needs no division, growing best when left alone.

CRIMSON PINCUSHION *(Knautia macedonica)*

Features: See-through plant; charming crimson red blooms on long, wiry stems all summer.
Hardiness: Zones 5 to 9
In-bloom size: 24- to 30-inch by 18-inch, weaving through other plants
Out-of-bloom size: 8-inch by 8-inch clump
Light: Full sun
Site: Well-drained, somewhat fertile, alkaline soil

DESCRIPTION AND USES: Crimson pincushion is a long-blooming perennial with cushion-shaped wine-red flower heads. The flowers appear on tall, wiry, branched stems above a low mound of slender leaves. It has an informal, untidy look well-suited to cottage gardens. Grow it in the mid border or surrounded by shorter plants, which will be visible through the airy stems. Instead of staking the stems, plant it with perennials that can support it, such as globe thistle, coreopsis, or 'Purple Rain' salvia. This short-lived perennial attracts bees and butterflies. It produces excellent cut flowers to use in fresh or dry arrangements.

CARE: This low-maintenance perennial prefers full sun and well-drained average garden soil. Deadhead to prevent self-sowing, and divide crowded clumps. Plants grown about 18 inches apart may look sparse in spring. By midsummer, however, the flower stems tend to flop and spread.

RECOMMENDATIONS:
'Mars Midget': 15 to 18 inches; ruby blooms from summer to fall. **'Melton Pastels' hybrids:** 24 to 30 inches; arching stems with pink, crimson, salmon, or light blue pincushions from early to late summer.

TORCH LILY (*Kniphofia uvaria*)

Features: Tall flower spikes in summer; colors graduate from red to orange and yellow. Tufts of upright, grassy leaves. Dramatic vertical accent.
Hardiness: Zones 6 to 9
In-bloom size: 3- to 4-foot by 3- to 4-foot upright spike
Out-of-bloom size: 1½- to 2-foot upright clump
Light: Full sun
Site: Moist, rich, well-drained, sandy soil with abundant organic matter

DESCRIPTION AND USES: Torch lily's hot-hued spikes bring a theatrical quality to the garden. Spikes, which narrow at the base, start out as red buds, open to orange flowers, and fade to yellow. The individual blossoms in the spike open over an extended period from the bottom up. With this staggered opening and the changing flower colors, the flowers appear two-toned with red to orange tops and yellow bottoms. The tall spikes, made up of 1- to 2-inch tubular, down-pointing flowers, are long lasting when cut and attract bees, butterflies, and hummingbirds. Group torch lily in a border with 'Cloud Nine' switch grass and 'Six Hills Giant' catmint, or use a single clump as an accent or specimen. Hybrids are available from 18 inches to 6 feet tall with red, yellow, orange, light green, and cream spikes that bloom from early summer to fall. Long, sword-shape blue-green leaves with toothed edges emerge from a basal rosette. The leaves are evergreen in warm climates.

CARE: Plant bare rhizomes or fleshy roots in spring 3 inches below the soil surface; if planting potted torch lilies, set them at the same level they were in the pot. Remove faded flowers from the bottom of the spike to extend bloom. Cut spikes to the base when they decline. Established plants resent disturbance and may take a couple of years to recover from division. Too much moisture may cause crown rot. Tie old leaves over the crown in fall to protect the plant in winter.

RECOMMENDATIONS:
'Alcazar': 3½ to 5 feet; salmon flowers. Reblooms. Zones 5 to 9.
'Bressingham Comet': 24 inches by 18 inches; oval scarlet to yellow flower spikes. Zones 5 to 9. **'Earliest of All':** 30 inches; rosy coral spikes in late spring to early summer. Zones 5 to 9. **'Prince Igor':** 72 inches; deep orangy-red bloom spikes from early to midfall.

LAVENDER (*Lavandula angustifolia*)

Features: Fragrant purple flower spikes. Aromatic, silver-green leaves.
Hardiness: Zones 5 to 8
In-bloom size: 3-foot by 3-foot mound topped with slender spikes
Out-of-bloom size: 2-foot rounded clump
Light: Full sun
Site: Well-drained, somewhat fertile, somewhat alkaline soil

DESCRIPTION AND USES: This evergreen shrub is a staple of herb gardens, Mediterranean gardens, and sunny perennial borders. Bees and butterflies like the fragrant two-lipped, tubular purple flowers growing on long, delicate spikes above the linear gray-green leaves. Both flowers and foliage produce a sweet, clean, lingering aroma. Lavender is a frequent ingredient in potpourri and fresh and dried flower arrangements. It appreciates the sharp drainage of rock gardens and makes a handsome short hedge or mass landscape planting. For an attractive combination, grow lavender with Knock Out roses and wall germander.

CARE: Lavender is heat- and drought-tolerant and needs full sun and excellent drainage to survive. On established plants, cut old shoots in spring after new growth begins, removing all but an inch of the last season's growth. Shear faded blooms after flowering for a denser shape and to promote reblooming. Division is not necessary. Root rot may occur when grown in wet conditions. To dry lavender, cut flower spikes when they are partly open. Bundle stems in groups up to 1 inch in diameter and hang them upside down in a dark, dry area that has good air circulation. Store dried lavender in an airtight container.

RECOMMENDATIONS:
'Blue Cushion': 16 inches; blue flowers, cushion form.
'Grosso': 24 inches; long spikes of dark violet flowers, grown for intensely fragrant essential oil. **'Hidcote':** 24 inches; deep purple flowers on a compact silver plant. **'Loddon Pink':** 18 inches; light pink flowers. **'Munstead':** 18 inches; blue-purple blooms. **'Nana Alba':** 12 inches; white flowers.
■ Hybrid lavenders **'Dilly Dilly':** 12 inches; purple-blue flower spikes.

TREE MALLOW *(Lavatera thuringiaca)*

Features: Spikes of pink or white trumpet-shape flowers similar to those of hollyhock in summer. Shallow-lobed grayish-green leaves.
Hardiness: Zones 6 to 9
In- and out-of-bloom size: 5- to 7-foot by 4-foot upright bush
Light: Full sun
Site: Well-drained soil

DESCRIPTION AND USES: This giant perennial is big, bushy, and lush with pink, white, or purplish-pink blooms all summer. Wide, branched stems produce loose spikes of five-petaled flowers up to 3 inches wide. Individual blooms resembling hollyhocks also appear in the upper angle where leaves meet stems. Tree mallow makes an impressive show in a container. It adds long-term color and stature to sunny perennial borders, where it belongs at the back, and looks good with Shasta daisies, bee balm, and coreopsis. For a flamboyant summer display, group three tree mallows, spacing them 3 feet apart.

CARE: Tree mallow grows best in continuously moist, fertile, well-drained soil. It tolerates heat and humidity and appreciates afternoon shade in hot climates. Remove Japanese beetles by hand.

RECOMMENDATIONS:
'**Barnsley**': 70 inches; fringed white blooms with a deep pink eye from June to frost. '**Lilac Lady**': 70 inches; lavender-violet flowers with deep purple veins. '**Red Rum**': 30 to 36 inches; long-blooming with deep red flowers, dark stems, and bushy growth. '**Sweet Dreams**': 70 inches; pale pink flowers with narrow petals; extra-hardy. Zones 5 to 8.

'GIBRALTAR' THUNBERG BUSH CLOVER *(Lespedeza thunbergii)*

Features: Purplish-pink blooms on arching stems in late summer and early fall. Blue-green leaves.
Hardiness: Zones 5 to 8
In- and out-of-bloom size: 3- to 6-foot by 3- to 10-foot fountain
Light: Full sun
Site: Light, well-drained soil

DESCRIPTION AND USES: Fast-growing bush clover can grow 6 feet tall in a season. Out of bloom, it has a columnar shape. In bloom the plant becomes a fountain of color when its long stems arch under the weight of lavish pink-purple blooms. Flowers, which attract bees, occur in droopy spikes along the stems and massive hanging clusters up to 24 inches long at the branch tips. Bush clover adds brilliant color to late-season borders. Plant it for contrast with tall yellow 'Herbstsonne' rudbeckia and 'Giraffe' maiden grass. Or let its long curving stems and vibrant blooms soften the harshness of a ledge or high wall.

CARE: Bush clover is a woody perennial or deciduous flowering shrub that grows easily in well-drained soils of average fertility. It tolerates heat, drought, and wind, but too much moisture can cause rot. Cut stems to the ground in late fall or early spring.

RECOMMENDATIONS:
'**Albiflora**': white flowers. '**Edo Shibori**': bicolor white and mauve-pink flowers.

SHASTA DAISY *(Leucanthemum ×superbum)*

Features: White daisies in early summer.
Hardiness: Zones 4 to 8
In-bloom size: 36-inch by 24-inch column
Out-of-bloom size: 9- to 12-inch by 24-inch mound
Light: Full sun to partial shade
Site: Well-drained, preferably alkaline soil

DESCRIPTION AND USES: This timeless white daisy with a yellow center looks good in early summer borders and bouquets combined with spiky 'May Night' blue salvia, 'Cerise Queen' yarrow, and yellow coreopsis. Flowers appear at the tips of stems emerging from a rosette of basal leaves. Individual blooms may be single or double, the latter resembling the cushion-shape flower heads of chrysanthemum. In bloom, Shasta daisy has a columnar shape, but when cut back to the leaves after blooming, it makes a low mound of shiny, lancelike dark green leaves.

CARE: Grow Shasta daisies 18 to 24 inches apart in a sunny spot in well-drained, alkaline soil. Stake with grow-through hoops. Deadheading extends flowering and prevents self-sowing. Removing faded flowers before they set seed also encourages reblooming. Cut plants back in fall after the foliage has died. Divide plants in spring or fall every two or three years to keep them healthy and blooming. Shasta daisies produce fresh offsets at the edges of the clump that are easy to transplant. Discard the center of the plant. Look out for aphids and four-lined plant bugs, which damage leaves before the flowers bloom. Shasta daisies planted in wet soils may be subject to rots, wilt, viruses, and nematodes.

RECOMMENDATIONS:
'Becky': 36 inches; 2- to 3-inch white single flowers all summer on deadheaded plants. Glossy, dark green leaves. **'Silver Princess':** 9 inches; creamy white flowers. **'Snow Lady':** 12 to 15 inches; dense 2½-inch clear white daisies on short stems from June to frost. **'Sonnenschein':** 24 inches; 3-inch blooms with pale yellow petals fading to white around a deep yellow center; blooms summer to fall when deadheaded; tolerates drought, heat, and humidity. **'Sunnyside Up':** 24 inches; double layer of white petals around a yellow center, disease-resistant, vigorous. **'White Knight':** 22 inches; 4-inch blooms that make good cut flowers from late spring to frost; good in containers.

SPIKE GAYFEATHER *(Liatris spicata)*

Features: Large purple or white flower spikes in midsummer. Grassy green leaves. Adds vertical interest.
Hardiness: Zones 3 to 9
In-bloom size: 30- to 60-inch by 24-inch spike
Out-of-bloom size: 12-inch clump
Light: Full sun
Site: Rich, moist soil with abundant organic matter

DESCRIPTION AND USES: Columnar in bloom, gayfeather has rosy-purple bottlebrush flowers and fine-textured leaves that make a useful vertical accent in perennial borders, containers, and cut flower arrangements. Gayfeather's long flower spikes are densely packed with flower heads that open from the top down. This native of North American prairies and moist meadows attracts bees and butterflies and is suitable for wildflower and wildlife gardens. Grow it massed with tree mallow, daylily, 'Goldsturm' rudbeckia, and purple coneflower, gayfeather's fine-textured grassy leaves make an attractive contrast to the larger, coarser foliage of these other perennials.

CARE: Drought-tolerant once established, easy-to-grow gayfeather thrives in average garden soil and is pH adaptable. Stake tall plants that are planted in average to dry soils in spring. Deadheading faded flowers will extend the bloom period. After flowering finishes, cut back stems to the larger, lance-shape basal leaves. Cut back old plants in late fall or early spring. Divide it every three to five years in spring as necessary to maintain the vigor of the plant. Few pests and diseases trouble spike gayfeather, though slugs and snails can cause problems.

RECOMMENDATIONS:
'Alba': 40 inches; white flowers. **'Floristan Violett':** 30 to 36 inches; violet spikes on strong stems, preferred by florists. **'Floristan White':** 30 to 36 inches; white spikes. **'Kobold':** 24 inches; rosy-purple spikes. **'Kobold Original':** 14 inches; thick rosy-purple spikes.

BIGLEAF LIGULARIA (*Ligularia dentata*)

Features: Clusters of brown-centered orange daisies from midsummer to early fall. Large heart-shape leaves on long reddish stems. Bold texture for the moist shade garden.
Hardiness: Zones 4 to 8
In-bloom size: 3- to 5-foot by 3- to 4-foot clump with stiff-stemmed flowers rising above
Out-of-bloom size: 3-foot mound
Light: Sun to shade, depending on the climate
Site: Continuously moist, fertile, well-drained soil

DESCRIPTION AND USES: Bigleaf ligularia's 12-inch leathery leaves bring a tropical flair to shady border and pondside plantings. Foliage is rounded with a deep heart-shape base, zigzag edges, and contrasting reddish stalks. It appears to be floating in horizontal layers. Orangy-gold flower heads arranged in flat red-stalked clusters are a butterfly-attracting bonus. Bigleaf liguria is a stunning accent in moist borders and bog gardens. Plant it as a specimen, or grow it massed for an exotic effect.

CARE: In cool climates, ligularia grows in sun as long as soil remains moist. In hot areas, it needs protection from heat and strong afternoon sunlight. Ligularia tends to wilt on hot, sunny days, even in cool regions and moist soil. It perks up when temperatures cool down and the soil is moistened. Add organic matter at planting, and set plants 2 to 3 feet apart. Division is rarely needed. Slugs and snails may eat the leaves.

RECOMMENDATIONS:
'Desdemona': 40 inches; shaggy orange daisies in loose, flat clusters; purplish-red young leaves turn bronzy green, dark maroon veins, undersides, and stems; good heat tolerance.
'Othello': 36 inches; like 'Desdemona' with orangy-yellow blooms and dark purple young leaves maturing to bronzy green; maroon stems and undersides.
■ **'Gregynog Gold'** (*L. hessei*) has pyramidal 6-foot spikes of 4-inch golden daisies in late summer to early fall and huge rounded leaves with toothed edges and a heart-shaped base.
■ **'The Rocket' narrow-spiked ligularia** (*L. stenocephala*) grows 72 inches tall and produces narrow spikes of yellow flowers in early and late summer. Its large triangular leaves are pointed at the tips and heart-shape at the base. **'Little Rocket' narrow-spiked ligularia:** 20 to 24 inches; short spikes of bright yellow flowers; shiny green leaves.

TURK'S-CAP LILY (*Lilium superbum*)

Features: Nodding green-throated orange flowers with maroon speckles in midsummer.
Hardiness: Zones 4 to 8
In-bloom size: 48- to 96-inch by 6- to 8-inch upright stems topped with airy flower clusters
Out-of-bloom size: 24- to 48-inch upright stems
Light: Full sun to partial shade
Site: Moist, acid, well-drained soil with abundant organic matter

DESCRIPTION AND USES: This eastern United States native grows on straight, rigid stems. Its whimsical nodding 3-inch flowers have six maroon-flecked orange to white petals that curve back on themselves, showing off projecting central stamens. Dozens of blooms may appear clustered above lance-shape whorled leaves. Use grouped or massed in cottage and wildflower gardens and meadows, or combined with hydrangeas and ornamental grasses in a mixed border. This lily attracts hummingbirds and butterflies and is good for naturalizing, for containers, and for cut-flower arrangements.

CARE: Plant bulbs 6 to 12 inches apart and 5 to 6 inches below the soil surface in spring or fall. Soil should be fertile, acid, and high in organic matter. Deadhead to reduce seeding; retain as much stem as possible on the main plant when cutting flowers for arrangements. Let leaves die on the plant after the flowers pass. Cut back stems to 4 to 6 inches in fall, and mulch with conifer boughs for winter protection. Plants may attract slugs, snails, deer, groundhogs, and rabbits.

RECOMMENDATIONS:
Asiatic and Oriental hybrid lilies, 12 to 42 inches by 6 to 10 inches, produce large, often fragrant blooms in summer. Those of Asiatic lily are cup-shaped and may face up, out, or down. Oriental lilies have bowl-shaped outward-facing blooms with recurved petals. In parts of the United States and Canada, red Asian lily beetles are a pest. Check with the cooperative extension about beetles in your locale. **'Petit Pink':** 12-inch Asiatic lily; pink flowers fading to white in the center, and darker spots. Good in containers. **'Reinesse':** 15-inch Asiatic lily; compact lily with white flowers from mid-June through July. Good in pots. **'Casa Blanca':** 48-inch Oriental lily; fragrant, ruffled white flowers in July. **'Stargazer':** 36-inch Oriental lily; fragrant up-facing blooms with a deep pink center, white edges, red spots, and a red center vein, in July.

LILYTURF (Liriope muscari)

Variegated lilyturf

Features: Evergreen ground cover with grassy leaves. Purple flower spikes in late summer to fall, followed by deep blue berries.
Hardiness: Zones 6 to 10
In-bloom size: 12- by 18-inch tufted mound
Out-of-bloom size: 8- by 10-inch tufted mound
Light: Sun to shade
Site: Moist, well-drained, somewhat fertile soil

DESCRIPTION AND USES: Lilyturf produces thick clumps of evergreen grassy to strap-shape leaves. In late summer through fall, it bears spikes of purple flowers, followed by attractive dark blue berries. Use lilyturf as a ground cover under trees and shrubs and as an edging or a grassy covering for shady slopes. Lilyturf works well in containers, alone or in mixed plantings. For singles, consider a decorative cultivar such as 'Okina', which has broad foliage that starts out white then acquires green tips with age.

CARE: Although blue lilyturf grows well in sun to shade, it prefers afternoon shade in the South. It also likes well-drained, acid, moderately fertile soil. Lilyturf needs regular deep watering after planting, but once established it is drought-tolerant and can grow in beds with shrubs and trees. Plant it 12 to 18 inches apart in spring or fall, and feed with slow-release fertilizer at planting. Water deeply when the soil feels dry about 3 inches below the surface. Deadhead faded flower spikes for tidiness. When grown as a ground cover, refresh the leaves in spring by mowing with a lawn mower at the highest setting. Divide in spring or fall.

RECOMMENDATIONS:
'Big Blue': 10 inches; lavender flowers. 'Monroe White': abundant white spikes. 'Pee Dee Gold Ingot': 10 inches; lavender flowers; grassy gold-and-chartreuse leaves year-round. 'Samantha': 12 to 15 inches; pink flowers. 'Variegata': 10 inches; lavender flowers; white-edged green leaves.
■ Creeping lilyturf (L. spicata), is an excellent ground cover with finer leaves than L. muscari. It grows 10 by 18 inches and has lavender or white flower spikes followed by dark blue berries. Plants adapt to full sun and full shade. Zones 5 to 10. 'Alba': white flowers. 'Silver Dragon': striped silver leaves.

CARDINAL FLOWER (Lobelia cardinalis)

'Sparkle Divine' big blue lobelia

Features: Red flower spikes in late summer.
Hardiness: Zones 3 to 9
In-bloom size: 36- to 48-inch by 12-inch upright
Out-of-bloom size: 20-inch clump
Light: Full sun to partial shade
Site: Moist to continuously moist, fertile, well-drained soil

DESCRIPTION AND USES: Cardinal flower looks attractive massed at the edge of lakes, streams, and ponds. Its tubular scarlet flowers, which attract bees, butterflies, and hummingbirds, occur in tall spikes from summer to early fall. Foliage is vivid green, sometimes tinged with bronze. Good companions for cardinal flower include gooseneck loosestrife and hybrid astilbe.

CARE: Give fast-growing cardinal flower full sun in cool climates and afternoon shade in warm ones, but the sunnier the location, the more water cardinal flower needs. It thrives in moist to wet, fertile, acid soil with abundant organic matter. Deadheading extends blooming. Prune back dead stems in late fall or early spring, and divide every few years. This trouble-free perennial is often short-lived, but because it self-sows it's not always lost from the garden.

RECOMMENDATIONS:
■ Hybrid cardinal flower 'Cranberry Crush': 20 to 24 inches; cranberry red spikes; tight form. 'Flamingo': 20 inches; pale pink spikes from July to September. 'Grape Knee-hi': 25 inches; deep purple blooms from midsummer to midfall; long blooming. 'Gladys Lindley': 48 inches; creamy white flowers.
■ 'Queen Victoria' Mexican lobelia (L. fulgens) grows 24 to 36 inches by 18 to 24 inches. It has mahogany leaves and scarlet spikes from July to September. Zones 6 to 8.
■ Big blue lobelia (L. siphilitica) produces 24- to 36-inch blue flower spikes all summer. It prefers abundant moisture and partial shade. Zones 4 to 8. 'Alba': 36 inches; white spikes; needs less moisture than the species.

ROSE CAMPION (Lychnis coronaria)

Features: Vibrant magenta flowers in early to midsummer. Fuzzy gray leaves.
Hardiness: Zones 3 to 8
In-bloom size: 24-inch by 12- to 24-inch irregular upright clump
Out-of-bloom size: 6-inch basal clump
Light: Full sun
Site: Lean, dry, alkaline soil

DESCRIPTION AND USES: Rose campion stands out for its contrasting silver foliage and loud magenta flowers. Its wooly gray 4- to 6-inch stalked leaves with wavy margins form a low basal rosette from which gray-branched stems emerge. Dry soils foster most silvery leaves. Plants bloom little the first year, heavily the second, and deteriorate the third, but they self-sow. Rose campion is charming in cottage gardens, where its short life and abundant seedlings add spontaneity to the garden. Grow it with lamb's-ears and prostrate rosemary.

CARE: This drought-tolerant perennial prefers dry conditions but appreciates watering during long dry spells. Even if rose campion does not survive a harsh, wet winter, it propagates itself by reseeding. Do not place mulch over the crown of the plant, and do not overwater or overfertilize; both actions will weaken the plant. Cut back dead stems in late fall.

RECOMMENDATIONS:
'Alba': 24 inches; white flowers. **'Gardener's World':** 24 inches; sterile 1- to 2-inch deep red double flowers from late June to early August. Does not self-sow. **'Oculata':** 32 inches; white flowers with a cherry pink eye.
■ 'Vesuvius' Arkwright's campion (*L. ×arkwrightii*) grows 18 inches tall and has Maltese-cross-shape blooms and red-tinged leaves.
■ Maltese cross (*L. chalcedonica*) has four-petaled brilliant scarlet flowers in dense clusters at the tips of 4-foot stems. It blooms briefly in early summer. Zones 3 to 10.
■ 'Nana' ragged robin (*L. flos-cuculi*) is a 4-inch dwarf with red flowers in spring and grassy gray-green leaves.

BEE BALM (Monarda didyma)

Features: Shaggy massed flower heads in scarlet, pink, purple, or white, with aromatic leaves.
Hardiness: Zones 3 to 9
In-bloom size: 36-inch by 36- to 48-inch upright
Out-of-bloom size: 24- to 30-inch spreading, bushy clump
Light: Full sun to partial shade
Site: Moist, well-drained, somewhat fertile soil with abundant organic matter

DESCRIPTION AND USES: Bee balm is a must for butterfly and hummingbird gardens with its tubular 1- to 2-inch whorls of red, pink, purple, or white flowers that are framed by reddish bracts. The plant has a lively appearance that is just right for prairie gardens and naturalized areas. You can also use bee balm in the middle of the border, but you'll have to keep its aggressive spread in check. Bee balm's fragrant, minty leaves grow on square stems.

CARE: Bee balm tolerates most soils and grows well in sun to partial shade. It blooms in midsummer and may need staking in rich garden soils. When deadheaded or sheared after flowering, it may bloom again. Plant mildew-resistant cultivars, and give the plant plenty of air circulation and moist (not dry or waterlogged) soil. If mildew affects the leaves, cut down old stems, leaving the fresh growth, and discard the mildewed parts. Avoid planting close to other perennials; it spreads freely. Divide every three years when the center dies out.

RECOMMENDATIONS:
'Blue Stocking' (also sold as 'Blaustrumpf'): 2 to 4 feet; whorled violet-blue flowers; mildew-resistant. **'Colrain Red':** 36 inches; red flowers; mildew-resistant. **'Gardenview Scarlet':** 3 feet; rosy red blooms; mildew-resistant. **'Jacob Cline':** 5 feet; big red flowers; mildew-resistant. **'Marshall's Delight':** 3 to 4 feet; rose-pink flowers; longer blooming than most, from July to September; mildew-resistant. **'On Parade':** 30 inches; rich purple-red flowers set in nearly symmetrical rows; blooms in July and may rebloom when cut back; mildew-resistant. **'Petite Delight':** 15 to 18 inches; bright lavender-pink flowers.

CATMINT (Nepeta ×faassenii)

Features: Billowing blue spikes beginning in early summer and lasting for several weeks. Small fragrant gray-green leaves.
Hardiness: Zones 3 to 8
In-bloom size: 18 inches by 18 inches spreading to upright
Out-of-bloom size: 10- to 12-inch by 36-inch spreading to rounded to upright clump
Light: Full sun; afternoon shade in warm climates
Site: Well-drained soil

DESCRIPTION AND USES: In full bloom, catmint creates cool blue swells in the summer landscape. Used as edging, its long-blooming flowers and aromatic leaves soften paths and bring cool hues to the herb garden. Catmint looks wonderful massed as a low-maintenance, drought-tolerant ground cover or repeated along the front of borders to tie together multihued perennials. When not in flower, catmint forms an attractive shrubby mound of branching stems covered in small scented gray-green leaves. Grow catmint with 'Creme Brulee' coreopsis, roses, 'Happy Returns' daylily, and 'Biokovo' cranesbill.

CARE: Catmint thrives in full sun and well-drained soil. Set plants about 18 inches apart. Cutting stems back by one-third to one-half after the first flush of bloom makes plants more compact and encourages rebloom later in the season. Divide in spring or fall every three years.

RECOMMENDATIONS:
'Blue Wonder': 12- to 15-inch ground cover with 6-inch flower spikes; more flowers and bigger leaves than the species. **'Dropmore':** 12- to 18-inch mounds; deep lavender flowers larger than the species in June and July. **'Six Hills Giant':** 30-inches; foot-long violet-blue flower spikes; leaves and flowers bigger than the species. **'Snowflake':** 12 to 15 inches; white flowers all summer. **'Walker's Low':** 18-inch mound; lavender-blue spikes; drought- and heat-tolerant.
■ **'Dawn to Dusk' giant catmint** (*N. grandiflora*) grows to 3 feet tall and has light salmon-pink flower spikes.
■ **'Souvenir d'Andre Chaudron' Siberian catmint** (*N. sibirica*) grows 2 to 3 feet tall and has abundant spikes of large blue flowers. Zones 3 to 7.

EVENING PRIMROSE (Oenothera fruticosa)

Features: Big bright yellow flowers on strong leafy stems in early to midsummer.
Hardiness: Zones 4 to 9
In-bloom size: 12- to 36-inch by 18- to 24-inch upright
Out-of-bloom size: 6-inch basal clump
Light: Full sun
Site: Moist, well-drained, somewhat fertile soil

DESCRIPTION AND USES: From early to midsummer rich yellow cups up to 2 inches wide bloom at the tops of robust reddish stems. Low basal leaves turn mahogany red in the cold and make an appealing ground cover after the growing season. Grow evening primrose in wildflower gardens, meadows, and mixed or perennial borders. They look striking with catmint, bigroot cranesbill, blanket flower, and 'Karl Foerster' feather reed grass.

CARE: Deadheading extends flowering and prevents excessive self-sowing. After flowering, cut back clumps by one-third to stimulate fresh, leafy growth, or cut back all the way to the evergreen basal rosette. To control spreading, lift surplus plants each year and give them to friends. Divide plants every four or five years in spring or early fall; discard the old central portion of the clump. Evening primrose is pest-free but may have occasional problems with mildew and may develop root rot when soils are too moist.

RECOMMENDATIONS:
'Fruhlingsgold': 15 inches; pink and white spring foliage expanding to variegated green leaves with creamy white edges; 1½-inch fragrant gleaming yellow flowers in early summer. **'Highlight':** 15 inches; lightly fragrant yellow flowers in clusters from June to August. **'Fireworks':** 18 inches; red stems with big yellow flowers in June and July.
■ **Ozark sundrops** (*O. macrocarpa*) grows 6 inches tall with ruddy creeping stems that spread aggressively. It produces golden cupped blooms up to 5 inches wide from late spring to early fall.
■ **'Siskiyou' showy evening primrose** (*O. speciosa*) grows 10 to 12 inches tall and has fragrant 2-inch light pink blooms from late spring through summer. It spreads fast and needs excellent drainage.

'HERRENHAUSEN' ORNAMENTAL OREGANO (Origanum laevigatum)

Features: Lavish sprays of maroon buds opening to dark pink flowers from July to October. Scented purple-tinged deep green leaves. Attracts butterflies.
Hardiness: Zones 5 to 9
In-bloom size: 18- to 30-inch by 18- to 24-inch spreading clump
Out-of-bloom size: 18-inch spreading clump
Light: Full sun
Site: Average, well-drained soil

DESCRIPTION AND USES: Although its leaves are fragrant, this plant is grown for its beautiful flowers and not to eat. Its deep pink flowers bloom all summer against a backdrop of small purplish-green leaves on reddish-purple stems. 'Herrenhausen' ornamental oregano is perfect for containers and Mediterranean gardens. Grow it at the front of perennial borders, where its wiry stems interlace with other plants. Good companions are baby's breath, lavender, Russian sage, white and purple forms of purple coneflower, and 'Moonbeam' coreopsis.

CARE: This woody perennial grows in average garden soil but thrives in very well-drained, lean to somewhat fertile, alkaline soils. To keep it from sprawling, cut it back by half in early summer. Plants are heat- and drought-tolerant and can rot in overly moist soils. Wait until early spring to clean up plants and remove the previous summer's growth.

RECOMMENDATIONS:
'Hopleys': 18 to 24 inches; long flowering with large deep purple blooms. Zones 6 to 9. 'Kent Beauty': 4 inches; small light pink blooms with big rosy pink bracts on a prostrate plant. 'Norton Gold': 8-inches; mounds of golden leaves with pinkish-purple flowers in late summer; may need afternoon shade in extreme heat. 'Rosenkuppel': 12 inches; erect plant with bright pink to lavender-pink blooms in summer.
■ Hybrid ornamental oregano 'Red Ball': 12 to 15 inches; low ball of fall-blooming pink and purple flowers; leaves larger than the species.

PEONY (Paeonia hybrids)

Features: Pink, red, white, and cream blooms, some intensely fragrant, from late spring to early summer. Handsome divided leaves.
Hardiness: Zones 3 to 7
In-bloom size: 3-foot by 3-foot upright clump
Out-of-bloom size: 24- to 30-inch upright clump
Light: Full sun to partial shade
Site: Moist, well-drained soil with abundant organic matter

DESCRIPTION AND USES: Grown for huge, romantic flowers with an irresistible scent, peony blooms from late spring to early summer. Most have double flowers in shades of pink or white. Use peonies as cut flowers, a low hedge, and a backdrop for later-blooming perennials. The attractive leaves grow lush enough to cover dying spring bulb foliage. Late-blooming double peonies pair well with early-blooming double-flowered old garden roses. Although individual peonies have a relatively short flower season, extend blooming for five to seven weeks by planting several varieties. Peonies are a must for cottage gardens.

CARE: Most root growth is in fall, the best time for planting. Fertilize in spring when shoots appear, or top-dress with compost around, not on, the plant. Deadhead to reduce the weight on the stems. Stake with hoop supports.

Plant peonies 3 feet apart. Make sure the eyes (or reddish buds) are just 1 inch underground, or your peony won't bloom. When planting potted peonies, keep them at the same level they were growing in the pot. They may take three years to flower and need no dividing. Ants love peonies and do not hurt them; brush them off when cutting flowers to bring indoors. Cut stems to 2 to 3 inches in late fall and discard.

RECOMMENDATIONS:
'Cheddar Charm': 30 to 36 inches; gold center against overlapping white outer petals; fragrant; midseason. 'Festiva Maxima': classic big white double blooms flecked with crimson, very fragrant. 'Pink Hawaiian Coral': 36 inches; yellowish-pink semidouble flowers with yellow stamens; fragrant. 'Red Charm': 30 inches; deep red double blooms with a ruffled central ball; sturdy stems; early. 'Sarah Bernhardt': 30 inches; soft pink double flowers; very fragrant; late-season. 'Vivid Rose': 34 inches; late-midseason deep pink double blooms; fragrant.

ORIENTAL POPPY *(Papaver orientale)*

Features: Spectacular dark-centered flowers with crepe-papery petals of red, orange, pink, or white in late spring to early summer.
Hardiness: Zones 3 to 7
In-bloom size: 2- to 3-foot by 2-foot airy, upright oval
Out-of-bloom size: 18-inch mound
Light: Full sun
Site: Moist, deep, well-drained soil rich in organic matter

DESCRIPTION AND USES: Surround these stars of spring beds and borders with late-blooming perennials; poppies die down by midsummer, and nearby plants will plug the hole. Oriental poppy flowers face upward on sturdy stems. White bristles coat the coarse green leaves, making them rough to the touch. Grow Oriental poppies in groups for a bigger effect. They look good with shrubby 3-foot 'Red Rum' tree mallow or 'Kopper King' hibiscus.

CARE: Poppies need good drainage year-round and a location away from strong winds. They prefer cool climates and can't bear heat and humidity. Deadhead for tidiness, or let seedpods develop for dried flower arrangements. Once the old leaves have died, new growth begins in mid- to late summer, persists through the winter, and continues to grow in spring. Divide poppies during their summer dormancy, if necessary.

RECOMMENDATIONS:
'Turkenlouis': 30 inches; brilliant orangy-red flowers with fringed edges and a dark basal mark. **'Helen Elizabeth':** 24 inches; crinkled salmon-pink blooms. **'Royal Wedding':** 30 inches; clean white petals with a black eye.

PATRINIA *(Patrinia scabiosifolia)*

Features: Lime-tinged yellow flowers clustered on towering stems; late-season back-of-the-border color.
Hardiness: Zones 5 to 8
In-bloom size: 48 to 72 inches by 24 inches
Out-of-bloom size: 12 to 18 inches, basal clump
Light: Full sun to partial shade
Site: Moist, well-drained, fertile soil that has abundant organic matter

DESCRIPTION AND USES: This tall perennial creates a bright greenish-yellow haze at the back of borders in late summer to fall. Delicate flat-topped flower clusters cap branched see-through stems, growing from a clump of basal leaves. The chartreuse-yellow flowers combine well with Russian sage, Joe-Pye weed, plume poppy *(Macleaya cordata)*, and 'Zebrinus' maiden grass. Long-blooming patrinia creates a lacy effect that suits lightly shaded woodland gardens and sunny borders. It is a long-lasting cut flower. Clumps spread at a moderate pace, and plants self-sow but are not invasive.

CARE: Patrinia is largely pest- and disease-free and adapts well to heat, drought, wind, and humidity. It prefers average to continuous moisture during the growing season but does not tolerate excessive winter wetness. Tall stems may require staking. Deadheading extends flowering and prevents self-sowing. Cut tall stems down to the basal clump after flowering has ended.

RECOMMENDATIONS:
'Nagoya': compact 36 inches by 18 inches; yellow flowers rise from a 12- to 18-inch mound of basal leaves.

'HUSKER RED' SMOOTH WHITE PENSTEMON
(Penstemon digitalis)

Features: Pink-tinged white flowers in loose branched clusters on dark maroon stems from early to late summer. Maroon leaves turn reddish green.
Hardiness: Zones 2 to 8
In-bloom size: 24- to 30-inch by 12- to 24-inch upright
Out-of-bloom size: 8-inch basal clump
Light: Full sun to partial shade
Site: Moist, fertile, well-drained soil

DESCRIPTION AND USES: Red tints the flowers, stems, and leaves of 'Husker Red' penstemon. The basal foliage starts spring as a deep maroon, turning to reddish green as the season progresses. Stems are also dark maroon, and the tubular flowers, which attract bees and butterflies, have a pinkish tint. Individual flowers look like bells and appear in clusters at the tips of long branches that are good for cutting. Airy flower stems emerge from a dense, low basal mound of semi-evergreen lancelike leaves. 'Husker Red' penstemon looks good with purple coneflower and 'Goldsturm' black-eyed Susan.

CARE: This penstemon tolerates extreme heat and humidity, but waterlogging in any season can kill it. Water it deeply during dry spells. Deadheading promotes rebloom. If not deadheaded, flower stems develop a rich bronze color, but seedlings will pop up all over the garden. Stake plants with floppy flower stems, especially those grown in partly shaded locations. Divide plants every three years in spring or fall.

RECOMMENDATIONS:
'Rachel's Dance': 20 inches; white flowers tinted pink on maroon stems; bright purplish-red leaves.
■ **Common beard-tongue** *(P. barbatus)* is a western United States wildflower producing 30-inch open spikes of red, pink, purple, blue, or white flowers in early summer. **'Coccineus':** 12 to 18 inches; scarlet flowers from midspring to early summer; narrow leaves. Zones 4 to 9.
■ **Hybrid penstemon 'Elfin Pink':** 12 to 14 inches; narrow spires of rosy-pink flowers; grayish-green leaves. Zones 4 to 9. **'Prairie Dusk':** 20 inches; rosy-purple flowers from May to September; green basal leaves.

RUSSIAN SAGE *(Perovskia atriplicifolia)*

Features: Small, fuzzy lavender-blue flowers on airy stems in mid- to late summer. Silver-green leaves.
Hardiness: Zones 3 to 9
In- and out-of-bloom size: 4-foot by 4-foot upright to oval
Light: Full sun
Site: Well-drained, somewhat fertile soil

DESCRIPTION AND USES: Russian sage is valued for its pungent gray-green leaves on white stems and tiny bluish-purple flowers in long, 12 inches or more clusters at the tips of each stem. The bruised foliage smells like sage. Russian sage tolerates drought, heat, and humidity. Grow it with evening primrose, white 'David' garden phlox, and 'Herrenhausen' ornamental oregano.

CARE: Russian sage is easy to grow in average, well-drained garden soil but prefers light, alkaline, somewhat dry soils. Because of its height and thin woody stems, it usually needs staking as the season progresses. It has no serious pests or diseases if grown in full sun and very well-drained soil. Cut back the woody stems to about 6 inches in spring; in cold climates where only the roots survive the winter, cut the plant to the ground.

RECOMMENDATIONS:
'Blue Spire': 12- to 15-inch-long violet-blue flower spikes from July to September; 2- to 3-foot stems; more upright than the species. **'Little Spire':** 24 inches; lavender flowers; grayish leaves. **'Filigran':** 3 to 4 feet; airy bluish-purple flowers all summer; finely cut, delicate gray-green leaves.

GARDEN PHLOX (Phlox paniculata)

Features: Clusters of fragrant pink, magenta, white, or lavender-blue flowers in mid- to late summer. Backbone of the border.
Hardiness: Zones 4 to 8
In-bloom size: 36- to 50-inch by 24- to 36-inch upright with domed clusters
Out-of-bloom size: 24- to 36-inch upright clump
Light: Full sun to partial shade
Site: Moist, well-drained, fertile, slightly acid soil with abundant organic matter

DESCRIPTION AND USES: This delightful heavy-flowering perennial attracts bees and butterflies. It belongs in cottage gardens, meadow plantings, and vases. Hybrids come in a wide range of colors and have improved disease resistance. Good partners include deep pink 'Red Fox' or dark blue 'Royal Candles' speedwell, repeat-blooming 'Stella de Oro' or 'Happy Returns' daylilies, Shasta daisy, and fountain grass.

CARE: Garden phlox is prone to powdery mildew, so plant only mildew-resistant varieties such as the ones listed below. Good air circulation helps prevent mildew. Water phlox deeply and fertilize regularly. Deadheading encourages more blooms and prevents self-sowing. (Self-sown phlox does not come true from seed.) Divide every three or four years.

RECOMMENDATIONS:
■ **Woodland phlox** (*P. divaricata*) has lightly scented blue or white flowers in late spring. It grows 1-foot tall and likes partial to full shade. Good woodland ground cover.
■ **Creeping phlox** (*P. stolonifera*) is a shade-loving ground cover with trailing stems and blue, pink, white, or purple flowers in spring. It grows into a 6-inch-tall mat.
■ **Moss phlox** (*P. subulata*) makes a dense 3- to 6-inch tall mat in sunny rock gardens and hillsides. It has blue, pink, white, or purple flowers in early to midspring. Zones 3 to 9.
■ **Hybrid garden phlox 'David':** 4 to 5 feet; fragrant white flower clusters; strong stems; mildew-resistant; a classic that blooms into fall with deadheading. **'Goldmine':** 30 inches; deep magenta flowers; variegated green leaves with wide gold borders; tolerates heat and humidity; mildew-resistant. **'Katherine':** 3 to 4 feet; lavender flowers with a white eye; extremely mildew-resistant. **'Shortwood':** 4 to 5 feet; bright pink with a deep pink eye; extremely mildew-resistant.

OBEDIENT PLANT (Physostegia virginiana)

Features: Dense spikes of pink, purple, or white flowers from late summer to fall. Adds vertical interest.
Hardiness: Zones 3 to 9
In-bloom size: 2- to 4-foot by 3-foot or more upright
Out-of-bloom size: 1½-foot by 3-foot upright spreading clump
Light: Full sun to partial shade
Site: Moist, fertile, acid soil

DESCRIPTION AND USES: This plant brings welcome color and vertical interest to late summer gardens and flower arrangements. Its rampant spreading makes it ideal for naturalizing in moist meadows and wildflower gardens. During the growing season, its smooth dark green leaves are an attractive backdrop for short, mounded perennials such as lady's mantle, Mariesii or 'Sentimental Blue' balloon flower, and variegated Japanese sedge.

CARE: Obedient plant grows in most soils and conditions. It is invasive, particularly in moist, fertile soils high in organic matter. To control its spread in beds and borders, grow a less invasive cultivar such as 'Miss Manners', or pull out excess stems and divide plants frequently. Tall forms need staking, particularly when grown in shade and fertile or moist soils.

RECOMMENDATIONS:
'Eyeful Tower': 80 inches; pink flowers; shiny green leaves; good vertical accent. **'Miss Manners':** 30 inches; pure white flowers; less invasive than the species. **'Olympus Gold':** 30 inches; pink flowers; variegated green leaves with wide gold margins fading to creamy yellow at maturity. **'Variegata':** 2 feet; pink flowers; green leaves with broad creamy margins. **'Vivid':** 20 inches; bright deep pink dwarf; invasive.

BALLOON FLOWER (Platycodon grandiflorus)

Features: Lovely long-lasting color in beds and borders, intense blue-violet, white, or pink flowers from summer to fall. Balloonlike buds.
Hardiness: Zones 3 to 8
In-bloom size: 24-inch by 12-inch upright
Out-of-bloom size: 12-inch clump
Light: Full sun to partial shade
Site: Well-drained, slightly acid soil

DESCRIPTION AND USES: Balloon flower takes its name from its puffy colorful buds, which open into five-petaled saucer-shaped, pointed stars that are long lasting in the garden and in a vase. They look enchanting at the front of beds and borders and pair well with fleabane, blanket flower, and butterfly weed. Low, mounded varieties are good for rock gardens and edging.

CARE: The only condition necessary for healthy balloon flowers is good drainage. Some need staking, especially tall plants in hot climates or those planted in shade. Short varieties form dense mounds and need no support. Deadhead flowers individually. Mark the plants' location in fall; they emerge later than many perennials in spring. Transplanting them is difficult, and division isn't necessary. They are pest- and disease-free and may self-sow.

RECOMMENDATIONS:
'Fairy Snow': 12 inches; white blooms and blue veins. **'Hakone Blue':** 20 inches; blue double flowers. **'Hakone White':** 20 inches; white double flowers. **'Hime Murasaki':** 15 to 18 inches; big blue-violet blooms. **'Sentimental Blue':** 6 to 8 inches; long-lasting 3-inch blue flowers.

JACOB'S LADDER (Polemonium caeruleum)

Features: Blue-violet or white flowers clustered at the stem tips in mid- to late spring. A mound of divided leaves that give the effect of a ladder.
Hardiness: Zones 3 to 8
In-bloom size: 18- to 24-inch by 18- to 24-inch upright
Out-of-bloom size: 8- to 12-inch mounded clump
Light: Full sun to partial shade
Site: Moist, well-drained soil rich in organic matter

DESCRIPTION AND USES: The leaves of this handsome, fine-textured plant resemble rungs on a ladder. Clustered blue-violet or white blooms top narrow flowering stems that rise above the dense mound of basal foliage in mid- to late spring. Jacob's ladder looks lovely in lightly shaded beds, borders, and woodland gardens planted in groups with hosta, Bethlehem sage, and lady's mantle.

CARE: Jacob's ladder needs moisture and good drainage. It may decline in extreme heat, drought, and high humidity but tolerates shade and alkaline soils. It may need staking. Remove flower stems after blooming. Doing this promptly keeps the plant attractive, prevents excessive self-sowing, and may promote some later flowers.

RECOMMENDATIONS:
'Brise D'Anjou': 24 inches; violet-blue flowers in early summer; variegated ferny leaves edged in cream. Zones 4 to 8. **'Bressingham Purple':** 15 inches; lavender-blue flowers; 8-inch mound of purple leaves in spring and fall. **'Stairway to Heaven':** lavender-blue spring flowers; variegated green leaves with white margins broader than 'Brise D'Anjou'. Zones 4 to 9.
■ **'Purple Rain'** Jacob's ladder (*P. yezoense*) produces a 24-inch mound of ferny purple leaves with clustered blue flowers in late spring and early summer. Zones 6 to 9.

VARIEGATED SOLOMON'S SEAL
(Polygonatum odoratum 'Variegatum')

Features: Nodding fragrant white flowers in spring. Graceful curving stems with variegated green-and-white leaves turning yellow in fall.
Hardiness: Zones 4 to 9
In- and out-of-bloom size: 2-foot by 1-foot upright arches
Light: Partial to full shade
Site: Moist, well-drained soil with abundant organic matter

DESCRIPTION AND USES: For a garden spot that's shady and a little moist, you can't do better than variegated Solomon's seal. You'll love this plant for its beauty throughout the growing season. It has variegated green-and-white leaves and yellow fall color. In spring, tiny fragrant creamy bells hang from the leaf angles, followed by dark blue berries. Its elegant structure of arched stems can brighten the darkness, whether grouped in a shade border with hosta and Japanese painted fern or massed with barrenwort in a grove of dogwoods or small maples.

CARE: Variegated Solomon's seal adapts to dry shade but prefers partial shade and moist soil with abundant organic matter. Space plants 1 foot apart when massing. Don't deadhead, and don't cut stems back in fall. Divide every five years in spring or fall. Except for the occasion slug, it is pest-free.

RECOMMENDATIONS:
■ Small Solomon's seal *(P. biflorum)* is 2 to 3 feet with arching stems that bear greenish-white flowers in late spring and dark blue berries in fall.

NEPAL CINQUEFOIL *(Potentilla nepalensis)*

Features: Saucer-shape magenta flowers from late spring to summer.
Hardiness: Zones 5 to 8
In- and out-of-bloom size: 1- to 3-foot tall by 2-foot wide sprawling clump
Light: Full sun
Site: Well-drained soil

DESCRIPTION AND USES: Valued for its 1-inch slightly cupped blooms, Nepal cinquefoil is perfect for rock gardens and raised beds, where it finds the excellent drainage it requires. The flowers appear in loose, branched clusters on wiry reddish stems, and the hairy leaves resemble the palm of a hand. Instead of staking the lax stems, grow Nepal cinquefoil in containers where it will trail over the rim, or mass it in borders, near rocks or on retaining walls, where its floppy form will soften and enhance the hard edges. It is better known for its cultivars than for the species itself.

CARE: Grow Nepal cinquefoil in full sun and well-drained soil. If stems look untidy after flowering, prune lightly to encourage branching and neaten the plant. Nepal cinquefoil is easy to grow and relatively untroubled by pests or diseases.

RECOMMENDATIONS:
'Miss Willmott': 10 to 12 inches; cherry pink flowers with a dark cherry eye. 'Rod McBeath': 10 to 12 inches; deep pink flowers with a darker center from late spring through summer.
■ Spring cinquefoil *(P. neumanniana* 'Nana') produces golden-yellow flowers in spring. It grows 3 to 4 inches by 20 inches and creates a robust ground cover on dry, sunny slopes. Zones 4 to 8.
■ Hybrid cinquefoil 'Gibson's Scarlet': 16 inches; flat 1-inch brilliant scarlet blooms with a dark center all summer. 'William Rollisson': 16 inches; 1½-inch vivid red-orange semidouble blooms.

SIEBOLD PRIMROSE (Primula sieboldii)

Features: Dainty woodland ground cover. Frilly pink, snow white, magenta, pale purple, or bicolor flowers in late spring. Hairy, scalloped light green leaves.
Hardiness: Zones 3 to 8
In-bloom size: 9- to 12-inch by 18-inch upright cluster
Out-of-bloom size: 4- to 6-inch clump
Light: Partial to full shade
Site: Moist, acid soil with abundant organic matter

DESCRIPTION AND USES: These late-spring lovelies look luscious under upright Japanese maples, massed around rhododendrons and azaleas, planted on the north side of your house, or tucked near a shady outcrop. Their delightful fuzzy light green leaves emerge in thick rosettes. A few weeks later, clusters of delicate 1-inch flowers open at the tips of erect 1-foot stems rising from the basal leaves. Blooms can be single or double, flat, fringed, starry, or slightly cupped. With summer heat and dryness, plants go dormant. Clumps will steadily increase over the years. Grow Siebold primrose with 'Black Magic' viola, 'Pink Bouquet' foamflower, and cowslips.

CARE: This carefree little primrose thrives in cool, moist, shady, acid soil with plenty of organic matter. In hot, dry summer weather, it goes dormant until the following spring. Plants prefer morning sun, afternoon shade, and they need protection in winter, either from consistent snow cover or a thick mulch. Divide plants when the leaves first appear in spring or after they bloom.

RECOMMENDATIONS:
'Lacy Snowflake': big white flowers with fringed petals.
■ Cowslip (P. veris) produces clusters of scented, nodding yellow flowers in spring on 10-inch stems above evergreen to semi-evergreen basal leaf rosettes. Zones 3 to 8.
■ English primrose (P. vulgaris) sends up clusters of pale yellow flowers on 8-inch stems. Its basal leaves are evergreen or semi-evergreen. Many vigorous, floriferous single- and double-flowered cultivars in purple, lavender, white, pink, and bicolor are available. Zones 4 to 8.

'MRS. MOON' BETHLEHEM SAGE
(Pulmonaria saccharata)

Features: Striking ground cover. Bold leaves splashed with white; simultaneous pink and blue flowers in spring.
Hardiness: Zones 4 to 8
In- and out-of-bloom size: 12-inch by 24-inch clump
Light: Partial shade to full shade
Site: Moist soil with abundant organic matter

DESCRIPTION AND USES: This enchanting early-blooming shade lover has two seasons of garden interest. In spring, fresh pink flowers clustered at the stem tips mature to blue while new pink buds continue to open. Yet Bethlehem sage saves its big WOW for summer, when old stems hide under a mound of huge white-splattered deep green leaves. Use this perennial to brighten the edges of shady paths, or mass it for a ground cover in woodland gardens. It looks wonderful in front of 'Taunton' yews in a foundation planting. Other good companions include trillium, dead nettle, and ferns.

CARE: This easy-to-grow plant needs partial to full shade and average garden soil rich in organic matter. Remove the flower stem after blooming for neatness and to prevent self-sowing. Deter powdery mildew by providing plants with good air circulation and adequate moisture during hot, dry spells. If mildew strikes, cutting down plants and watering them well will encourage a fresh crop of leaves to replace the old ones.

RECOMMENDATIONS:
'Excalibur': 10 by 20 inches; rosy pink to blue flowers; broad bright silver leaves with narrow dark green margins; very mildew-resistant.
■ Long-leafed lungwort (P. longifolia cevennensis) produces big blue flowers, narrow silver-marked leaves up to 26 inches long, and is an excellent pulmonaria for the South. It is extremely mildew-resistant. Mature plants grow into leaf clumps up to 18 inches by 40 inches.
■ 'David Ward' red lungwort (P. rubra) forms a compact 12-inch clump of variegated green leaves with white margins and salmon-pink flowers in early spring.
■ 'Sissinghurst White' common lungwort (P. officinalis) grows 10 to 12 inches tall with white flowers and white-spotted leaves, which are susceptible to mildew.
■ Hybrid lungwort 'Samourai': 12 inches by 15 inches; pink to blue blooms; long, narrow pure silver leaves with a dark green edge; more sun tolerant than the species.

PASQUE FLOWER (*Pulsatilla vulgaris*)

Features: Hair, hair, everywhere. Hairy purple bells opening in early spring; feathery seed heads; and delicate, downy light green leaves.
Hardiness: Zones 5 to 7
In-bloom size: 8- to 10-inch by 8-inch clump with erect solitary flower stems
Out-of-bloom size: 3-inch clump
Light: Full sun in the North; afternoon shade in the South
Site: Well-drained, fertile soil

DESCRIPTION AND USES: Silky up-facing or droopy purple blooms with a yellow center on downy stems, decorative puffy silken seed heads, and ferny, hairy leaves give little pasque flower an exotic look. Up to 3½ inches wide, the flowers look jumbo on the petite plant. Pasque flower is particularly charming at the front of raised beds, on top of stone retaining walls and terraces, and in rock gardens near eye level, where you can inspect its attributes.

CARE: Pasque flower needs well-drained soil and average moisture to thrive. It tolerates some drought in the North. In the South, it benefits from afternoon shade. Once established in the garden, it likes to stay put. If you must divide it, do so in spring after blooming.

RECOMMENDATIONS:
'Alba': 8 to 10 inches; yellow-centered white flowers. **'Papageno':** 12 inches; fringed single and semidouble blooms in pink, red, white, and blue. **'Rubra':** 8 to 10 inches; red bells. **'Red Clock':** 12 inches; yellow-centered rosy-red bells.

FEATHERLEAF RODGERSIA (*Rodgersia pinnata*)

Features: Bold scale. Massive, rough dark green leaves. Fuzzy plumes of tiny pink, red, or white flowers in mid- to late summer.
Hardiness: Zones 5 to 7
In-bloom size: 3- to 4-foot by 3- to 4-foot clump with upright flower clusters
Out-of-bloom size: 2-foot rounded clump
Light: Partial shade
Site: Fertile, continuously moist soil with abundant organic matter

DESCRIPTION AND USES: Everything about featherleaf rodgersia is big. The coarse leaves can measure 3 feet across, and the individual flowers, although small, come in clusters up to 2 feet long. From afar, the dark green compound leaves, bronzy in spring and fall, look like those of a giant horsechestnut. A plant this dramatic looks good as a specimen or grouped in a bog garden, a low spot, or a very moist, shady border. Suitable companions include royal fern, astilboides (*A. tabularis*), and all species of ligularia. Rodgersia also makes a lovely cut flower.

CARE: Given proper growing conditions, rodgersia is a robust plant. When growing it in groups, space plants 3 feet apart. Mulch to keep plants cool and moist. You can plant rodgersia in full sun, but it will need more water than in partial shade. Cut back plants in fall once the top growth dies.

RECOMMENDATIONS:
'Chocolate Wing': 2½ feet; chocolate-bronze foliage; pink flowers with a red eye. **'Alba':** white flowers. **'Elegans':** creamy flowers tinged with pink. **'Firework':** deep red blooms. **'Superba':** rosy pink blooms; attractive bronze new growth.
■ **Fingerleaf rodgersia** (*R. aesculifolia*) produces spikes of creamy or pink-tinted blooms rising on bronze stems 4 to 5 feet above big, fingerlike bronzy foliage.

'AUTUMN SUN' CONEFLOWER
(Rudbeckia nitida)

Features: Large yellow daisies. Giant size.
Hardiness: Zones 4 to 9
In-bloom size: 6- to 8-foot by 3-foot upright
Out-of-bloom size: 30-inch clump
Light: Full sun
Site: Average to moist, well-drained soil

DESCRIPTION AND USES: 'Autumn Sun' coneflower stands out for its handsome flowers, vigorous green foliage, and towering height. Flowering begins in mid- to late summer and extends to fall. 'Autumn Sun' produces blooms with droopy yellow rays around a green center. Butterflies visit this outstanding plant when it's in bloom, and songbirds enjoy the seed heads later in the year. 'Autumn Sun' coneflower belongs in wildflower gardens, at the back of informal borders, and in prairie plantings; it makes a handsome cut flower. This cultivar is also sold as 'Herbstsonne'.

CARE: This coneflower thrives in garden soil of average fertility and moisture. Water regularly until it is established. Depending on climate, wind exposure, and soil fertility, you may need to support the plant with stakes and string, or let nearby shrubs and ornamental grasses do the job.

RECOMMENDATIONS:
■ **Gloriosa daisy** (*R. hirta*), a drought-tolerant short-lived perennial or biennial, grows 12 to 36 inches. Zones 3 to 7. **'Becky':** 12 to 15 inches by 12 to 15 inches; assortment of yellow, gold, orange, reddish-bronze, and bicolor daisies with a black central cone; heat- and drought-tolerant; good in containers. **'Prairie Sun':** 30 inches by 12 to 18 inches; orange rays with lemon yellow tips and a green cone. **'Toto' hybrids:** 10 inches by 12 inches; 4- to 5-inch flowers of gold, lemon, or mahogany with gold tips; flowers from June to September.
■ **'Goldsturm' black-eyed Susan** (*R. fulgida*) is bushy and vigorous with long-blooming black-centered golden-yellow daisies. It grows 24 inches by 24 inches. Zones 3 to 8.
■ **Giant coneflower** (*R. maxima*) is a stunning plant with a mound of huge pale blue leaves and droopy yellow daisies with a huge persistent cone that attract goldfinches. They bloom on 6- to 8-foot stems that need no staking.

PERENNIAL SALVIA *(Salvia nemorosa)*

Features: Intense violet-blue spikes in summer; rough gray-green leaves.
Hardiness: Zones 3 to 8 (cultivars Zone 4)
In-bloom size: 24- to 36-inch by 18- to 24-inch upright
Out-of-bloom size: 8-inch basal mound
Light: Full sun
Site: Average, well-drained soil

DESCRIPTION AND USES: Tall, erect violet-blue flower spikes on square stems and furry, aromatic gray-green leaves form a medium-textured clump. This species looks stunning massed in the middle of the perennial border; small cultivars look good at the front of the border. Plant perennial salvia with light pink shrub roses, baby's breath or Shasta daisies. Or combine it with the clear yellow daisies of coreopsis. Perennial salvia makes an excellent container plant or cut flower. Bees, butterflies, and hummingbirds flock to it, whereas rabbits and deer usually leave it alone.

CARE: This easy-care plant grows in most soils and conditions but prefers moist, well-drained soil. Avoid planting it in sites that are wet in winter. Once established, it tolerates heat, humidity, and drought. Deadhead to extend blooming, cutting back stems to the basal leaves when flowering finishes. You can also prune back shabby clumps. Divide plants every three years in early spring.

RECOMMENDATIONS:
Blue Hill (also sold as 'Blauhugel'): 20 inches; lilac-blue spikes from late spring to fall. **'Marcus':** 8 to 12 inches by 10 to 12 inches; 4-inch dark violet spikes all summer, especially when deadheaded. **'May Night'** (also called 'Mainacht'): 18 to 24 inches by 18 to 24 inches; stiff blue-violet spikes in early to midsummer. **'East Friesland'** (also known as 'Ostfriesland'): 18 by 36 inches; deep purple flower spikes from early to midsummer. **'Snow Hill':** 20 inches; long-flowering white spikes from late spring through summer.
■ **Common sage** (*S. officinalis*) is 2 feet by 2 feet and is grown mainly for its edible leaves. It produces blue flower spikes in early summer. Some cultivars make fine ornamental plants. **'Purpurascens':** leaves flushed red. **'Tricolor':** gray-green leaves with irregular cream margins, some tinged red. Zones 4 to 8.
■ **'Purple Rain' lilac salvia** (*S. verticillata*), is 24 by 24 inches, with mauve spikes from mid- to late summer. Zones 5 to 8.

LAVENDER COTTON
(Santolina chamaecyparissus)

Features: Shrubby mound of evergreen aromatic silvery foliage; tight, round yellow blooms in summer.
Hardiness: Zones 6 to 8
In-bloom size: 18-inch by 24- to 36-inch mound
Out-of-bloom size: 12-inch mound
Light: Full sun
Site: Average garden soil

DESCRIPTION AND USES: Grown for its silvery evergreen leaves, lavender cotton resists deer and rabbits and looks good year-round. The foliage, which is edible, is fuzzy, fragrant, and fine-textured with tiny, toothed edges. Use this woody perennial as an edging in rock gardens or perennial borders. Mass it as a ground cover. Or shear it to make a low, dense formal hedge in herb and knot gardens. Lavender cotton does especially well in dry, low-maintenance gardens. Its round, flat brilliant yellow flower heads bloom in summer on the tips of stems. Good companions include yucca, heart-leaf bergenia, and Japanese blood grass.

CARE: Well-drained soil year-round is a must. Lavender cotton tolerates heat, drought, and salt spray but dislikes high humidity. Prune it back to 6 to 8 inches in early spring to keep plants dense and compact. For hedges, forego the flowers and clip the foliage as often as necessary to maintain a clean shape. If you like the button flowers, trim plants right after they bloom.

RECOMMENDATIONS:
'Nana': 10 inches; strong aroma.

COMPACT PINCUSHION FLOWER
(Scabiosa columbaria)

Features: Light blue blooms on wiry stems in summer and fall; low mound of basal leaves.
Hardiness: Zones 5 to 8
In-bloom size: 18- to 24-inch by 18- to 24-inch round clump with long flower stems
Out-of-bloom size: 6- to 8-inch mound
Light: Full sun
Site: Fertile, well-drained soil with abundant organic matter

DESCRIPTION AND USES: Pincushion flower is grown for its attractive tufted blooms and airy habit. Delicate stamens rise above the tufts like pins stuck in a pincushion. Basal leaves form a low mound; the stem leaves are ferny and finely cut. The flowers, growing on long, wiry stems over the low-mounded leaves, are perfect for the front of the perennial border. They attract bees and butterflies. They also make excellent long-lasting cut flowers and grow well in containers. Grow pincushion flower with miniature hollyhocks and 'Sweet Dreams' coreopsis.

CARE: Deadheading extends the bloom season of pincushion flower. It can take light frost and may bloom into December, although the typical bloom season is from June to November. The wiry flower stems need no support. Compact pincushion flower tolerates many types of soil but prefers fertile, well-drained, neutral to slightly alkaline soils, and cool, humid climates. Cut back remaining flower stems but not the basal leaves before winter. Clean up the clump in spring.

RECOMMENDATIONS:
'Butterfly Blue': 12 to 18 inches; abundant lavender-blue pincushions from late spring to fall. **'Misty Butterflies':** 10 inches; mix of lavender-blue and dusky pink flowers. **'Pink Mist':** 12 to 18 inches; purple-pink flowers from late spring to fall.
■ Pincushion flower (*S. caucasica*) grows 2 feet by 2 feet, producing long-stemmed light blue pincushions all summer, similar to those of compact pincushion flower. Zones 5 to 9. **'Fama':** 24 to 30 inches; larger and deeper blue flowers than the species. **'Kompliment':** 18 to 24 inches; large lavender-blue flowers.

'AUTUMN JOY' SEDUM
(Sedum hybrid)

Features: Four seasons of garden interest from developing stems, changing flower colors, and winter form. Rose to burgundy blooms in late summer to fall.
Hardiness: Zones 3 to 9
In-bloom size: 24-inch by 24-inch upright
Out-of-bloom size: 12- to 18-inch rounded clump
Light: Full sun to partial shade
Site: Moderately fertile, well-drained soil

DESCRIPTION AND USES: This classic border perennial has four seasons of garden interest. In spring, attractive, bushy stems develop from a mound of frosty blue-green fleshy nubs emerging from the soil. Summer brings the flowering stems, which are topped by dense, flat clusters of light green buds. With cooler fall weather, flowers open, attracting bees and butterflies as they deepen in hue to rose, then burgundy. In winter, the now-chocolate blooms and tan stems maintain their form even under a blanket of snow. Use 'Autumn Joy' as a specimen or massed with 'Chocolate' Joe-Pye weed, giant coneflower, and 'Heavy Metal' switch grass.

CARE: Easy to grow and maintain, 'Autumn Joy' sedum thrives in well-drained soil and sun to partial shade. In shade and fertile soils, clumps may fall open and thus need some support. These drought-tolerant sedums rarely need division, but floppy plants may benefit from dividing every five years or so to maintain vigor and shape. Keep the plant intact through the cold weather; its striking form adds winter interest to the garden.

RECOMMENDATIONS:
■ **Hybrid sedums 'Autumn Fire':** 24 inches; improved 'Autumn Joy' with bigger flowers on stronger stems to reduce flopping. **'Bertram Anderson':** 12 inches; intense rosy-pink blooms in late summer; frosted purple leaves; shiny purple stems. **'Frosty Morn':** 12 inches; pink to white flower clusters in summer; variegated leaves with white edges. **'Lydia Windsor':** 16 inches; deep ruby blooms in late summer to fall; very dark brownish-purple leaves. **'Matrona':** 18 to 24 inches; big pink blooms on polished red stems in late summer; deep gray-green leaves with rosy margins.

CHECKERBLOOM *(Sidalcea malviflora)*

Features: Vertical accent. Low spikes of pink, white, or purplish flowers in early to midsummer. Rounded or lobed shiny dark green basal foliage.
Hardiness: Zones 4 to 8
In-bloom size: 15- to 60-inch by 18- to 24-inch upright spires
Out-of-bloom size: 8-inch mound
Light: Full sun to partial shade
Site: Moist, well-drained soil

DESCRIPTION AND USES: Like its big cousin the hollyhock, this short-lived perennial brings a vertical accent to beds and borders. Checkerbloom, however, is smaller by half, making it ideal for both small and large beds and borders. Dense spikes of long-lasting flowers with five silky-smooth petals, some fringed at the tips, top thin but rigid stems that are useful in flower arrangements. Most checkerblooms in garden centers are hybrids that grow from 15 to 60 inches tall and bloom in July and August. Good companions include 'Hameln' dwarf fountain grass and 'Goldrush' goldenrod.

CARE: Checkerbloom prefers climates with cool summers. It is easy to grow in moist, well-drained, average garden soil. Deadheading spikes extends flowering and reduces self-sowing. After blooming, cut checkerbloom to the ground, particularly if it wanes in summer's heat. Cutting after the first flush of bloom stimulates fresh basal growth and the prospect of more flowering. Pick off Japanese beetles by hand and discard.

RECOMMENDATIONS:
'Elsie Heugh': 36 inches; fringed pink blooms. **'Little Princess':** 15 inches; lavish light pink flowers. **'Party Girl':** 24 to 48 inches; spikes of 2-inch rosy pink flowers from midsummer to fall. **'Bianca':** 3 feet; white flowers. **'Brilliant':** 28 inches; vivid red blooms on erect stems; shiny leaves with shallow lobes.

FALSE SOLOMON'S SEAL *(Smilacina racemosa)*

Features: Gracefully arching, leafy stems; showy creamy white flower plumes in spring.
Hardiness: Zones 3 to 8
In- and out-of-bloom size: 3 feet by 2 feet upright to arching
Light: Partial to full shade
Site: Moist, well-drained, moderately fertile soil with abundant organic matter

DESCRIPTION AND USES: In nature, false Solomon's seal grows densely clustered in rich woods. Its broad, pointed green foliage has smooth edges and parallel veins running lengthwise on the blade. Leaves turn yellow in fall. In April through May or June, showy pyramidal plumes of tiny, fragrant white flowers bloom at the stem tips. After flowering, dense clusters of small berries appear at the stem tips, ripening from mottled green to bright red. Grown in masses, false Solomon's seal beautifies wild gardens, woodland edges, the banks of shady ponds and streams, and shady borders. Grow it with ferns, hosta, and snowy woodrush, a shade-tolerant ornamental grass. Both Solomon's seal and false Solomon's seal produce leaves along curving stems. You can tell the plants apart by the way they bloom.

CARE: Grow false Solomon's seal in somewhat fertile, acid soils rich in organic matter. It prefers a cool location, uniform moisture, good drainage, and partial to full shade. To propagate plants, divide in spring.

RECOMMENDATIONS:
■ **Starry false Solomon's seal** *(S. stellata)* produces small clusters of starry greenish-white flowers at the tips of leafy stems. It grows 1 to 2 feet tall and wide and does best in partial shade and dry, sandy soils. Zones 3 to 7.

'GOLDEN FLEECE' GOLDENROD *(Solidago sphacelata)*

Features: Plumes of bright golden-yellow flowers on arching stems in late summer to fall; compact form.
Hardiness: Zones 4 to 9
In-bloom size: 18-inch by 24-inch upright, airy clump
Out-of-bloom size: 15-inch clump
Light: Full sun
Site: Sandy, lean to somewhat fertile, well-drained soil

DESCRIPTION AND USES: This fast-spreading perennial brings brilliant gold flowers, not hayfever, to late summer and fall gardens. Its 10-inch yellow flower clusters arc at the stem tips, creating a mass of color. This named cultivar is not invasive, as many goldenrod species can be. Stunning at the front of late-season perennial borders and able to grow in just about any soil, this dwarf ornamental is also appropriate for butterfly, meadow, and wildflower gardens. Grow with long-blooming 'Alba' or 'Floristan Violett' gayfeather, Russian sage, 'Purple Dome' asters, or ornamental grasses.

CARE: 'Golden Fleece' is deer-resistant and tolerates drought. It prefers sandy, well-drained soils and full sun, although it can take some light shade. Fungal diseases may sometimes bother goldenrod, but it is mostly a sturdy, healthy, easy-to-grow plant. Division may be necessary to manage its spread.

RECOMMENDATIONS:
■ **'Goldrush' goldenrod** *(S. cutleri)* grows 12 to 14 inches tall with masses of bright yellow flowers from early August to September. It is suitable for the front of the garden, and the flower stems are good weavers. Zones 4 to 9.
■ **'Fireworks' rough-stemmed goldenrod** *(S. rugosa)* has 18-inch tapering clusters of bright yellow flowers that arch over 3-foot leafy green stems. Zones 5 to 9.
■ **Hybrid goldenrods 'Golden Baby':** 20-inch mound; arched bright yellow flower plumes from late summer into fall. The plumes make excellent cut flowers. Zones 4 to 8.

LAMB'S-EARS *(Stachys byzantina)*

Features: Lamb's-wool texture and color; woolly gray leaves; furry gray spikes of purple blooms in early summer.
Hardiness: Zones 3 to 8
In-bloom size: 18-inch by 24-inch spike
Out-of-bloom size: 8-inch low rosette
Light: Full sun
Site: Dry, sandy to loamy, well-drained soil

DESCRIPTION AND USES: Most folks remember the first time they touched lamb's-ears—their feelings of surprise that something so soft and furry and almost white is a common garden plant. Everything about lamb's-ears but the flowers wears a thick, furry whitish coat. Pinky-purple bloom spikes cap thick, rigid whitish stems. Some people like the flower spikes for their vertical interest. Others remove the stalks before they have time to grow for the sake of the wonderful leaves. Grow this rather drought-tolerant plant in dry, sunny borders and on top of terraces and retaining walls. Lamb's-ears makes a good ground cover that many weeds find hard to penetrate. Good companions include 'Biokovo' cranesbill and 'Crème Brulee' coreopsis.

CARE: Lamb's-ears grows best when you meet its needs, which include full sun and very well-drained soil. Divide every five years or so to control vigor and keep it in check. In moist soils, the 4-inch leaves of lamb's-ears may start rotting and need some deadleafing by midseason.

RECOMMENDATIONS:
'Big Ears' (also sold as 'Helene Von Stein'): 8 to 10 inches; few to no flowers; superb ground cover with leaves twice as big as the species. Heat-tolerant; very desirable. **'Primrose Heron':** 6 to 8 inches; dense clump of cream-yellow leaves that are rather cupped. **'Silver Carpet':** 8 inches; no flowers; dense carpet of silvery leaves.

STOKES' ASTER *(Stokesia laevis)*

Features: Shaggy blue, pink, white, or yellow daisies with a lighter or darker center from summer to fall; basal rosette of lance-shaped evergreen leaves.
Hardiness: Zones 5 to 9
In-bloom size: 18- to 24-inch by 18-inch round mound
Out-of-bloom size: 8- to 10-inch low rosette
Light: Full sun to light shade
Site: Moist, well-drained, acid soil rich in organic matter

DESCRIPTION AND USES: Big, cheery 3- to 5-inch flowers that last many weeks and attractive evergreen basal leaves make this native southern belle stand out in flower beds, borders, containers, and cottage gardens. The blooms have fringed petals and a fluffy center, and they attract butterflies. The long-lasting flowers are excellent for cutting. Grow Stokes' aster with baby's breath, 'Happy Returns' daylily, and blanket flower.

CARE: Stokes' aster prefers full sun and winter mulch in the North and a little afternoon shade in the South. Deadheading extends blooming. Blooming clumps tend to open in the center and may need staking. Divide crowded clumps every three or four years.

RECOMMENDATIONS:
'Blue Danube': 18 to 24 inches; lavender-blue flowers. **'Colorwheel':** 24 inches; flowers open white, change to lavender, then to purple. **'Mary Gregory':** 12 inches; yellow flowers. **'Klaus Jelitto':** 18 inches; 4- to 5-inch light blue flowers. **'Peachie's Pick':** 12 to 18 inches; blue flowers; less floppy than most Stokes' asters; dense mound of evergreen leaves.

GERMANDER *(Teucrium chamaedrys)*

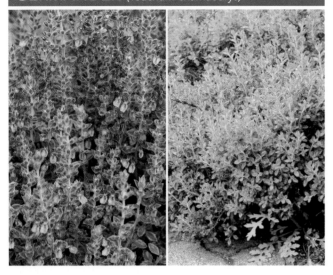

Features: Upright and bushy plant with shiny evergreen leaves; pinky-purple blooms in early summer.
Hardiness: Zones 5 to 9
In-bloom size: 12- to 20-inch by 12- to 18-inch upright
Out-of-bloom size: 10- to 12-inch rounded clump
Light: Full sun
Site: Well-drained, moderately fertile, neutral to alkaline soil

DESCRIPTION AND USES: Grown mostly for low evergreen to deciduous hedging, germander has dense, lustrous, fine-textured dark green leaves that make a handsome frame for other plants. It can outline patterns in knot gardens and formal gardens or bring welcome structure and definition to the jumble of a cottage garden. Once established, germander can tolerate some drought, and it grows well in containers. If you choose to let it flower, the blooms will attract bees and butterflies. Grow germander with cranesbill and 'Snowcap' Shasta daisy, or use it as a miniature hedge to edge a bed filled with lavender or ornamental oregano.

CARE: Plant germander 12 to 18 inches apart in spring or fall. In cool climates, choose a protected location for planting. Feed with slow-release granular fertilizer in spring. Clipping stems in spring to 2 to 6 inches tall removes winter damage, reduces legginess, and keeps the shape neat and tight for hedging. Or wait until blooming ends to remove the top third of the stems to keep them dense. Many gardeners routinely shear germander; however, sheared plants tend to be less healthy than ones that receive minor pruning. Germander is relatively free of pests and diseases, as long as you meet its cultural needs. Divide in spring or fall.

RECOMMENDATIONS:
'Summer Sunshine': 6 to 8 inches by 15 inches; short pink flower spikes in late summer; yellow to chartreuse leaves.

'LAVENDER MIST' MEADOW RUE *(Thalictrum rochebrunianum)*

Features: Airy clusters of dainty lavender-pink flowers on tall purplish stems from mid- to late summer; mound of leaves like maidenhair fern.
Hardiness: Zones 4 to 9
In-bloom size: 6- to 8-foot by 2- to 3-foot upright
Out-of-bloom size: 3-foot airy clump
Light: Full sun to partial shade
Site: Moist, rich, well-drained soil rich in organic matter

DESCRIPTION AND USES: Although 'Lavender Mist' meadow rue towers above many garden plants, it is no garden bully. Its presence is magical and harmonious, like a giant lacy fern capped with sprays of blooms. Each little flower, which is lavender-pink in bud, opens to reveal a big tuft of yellow stamens. The leaves and flowers are lovely in bouquets. 'Lavender Mist' meadow rue makes a graceful accent grown among Fox Valley birches. It is deer-resistant. A group of three meadow rues looks stunning in woodland gardens or the middle or back of beds and borders with 'Brunette' bugbane and 'Morning Light' maiden grass.

CARE: Set plants about 2 feet apart in partial shade, except in the North where it can take full sun. 'Lavender Mist' meadow rue prefers deep, consistently moist, fertile soil with abundant organic matter. Although tall, it needs no staking. Divide every five years if crowded; otherwise, division is rarely necessary.

RECOMMENDATIONS:
■ Columbine meadow rue (*T. aquilegifolium*) has leaves that resemble columbine and clouds of pink flowers. Zones 5 to 7.
■ Yellow meadow rue (*T. delavayi*) produces sprays of tiny lilac single blooms. It grows 3 to 5 feet tall. Because of its see-through stems, you can plant it toward the front of the border. **'Album':** white flowers. **'Hewitt's Double':** lilac double blooms. Zones 4 to 7.
■ Hybrid meadow rues **'Black Stockings':** 6 feet by 2 feet; lavender flower puffs on near-black stems.

ALLEGHENY FOAM FLOWER
(Tiarella cordifolia)

FORMOSA TOAD LILY (Tricyrtis formosana)

Features: Starry white spring blooms; attractive green leaves from spring through fall; ruddy bronze fall color.
Hardiness: Zones 3 to 8
In-bloom size: 9-inch by 18-inch ground cover
Out-of-bloom size: 6-inch ground cover
Light: Partial to full shade
Site: Moist, well-drained, humusy soil

DESCRIPTION AND USES: Allegheny foam flower thrives in shade and woodland conditions. This vigorous plant spreads fast, forming a handsome ground cover with good red to yellow fall color; the foliage may stay evergreen in temperate areas. In spring, petite star-shaped white flowers appear in fluffy spikes above the leaves. Although the species itself is attractive, showy new, often fragrant hybrids frequently come on the market, some with long-lasting pink blooms and others with variegated or multihued leaves. Grow with ferns, bleeding heart, and yellow waxbells.

CARE: Space plants about 12 to 15 inches apart. Although removing spent flowers may stimulate more blooming, this ground cover has such appealing lobed foliage that it looks good if you leave it alone. It's easy to keep foam flower in check by pulling out runners, which you can pot up and give to your friends.

RECOMMENDATIONS:
■ **Wherry's foam flower** (T. wherryi) forms a nonspreading clump of evergreen leaves with attractive 10-inch white bloom spikes. **'Heronswood Mist':** 12 inches; white bloom spikes with pink stems; mottled cream-and-green foliage with pinkish new growth.
■ **Hybrid foam flowers 'Black Snowflake':** 12 inches; dramatic semi-evergreen leaves with dark purple veins and nearly black new growth; coloring is stronger in cool weather; creamy white flowers. **'Elizabeth Oliver':** 12 inches; dense ground cover; pale pink spikes; deeply lobed foliage marked with maroon. **'Jeepers Creepers':** 12 inches; ground cover; creamy flower spikes; leaves have strong markings. **'Pink Skyrocket':** 12 inches; long-lasting pink flower spikes; deeply cut leaves with blackish central markings. **'Pirate's Patch':** 5-inch mound of leaves; profuse white flower spikes on 10-inch stems.

Features: Clusters of purplish-white flowers with purple spots in late summer and fall. Shiny dark green leaves, strong stems.
Hardiness: Zones 6 to 9
In- and out-of-bloom size: 24-inch by 18-inch loose upright clump
Light: Partial to full shade
Site: Moist, well-drained, humus-rich soil

DESCRIPTION AND USES: Toad lily brings subtle beauty to late summer and fall gardens with its funnel-shaped spotted flowers and glossy leaves. The up-facing 1- to $1\frac{1}{2}$-inch blooms look like little orchids loosely clustered at the stem tips. Unlike hairy toad lily, which browns toward late summer, this toad lily's leaves stay relatively fresh. Long, oval, shiny dark green leaves cover upright stems that spread quickly. Grow toad lily for cutting, or mass it in shady perennial borders and woodland gardens with Japanese painted fern and 'Frances Williams' hosta.

CARE: Toad lily prefers partial shade and moist, well-drained, acid soil rich in humus. Space plants about 18 inches apart. Use pine needles and shredded leaves for mulch.

RECOMMENDATIONS:
■ **Hairy toad lily** (T. hirta) produces lilac blooms with purple spots in late summer on long upright stems. This hairy plant grows 30 inches tall. Zones 4 to 8.
■ **Hybrid toad lilies 'Empress':** 29 inches; large flowers with deep purple spots; sturdy, handsome foliage. **'Gilt Edge':** 24 inches; starry white flowers with purple spots in early summer to fall; striking golden-edged glossy leaves. Zones 5 to 9. **'Lightning Strike':** 24 inches; lavender blooms; green-striped golden leaves. Zones 4 to 8. **'Moonlight Treasure':** 10 inches; small clusters of yellow flowers in late summer; spotted leathery leaves. **'Sinonome':** 36 inches; clustered purple-and-white spotted blooms in late summer; drought-tolerant once established. Zones 5 to 9.

NETTLE-LEAVED MULLEIN
(Verbascum chaixii)

Features: Strong vertical accent. Pointed spikes of yellow or white flowers with a purple center; rosette of big furry gray-green leaves.
Hardiness: Zones 5 to 8
In-bloom size: 3-foot by 2-foot erect spike
Out-of-bloom size: 8- to 12-inch basal mound
Light: Full sun
Site: Light, sandy, well-drained soil

DESCRIPTION AND USES: In shape, nettle-leaved mullein resembles a column on a broad, stable base. It creates an elegant vertical accent in shrub and perennial borders, where viewers can appreciate the subtle hues of its leaves and flowers. In masses, it looks best planted in mid border, but a random specimen (planted or self-sown) edging a cottage-garden path or at the front of a raised bed has a charming effect. Grow nettle-leaved mullein amid bigroot geranium or with the purplish blooms of 'Karley Rose' fountain grass.

CARE: This low-maintenance but short-lived perennial needs well-drained soil to survive. Although it prefers full sun and sandy alkaline soils, it tolerates many other situations. Space this drought-tolerant plant about 18 inches apart. Cutting off faded flower spikes prevents excessive self-sowing and encourages side branching and thus more blooms.

RECOMMENDATIONS:
'Album': 3 feet; white blooms with a purple center. 'Sixteen Candles': many-branched spikes of golden yellow blooms with violet stamens.
■ Olympic mullein (*V. olympicum*) has huge, branched spikes of yellow blooms on 6- to 7-foot gray stems.
■ Hybrid mulleins 'Jackie': 16 inches; light apricot blooms; big felty leaves. 'Jackie in Pink': 16 inches; pink blooms. 'Sugar Plum': 18 inches; deep plum flower spikes with excellent rebloom. Zones 5 to 9.

SPIKE SPEEDWELL
(Veronica spicata)

'Goodness Grows'

Features: Long-blooming, pointed blue flower spikes in summer; narrow, hairy dark green leaves.
Hardiness: Zones 3 to 8
In-bloom size: 12- to 24-inch by 18-inch spiky upright clump
Out-of-bloom size: 8- to 18-inch upright clump
Light: Full sun to partial shade
Site: Moist, well-drained, somewhat fertile soil

DESCRIPTION AND USES: Spike speedwell brings vertical interest and bright color to container plantings and perennial beds and borders. Cultivars produce upright, pointed spikes of star-shaped flowers in blue, pink, white, and violet. Speedwell, which attracts bees and butterflies, has an informal look well-suited to cottage gardens. Plant it with orange daylily, purple coneflower, and 'Goldsturm' black-eyed Susan.

CARE: Spike speedwell needs good winter drainage. Plant them 18 inches apart in spring or fall in full sun to partial shade. Removing faded flower spikes encourages more blooms. Cut back to new growth at the base after flowering to improve the plant's appearance. Divide as necessary in spring or fall every few years.

RECOMMENDATIONS:
'Goodness Grows': 12 to 18 inches; dark blue flower spikes all summer. 'Red Fox': 15 inches; rose-red flower spikes.
■ Woolly speedwell (*V. s. incana*) grows 12 to 18 inches tall and has violet-blue flowers and silver, furry foliage.
■ 'Georgia Blue' creeping veronica (*V. peduncularis*) is a low, mat-forming plant 4 to 6 inches high by 12 inches wide with round bright blue blooms in late winter or spring, depending on your climate. Dark green leaves are purple in winter. Good in a rock garden. Grow in full sun to partial shade. Zones 3 to 8.
■ Hybrid speedwells 'Baby Doll': 8 inches; uniform clump with bright pink flowers. 'Sunny Border Blue': 18 to 24 inches; deep violet-blue spikes; wrinkled deep green leaves. Zones 6 to 8. 'Waterperry Blue': 4- to 6-inch ground cover; round pale blue blooms in early summer; purple leaves in winter. Good in rock gardens or atop stone retaining walls.

HORNED VIOLET (Viola cornuta)

ADAM'S NEEDLE (Yucca filamentosa)

Features: Fragrant purple to pale purple flowers like little pansies in spring to early summer; tufted green leaves.
Hardiness: Zones 6 to 9
In-bloom size: 6-inch by 12-inch mounds
Out-of-bloom size: 3-inch tuft
Light: Full sun to partial shade
Site: Moist, well-drained, fertile soil

DESCRIPTION AND USES: These charming plants produce flowers that are rounded, sometimes fragrant, with lines in contrasting or darker hues. Horned violets grow in small, leafy tufts and have upright flower stems. They add whimsy to cottage gardens, woodland gardens, rock gardens, and stone walls, and at the front of perennial borders. Grow them in odd-numbered groups with Lenten rose, 'Georgia Blue' speedwell, or Christmas fern. Although the species is usually a light to dark purple, cultivars are available in red, white, yellow, blue, black, apricot, and multicolor.

CARE: This versatile perennial can survive in most places with good winter drainage. Plant 12 inches apart in early spring. Deadheading old flowers promotes continued blooming. Clip back after blooming to keep the plant neat and reduce self-sowing. Horned violets hybridize with other violas, creating new plants. Cultivars do not come true from seed and must be propagated by division in spring or fall.

RECOMMENDATIONS:
■ **Labrador violet** (V. labradorica) grows 3 inches high with an indefinite spread, making it an excellent ground cover. It has light bluish-purple flowers through the growing season and bronzy new growth. Zones 3 to 8.
■ **Sweet violet** (V. odorata) produces violet or white flowers in fall, winter, and spring in the South and spring in the North. Zones 6 to 8. **'Marie Louise':** ruffled lavender double flowers and a powerful perfume. Zones 6 to 8.
■ **Hybrid violets 'Arkwright's Ruby':** 6 to 8 inches; red pansy flowers. **'Baby Franjo':** 4 inches; copious pale yellow flowers. **'Molly Sanderson':** 6 to 8 inches; black blooms all summer. **'Rebecca':** fragrant white blooms with uneven dark violet edges. Cultivars hardy in Zones 5 to 8.

Features: Tall, architectural form; tufted, swordlike leaves and towering clusters of scented creamy bells in summer.
Hardiness: Zones 4 to 10
In-bloom size: 5- to 12-foot by 3-foot huge, upright, branched clusters
Out-of-bloom size: 18- to 24-inch spiky clump
Light: Full sun
Site: Light, sandy, well-drained soil

DESCRIPTION AND USES: For pure drama, you can't beat Adam's needle, with its evergreen tuft of sword-shaped gray-green foliage edged in wavy white threads. In summer, giant branched flower clusters loom up to 12 feet over leaves. Flowers are 2-inch long-lasting, fragrant creamy-white bells. Yucca, technically a drought-tolerant shrub, anchors borders, lines formal paths, and makes an excellent specimen plant. Grow it with roses, giant coneflower, or ornamental grasses.

CARE: Grow in full sun and light, sandy soil with good drainage. Plant 3 feet apart. Trim off dead or damaged leaves in spring and old flower stalks after blooming.

RECOMMENDATIONS:
'Bright Edge': 20-inch mound of sword-shape dark green leaves with narrow golden edges. **'Color Guard':** 20-inch tuft of bold yellow-centered leaves with deep green edges. Foliage flushed coral in winter. **'Variegata':** bluish-green leaves with white edges and a pinkish winter flush.
■ **'Golden Sword' weakleaf yucca** (Y. flaccida) has foliage with a yellow center and green edges.

Northern maidenhair fern

Japanese painted fern

Features: Handsome textural accents. Foliage colors vary from deep to light green, some with hints of rust or brown and some with silvery variegations.
Hardiness: Zones 3 to 8, depending on species
Size: Less than 1 foot to 6 feet, depending on species
Light: Partial to full shade
Site: Rich, well-drained soil

DESCRIPTION AND USES: Ferns go well in woodland gardens and shady beds and borders when planted with other shade-loving perennials such as hosta, astilbe, Solomon's seal, and Bethlehem sage. Individually, they are graceful in form. Massed as a ground cover under high-canopied trees, they add drama and refinement to the landscape.

CARE: Most ferns grow easily in partial to full shade and moist, well-drained, slightly acid soil rich in organic matter, but a few prefer wetter sites. Divide ferns in spring or fall, and keep divisions well watered.

RECOMMENDATIONS:
■ Maidenhair ferns (*Adiantum* spp.) are delicate-, airy-looking ferns with broad leaflets on slender stalks. They are lovely grouped in a shady border, rock garden, or woodland garden. Northern maidenhair ferns (*A. pedatum*) have upright blackish-purple stems topped by arching branchlets arranged like fingers on a hand. This tough but dainty deciduous fern grows about

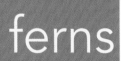

ferns

2 feet tall and wide and prefers dappled shade. It is hardy in Zones 3 to 8. **'Miss Sharples':** light yellow-green leaflets. Himalayan maidenhair fern (*A. venustum*) grows 8 to 12 inches tall with purplish-black stems, light bluish-green fronds in summer, and yellowish-brown fall color. Zones 5 to 8.

■ Lady ferns (*Athyrium* spp.) are deciduous, upright to spreading ferns. **Japanese painted fern** (*A. nipponicum* 'Pictum') is grown for its burgundy red stems and silver fronds licked with red and blue. It grows 12 to 18 inches tall and up to 24 inches wide, and makes an elegant and colorful garden or container accent. It brightens dark garden corners but is at its most colorful with a few hours of morning light. Zones 4 to 9. **'Pewter Lace':** 12 inches; dark-centered silvery gray leaves. Zones 5 to 8. **'Red Beauty':** 12 to 18 inches; silver, red, and green fronds with red stems and a red central vein. Lady fern (*A. filix-femina*) grows 2 to 3 feet tall and is evergreen in mild climates. Easy to grow, it has delicate, lacy fronds and tolerates dry soil. It will grow in full sun if given plenty of moisture. Zones 4 to 9. **Tatting fern** (*A. f.* 'Frizelliae') looks like strings of green pearls. This odd plant grows about 1 foot tall. Zones 3 to 8. **Hybrid lady ferns 'Ghost':** 2 to 3 feet tall; erect silver fronds.

■ Hay-scented fern (*Dennstaedtia punctilobata*), named for the scent of its bruised fronds, increases fast, making it excellent for naturalizing moist, slightly acid soils in sun or shade. This native fern grows 30 to 36 inches by 30 to 36 inches and tolerates many soil conditions. Zones 3 to 8.

■ Wood ferns (*Dryopteris* spp.) are medium-size woodland ferns. They are tough, adaptable ferns with strong forms and bold texture. Some species are evergreen; others are deciduous. **Male wood fern** (*D. filix-mas*) forms a 3-foot by 3-foot clump of fronds. In protected places, it may remain evergreen through the winter. Zones 3 to 8. **Autumn fern** (*D. erythrosora*), an evergreen, produces coppery new growth that turns green with age; it has ruddy fall color. It grows about 18 inches tall and wide. **Goldie's fern** (*D. goldiana*) forms 4-foot by 2-foot clumps of light green fronds. Zones 6 to 8. **Marginal shield fern** (*D. marginalis*) has evergreen fronds. It grows about 18 inches tall and 24 inches wide. Zones 3 to 8.

Male wood fern

Ostrich fern

■ **Ostrich fern** (*Matteuccia struthiopteris*) grows in a vaselike form up to 6 feet tall and 3 feet wide. Use this spreading fern to create drama in primeval settings and backgrounds. It also makes a tall, vigorous ground cover. Zones 3 to 8.

■ **Sensitive fern** (*Onoclea sensibilis*) is a wide-spreading 2-foot-tall fern with light green fronds. It makes an excellent ground cover for moist shade and is frequently found growing at the edge of moist woods.

■ **Osmundas** (*Osmunda* spp.) are among the largest ferns suited to home gardens. They require very moist soil to survive. **Cinnamon fern** (*Osmunda cinnamomea*), a deciduous fern, grows wild in moist to wet soils in sun or shade. Its sterile light green fronds on the outside of the clump can reach 5 feet tall and 2 feet wide, while erect fertile reddish-brown fronds in the center of the plant, from which the plant gets its name, grow 3 feet tall. This fern looks striking at the edge of ponds and woodlands. Zones 4 to 9. **Interrupted fern** (*O. claytoniana*) can form a clump up to 3 feet tall and twice as wide. This fern produces upright stems that bow at the top. Brown leaflets in midfrond interrupt the progression of the sterile green leaflets. Interrupted fern looks particularly striking in spring when its fertile leaflets turn rich blackish brown. Zones 3 to 6. **Royal fern** (*O. regalis*) forms a 2- to 6-foot tall well-shaped clump in wet, boggy, or lakeside soils. The deciduous foliage is leathery light green, turning an attractive gold tone in fall. Zones 4 to 9.

Cinnamon fern

■ **Christmas, sword, and shield ferns** (*Polystichum* spp.) are upright, evergreen ferns with medium to bold texture. They tolerate slightly alkaline soils. **Christmas fern** (*P. acrostichoides*) produces fronds up to 3 feet long. Although new fronds are erect, they sprawl on older growth to form a striking, slightly glossy mound. Because of its compact, mounded shape and evergreen foliage, this fern looks good in woodland settings and shines in partly shaded borders. Zones 3 to 8. **Western sword fern** (*P. munitum*) has glossy dark green evergreen fronds that make an erect, arching clump of medium texture about 3 to 4 feet tall and wide. This fern looks outstanding planted in moist, shady woodland gardens in soil rich in organic matter. Zones 3 to 8. **Soft shield fern** (*P. setiferum*) produces feathery, dark evergreen fronds that grow in a whirl, giving plants a shuttlecock shape. It grows about 3 to 4 feet tall

Soft shield fern

and 3 feet wide. This erect fern adds an exotic touch to woodland gardens and shady borders. Plant it in beds with hosta under ornamental trees. Soft shield fern dies back in cold-winter climates. Zones 6 to 9. **'Congestum':** 8 inches; crowded, overlapping segments give the grayish-green fronds an intricate texture. **'Herrenhausen':** 10 to 12 inches; lacy fronds; good for containers.

Feather reed grass

'Bowles Golden' tufted sedge

Features: Handsome textural accents. Upright to fountain-shaped plants. Among the best for winter interest.
Hardiness: Zones 3 to 11, depending on species
Size: Less than 1 foot to more than 6 feet, depending on the species
Light: Full sun to light shade
Site: Well-drained soil

DESCRIPTION AND USES: Ornamental grasses are year-round plants for the senses. Some whisper in the breeze. Some look like moving sculptures with erect, mounded, or fountainlike forms. Some change hues with the seasons.

In summer, ornamental grasses pair with flowering perennials, create textural contrast in shrub borders, and make stunning landscape accents whether used singly or in groups. Many bear striking flowers in summer or fall. Sometimes plumy, sometimes dangling, the blooms are pink, rose, green, silver, or yellow.

Grass foliage comes in hues ranging from bright yellow, red, and chartreuse to blue, clear green, and variegated green and white or green and yellow. Some grasses have brilliant red or golden fall color before changing to subtle buff or tan. Others shine in winter, when morning sunlight dances on their ice-slicked leaves, and their architectural shapes remain distinct through ice and snow. Although you cut deciduous grasses back in spring and let spring bloomers take the stage, evergreen and grasses look good year round.

grasses

There's a grass that's right for every site. Grasses can be large or small. You can find them for sun or shade, wet or dry sites, and sandy or clay soils.

CARE: Plant ornamental grasses throughout the growing season, especially in warm climates. In cold climates, spring or summer planting is best. Cut deciduous grasses close to the ground in spring just before new growth begins. Trim dead and damaged parts off evergreen to semievergreen grasses. Division is not necessary, but you can do it to make more plants or revive a waning clump. Note, however, that digging and dividing clumps of large, well-established grasses may require great strength and a chain saw.

RECOMMENDATIONS:

■ **Sweet flags** (*Acorus* spp.) are not grasses, but they look like grasses, growing into short arching clumps of slender foliage. Grow sweet flag for its leaves; its flowers are not showy. Acorus cultivars look good in containers, massed by streams and ponds, and softening the edges of shady woodland paths. **Dwarf sweet flag** (*A. gramineus*) makes a 1-foot tuft of grassy green leaves. This slow-growing evergreen to semi-evergreen species thrives in continuously moist to wet soils and sun to partial shade. The crushed leaves are fragrant. Zones 5 to 11. **'Minimus Aureus':** 4 inches by 6 to 12 inches; golden leaves. **'Ogon':** 6 to 12 inches tall and wide; yellow stripes. **'Argenteostriatus':** green leaves striped with creamy white. **Variegated sweet flag** (*A. calamus* 'Variegatus') can grow in several inches of water in full sun to partial shade. It grows 3 to 5 feet tall and about 2 feet wide. Zones 4 to 11.

■ **Big bluestem** (*Andropogon gerardii*) is the native grass that greeted settlers when they first arrived in the tallgrass prairie of the central United States. It forms a bluish-green column of grass that turns bronzy red in fall. The plants grow 5 to 8 feet tall in soils with average moisture; they tolerate heavy clay. They also will grow in poor, dry soil but are shorter in such conditions. Space plants 2 feet apart. Zones 3 to 10.

■ **Feather reed grass** (*Calamagrostis acutiflora*) is an adaptable, upright grass that makes a fine garden accent. **'Karl Foerster'** forms a stiff 5-foot by 1½- to 2-foot column when in flower. It has lustrous dark green deciduous leaves that emerge in spring

Dwarf blue fescue

Golden hakone grass

and last into winter. In June the plant produces pale pink flowers that develop into tan seed heads. The grass maintains its erect architectural form through the winter. Use it singly or grouped in prairie gardens, perennial beds, mixed borders, and containers as a vertical accent, or cut it for fresh or dried arrangements. It prospers in sun to partial shade and moist, well-drained soil rich in organic matter but tolerates a variety of soils and conditions. Zones 5 to 9. **'Avalanche':** 4 to 5 feet; variegated leaves with a white streak down the center; similar to 'Karl Foerster' but shorter. **'Overdam':** 3 feet; variegated leaves with white stripes around a green center.

■ **Sedges** (*Carex* spp.) may be best known as water garden plants. They thrive in moist to well-drained soil and in light to partial shade. The colorful foliage is evergreen in hot regions, semievergreen in colder ones. Plants grow in clumps and have a low arching form. Like sweet flags, sedges are not true grasses. **Golden tufted sedge** (*Carex elata* 'Aurea') lights up the dark with its yellow-edged bright green leaves. It grows about 2 feet tall and wide in sun to partial shade, but plants in full sun need more water to flourish than those in darker sites. It thrives in fertile, moist to waterlogged soils at the edge of ponds, in bogs, and in containers. Zones 5 to 9. **'Bowles Golden' tufted sedge:** 2 feet tall; bright golden-yellow leaves with a thin green margin. **Weeping brown sedge** (*C. flagellifera*) forms an arching 18-inch clump of linear reddish-bronze evergreen foliage resembling a tuft of hair. Grow it in sun to partial shade in moist, fertile soil. It looks spectacular grouped at the front of a border or softening the edge of a container. Cut out dead or winter-damaged leaves in late spring or summer. Zones 6 to 9. **'Bronzita':** 12-inch tannish-bronze tuft.

Japanese grass sedge (*C. morrowii*) prefers moist, well-drained, fertile soil in sun to shade. Zones 5 to 9. **'Goldband':** a 1- by 2-foot clump of white-edged green grass that stays evergreen in the South and looks handsome planted under hollies or with hosta and ferns. **'Ice Dance':** leaves with narrow white edges and a spreading habit suitable for a ground cover. **'Variegata':** silvery-edged foliage. **'Island Brocade' broad-leaf sedge** (*C. siderosticha*) grows 6 to 10 inches tall. It has a spreading form with broad bowed, straplike green leaves that have creamy yellow margins. It is well-suited for use as a ground cover under trees, a path

edging, or in containers. Grow broad-leaf sedge in moist to continuously moist soil in sun to partial shade. Zones 6 to 9.

■ **'Elijah Blue' dwarf blue fescue** (*Festuca glauca*) forms an 8- to 10-inch compact, rounded tuft of fine blue leaves. It is evergreen except in its northernmost range, but it looks best in spring and early summer, when the foliage is fresh. Plant it in average to dry, lean to somewhat fertile, well-drained soil in full sun. Cut out dead leaves in spring, and divide it every few years to freshen the clump. Its linear blue foliage adds elegance in flower borders. Zones 3 to 8. Other cultivars include **'Blue Fox':** 12-inch tufts of silvery blue leaves. **'Blue Sea':** 6-inch grayish-blue tufts. **'Sea Urchin':** 10-inch dense blue tuft.

■ **Golden hakone grass** (*Hakonechloa macra* 'Aureola') produces an elegant 12- to 18-inch by 18- to 24-inch mound of curving, narrow vivid yellow leaves marked with skinny green stripes. It prefers partial shade and moist, well-drained soil rich in organic matter. Use it singly in a container or massed for bold effect at the front of shady borders. Its graceful habit softens the hard edges of architectural features and brings bright color and contrast to rock and woodland gardens. Good companions include shiny green 'Jade Cascade' hosta and glossy-leaved dark green 'Invincible' hosta. Zones 4 to 8.

■ **Blue oat grass** (*Helictotrichon sempervirens*) forms a fine-textured 2-foot thick round tuft of grayish-blue evergreen grass perfect for dry areas. Airy flowers sway on tall tan stalks from early summer. This grass looks beautiful with the powdery blue-green foliage of giant coneflower and 'Chocolate' Joe-Pye weed. Grow it in full sun and lean to moderately fertile, well-drained soil. Zones 4 to 9. **'Sapphire':** bluer than the species; excellent specimen.

■ **Snowy woodrush** (*Luzula nivea* 'Lucius') has evergreen foliage edged with silky white hairs. It spreads slowly and grows up to 2 feet tall by 1½ feet wide. It makes a good ground cover for damp shade. In summer it bears fluffy white flower clusters like falling snow above the flat, narrow dark green leaves. Zones 4 to 9. **'Star Maker':** 12 inches; upright with wide green leaves and white flowers; most effective when massed. **'Ruby Stiletto':** 12 inches; leaves with reddish-bronze tips and edges in cold weather; deep green summer color.

Blue oat grass

■ **Miscanthus** (*Miscanthus sinensis*), a Japanese native, is a versatile perennial. It is probably also the grass used most often in gardens. Dozens of cultivars exist, varying in foliage color, flower shape and plant form. Starting in late summer or fall, showy pink, tan, silver, or bronze floral plumes rise above the leaves and persist with the foliage into winter. This sensual grass attracts birds, shimmers in strong sunlight, and quivers and rustles in wind. Use short cultivars for beds, borders, waterside plantings, and small garden spaces. Tall forms look good at the back of borders, next to ponds, and as garden specimens. You can also use them for privacy screening or to block unpleasant views. They suit informal gardens, where they harmonize with purple coneflower, black-eyed Susan, and gayfeather. Plumes make attractive, long-lasting cut flowers.

Miscanthus prefers moist, well-drained, fertile soil in full sun to partial shade. Plants are robust, and once established, they will tolerate some drought and road salt spray. The species and some cultivars, particularly ones that bloom early in the growing season, may self-sow and become invasive. Weed out seedlings or dig them up to share with your friends. A clump that is dying in the center needs to be divided. If the clump is big and old, the task requires a very sharp spade for digging, a saw to part the clump, and enough physical strength to carry out the job. Zones 5 to 9. Hardiness depends on cultivar, and some cultivars are more or less hardy.

'Adagio': 3 to 4 feet; narrow green leaves with a white midrib; pink-tinted flowers in August aging to white. **'Graziella':** great fluffy white plumes in August on 5- to 6-foot stems over an arching clump of fine, graceful leaves. **'Little Kitten':** 30-inch silver flowers above 15-inch foliage in late summer. **'Herkules':** 5 to 6 feet; strong-growing; ruddy fall color. **'Silver Feather':** 6 to 9 feet; tall, dense, arching form for screening; lavish silver flowers from September through winter. **Porcupine grass ('Strictus'):** 6 to 8 feet; erect flowers in September above a columnar clump of green leaves with broad yellow horizontal bands. **Maiden grass ('Gracillimus'):** 3 to 4 feet tall by 3 feet wide; narrow leaves; arching habit; large silvery plumes. **Zebra grass ('Zebrinus'):** tall, upright habit and yellow horizontal bands on leaves.

Hardier miscanthus: Flame grass (the variety *purpurascens*): red-tinged 4-foot tall foliage that turns red-orange in fall; fluffy white flowers in July and August; blooms on 5-foot stalks appear earlier than many miscanthus; seldom self-sows.

Zones 3 to 9. **'Autumn Light':** 7- to 9-foot deep bronze plumes in mid-September on an upright 6-foot clump of foliage that arches at the top and turns yellow in fall. Zones 4 to 9.

Less hardy miscanthus: 'Cabaret': 6 to 8 feet; bold, wide, variegated foliage with a large creamy white center and deep green edges; pink blooms. Zones 6 to 9. **'Little Nicky'** (also sold as 'Hinjo'): 3 to 4 feet; red flowers in September and October; arching light green foliage with horizontal yellow bands. Zones 6 to 9.

■ **Black mondo grass** (*Ophiopogon planiscapus* 'Niger') produces grasslike leaves in a spreading clump about 6 inches high and 12 inches wide. In summer, clusters of lavender flowers on leafless stalks contrast with the short, arched black to violet-black leaves. Massed in shade, this grassy member of the lily family creates a dark background that makes plants with bright flowers or variegated leaves stand out. Black mondo grass prefers a shady site in moist, well-drained soil rich in organic matter. Zones 6 to 9.

■ **Switch grass** (*Panicum virgatum*) is valued for its airy flowers, upright narrow form, and multiseason interest. It prefers moist, well-drained soil in full sun. It is easy to grow, and once established it tolerates salt spray and drought. Some switch grasses have spectacular fall color before turning tan; others change from their original color to an attractive muted tan. Switch grass may remain erect for winter interest, but it is more often crushed under the weight of heavy snow. Plants may self-sow if they are growing in ideal conditions. Check with your cooperative extension to see if self-sowing is a nuisance in your area. Zones 5 to 9. **'Cloud Nine':** 6 feet; fine-textured clump of skinny icy blue leaves and clouds of rust-colored blooms in late summer and fall. **'Dallas Blues':** 5 feet; clump of drooping pale blue leaves accented in early fall by huge rosy purple seed heads ripening to tan. **'Haense Herms':** 5 feet; red to orange fall color on an arching clump of leaves topped with open floral plumes. **'Heavy Metal':** 3 to 4 feet; stiff, upright clump of fine powder blue leaves that turn yellow in fall. **'Rotstrahlbusch':** 3 to 4 feet; outstanding red fall color. **'Shenandoah':** 3 feet; clump of purple-tinged green leaves that turn deep wine-red in autumn.

■ **Fountain grass** (*Pennisetum alopecuroides*) forms a 3- to 4-foot

Zebra grass

'Heavy Metal' switch grass

Fountain grass

Mexican feather grass

graceful clump with slim, arching green foliage that turns tan in winter. Fuzzy, long spikes of mauve to buff flowers bloom from August to October and last until walloped by winter ice and snow. Grow large fountain grass cultivars with tall asters at the back of the border or in the middle of the garden for an attractive late-season display. Small cultivars look charming in containers and around mailboxes or lampposts mass-planted with 'Happy Returns' or 'Black-Eyed Stella' daylilies. They add an airy, fine texture to the front of beds and borders and can be grouped for maximum effect. The bottlebrush blooms are excellent for cutting. Fountain grass prefers full sun and moist, well-drained, somewhat fertile soil. In warm climates it may self-sow to the point of invasiveness. Before buying this grass, check with your local cooperative extension service to see which cultivars grow best in your area. Division is easy. Zones 5 to 8. **'Hameln':** 24 inches by 24 inches; creamy white blooms in midsummer; leaf blades thinner than the species; use in masses or as a ground cover. **'Little Bunny':** 8 to 12 inches; profusely flowering green-leaved miniature. **'Little Honey':** variegated version of 'Little Bunny'. **'Moudry':** 2 to 3 feet; dark brown to black bottlebrush flowers in late fall. **'National Arboretum':** 2 to 3 feet; dark brown flower spikes; dark green leaves.

■ **Little bluestem** (*Schizachyrium scoparium*) is a native grass once common on prairies. It produces 2- to 3-foot-tall upright clumps of blue-green grass that turn reddish brown in fall. Its lustrous seed heads glow in the autumn light. Plants do best in full sun and well-drained soil with dry to average moisture. Space them about 18 inches apart. Zones 3 to 10.

■ **Prairie dropseed** (*Sporobolus heterolepis*), another native grass, grows 2 to 4 feet tall in well-drained soil of dry to average moisture. It looks like a fountain of fine green grass and turns tan in fall. Plants are stunning when massed. The flowers, which appear in late summer, smell like cilantro, and the seed heads glisten in the fall sunlight, weighing down the arching stems. Plants tolerate heat and drought, and in spite of their name, they do not self-sow freely. Zones 3 to 9.

■ **Mexican feather grass** (*Stipa tenuissima*) grows 18 to 24 inches tall and 12 to 18 inches wide. Bright green tufts of foliage appear sleek and flowing. From May to August, the plant produces soft, refined plumes that turn from green to golden buff and sway gracefully with the leaves. Grow this drought-tolerant, self-sowing grass in groups or masses on slopes and in very well-drained or dry beds and borders. The feathery blooms make excellent cut flowers. This grass prefers light, average to dry, well-drained soil in full sun. Zones 6 to 9.

index

frost dates

Average frost dates are less critical to the activities associated with growing perennials than they are with other garden plants. Many perennials start peeking through the earth as soon as the snow is off the ground in spring; others, such as hibiscus and balloon flower, wait until late spring to make an appearance. In autumn, a light frost quickly ends the growing year for perennials such as hostas, while others sail through several hard frosts and continue to make a show until Arctic winter air arrives. As long as the plants are hardy in your region, they'll be back the next year.

Knowing frost dates, however, will help you prepare for the beginning and end of the perennial gardening season. Set out grid-style plant stakes when the first few plants pop up in spring. Order mulch and plants and have them ready to go. In fall before the first frost rolls around, ready your compost pile or have plenty of landscape bags on hand.

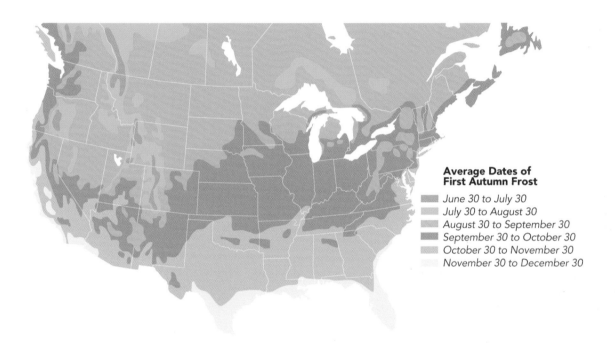

Average Dates of First Autumn Frost

- June 30 to July 30
- July 30 to August 30
- August 30 to September 30
- September 30 to October 30
- October 30 to November 30
- November 30 to December 30

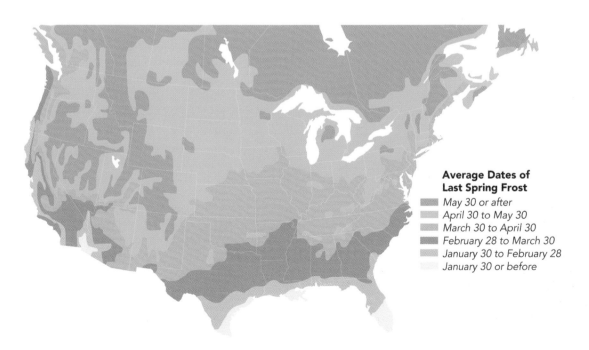

Average Dates of Last Spring Frost

- May 30 or after
- April 30 to May 30
- March 30 to April 30
- February 28 to March 30
- January 30 to February 28
- January 30 or before

USDA plant hardiness zone map

This climate zone map helps you select plants for your garden that will survive a typical winter in your region. The United States Department of Agriculture (USDA) developed the map, basing the zones on the lowest recorded temperatures across North America. Zone 1 is the coldest area and Zone 11 is the warmest.

Plants are classified by the coldest temperature and zone they can endure. For example, plants hardy to Zone 6 survive where winter temperatures drop to –10° F. Those hardy to Zone 8 die long before it's that cold. These plants may grow in colder regions but must be replaced each year. Plants rated for a range of hardiness zones can usually survive winter in the coldest region as well as tolerate the summer heat of the warmest one.

To find your hardiness zone, note the approximate location of your community on the map, then match the color band marking that area to the key.

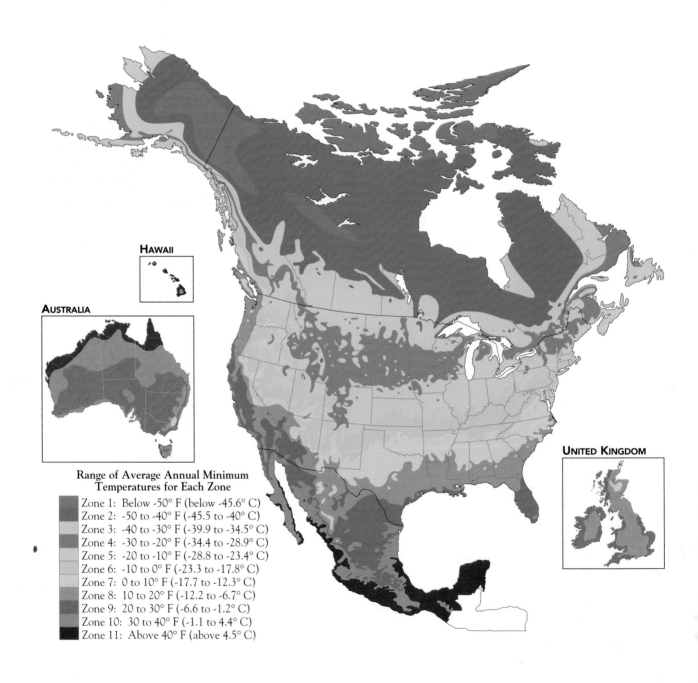

HAWAII

AUSTRALIA

UNITED KINGDOM

Range of Average Annual Minimum Temperatures for Each Zone

Zone 1: Below -50° F (below -45.6° C)
Zone 2: -50 to -40° F (-45.5 to -40° C)
Zone 3: -40 to -30° F (-39.9 to -34.5° C)
Zone 4: -30 to -20° F (-34.4 to -28.9° C)
Zone 5: -20 to -10° F (-28.8 to -23.4° C)
Zone 6: -10 to 0° F (-23.3 to -17.8° C)
Zone 7: 0 to 10° F (-17.7 to -12.3° C)
Zone 8: 10 to 20° F (-12.2 to -6.7° C)
Zone 9: 20 to 30° F (-6.6 to -1.2° C)
Zone 10: 30 to 40° F (-1.1 to 4.4° C)
Zone 11: Above 40° F (above 4.5° C)

Miracle-Gro Beautiful Perennials
Editor: Marilyn Rogers
Contributing Writer: Penelope O'Sullivan
Contributing Designer: Crowley Design LLC
Copy Chief: Terri Fredrickson
Publishing Operations Manager: Karen Schirm
Senior Editor, Asset and Information Manager:
   Phillip Morgan
Edit and Design Production Coordinator: Mary Lee Gavin
Editorial and Design Assistant: Kathleen Stevens
Book Production Managers: Pam Kvitne,
   Marjorie J. Schenkelberg, Rick von Holdt, Mark Weaver
Contributing Copy Editor: Barbara Feller-Roth
Contributing Proofreaders: Susan Brown, Pamela Elizian, Terri Krueger
Contributing Map Illustrator: Jana Fothergill
Indexer: Richard T. Evans, Infodex Indexing Services Inc.
Other Contributors: Janet Anderson, Susan Ferguson

Contributing Photographers:
David Cavagnaro: 123L, 124R, 142L, 161L
Alan & Linda Detrick: 141R, 170L, 170R
Catriona Tudor Erler: 150L, 172L, 174C
John Glover: 41, 76, 133C, 167R, 168R, 179L, 179RT, 179BR
John Glover/Positive Images: 131C, 133L
Marcus Harpur: 167C
Saxon Holt: 21B, 145R, 152BR, 166R
Andrew Lawson: 140L, 153LC, 163R, 164R, 165R, 171R, 173R, 177L
Andrew Lawson/Jill Walker, Designer: 77
Janet Loughrey: 157L
J. Paul Moore: 125L, 155R
Jerry Pavia: 4BL, 131L, 139L, 141C, 145L, 145C, 162R, 169L, 172R, 174L, 175R,
Howard Rice/Garden Picture Library: 179CR
Ron Sutherland/Garden Picture Library/Stephan Woodhams, Designer:
   40
Michael Thompson: 180R
Martien Vinkesteijn Photography/Positive Images: 146L

Meredith® Books
Executive Director, Editorial: Gregory H. Kayko
Executive Director, Design: Matt Strelecki
Managing Editor: Amy Tincher-Durik
Executive Editor/Group Manager: Benjamin W. Allen
Senior Associate Design Director: Ken Carlson
Marketing Product Manager: Isaac Petersen

Publisher and Editor in Chief: James D. Blume
Editorial Director: Linda Raglan Cunningham
Executive Director, New Business Development:
   Todd M. Davis
Executive Director, Sales: Ken Zagor
Director, Operations: George A. Susral
Director, Production: Douglas M. Johnston
Director, Marketing: Amy Nichols
Business Director: Jim Leonard

Vice President and General Manager: Douglas J. Guendel

Meredith Publishing Group
President: Jack Griffin
Executive Vice President: Bob Mate

Meredith Corporation
Chairman and Chief Executive Officer: William T. Kerr
President and Chief Operating Officer: Stephen M. Lacy

In Memoriam: E.T. Meredith III (1933–2003)

All of us at Meredith® Books are dedicated to providing you with the information and ideas you need to enhance your home and garden. We welcome your comments and suggestions about this book. Write to us at:
   Meredith Corporation
   Meredith Gardening Books
   1716 Locust St.
   Des Moines, IA 50309–3023

If you would like more information on other Miracle-Gro products, call 800/225-2883 or visit us at www.miraclegro.com

Note to the Readers: Due to differing conditions, tools, and individual skills, Meredith Corporation assumes no responsibility for any damages, injuries suffered, or losses incurred as a result of following the information published in this book. Before beginning any project, review the instructions carefully, and if any doubts or questions remain, consult local experts or authorities. Always read and observe all of the safety precautions provided by manufacturers of any tools, equipment, or supplies, and follow all accepted safety procedures.

Guide to Growing Beautiful Flowers

Encyclopedia of Plant Care

NEW

THE COMPREHENSIVE GUIDE TO GROWING MORE THAN 2000 PLANTS FOR YOUR GARDEN AND HOME

Instant GARDENS

High-Impact Makeovers That Look Great Right Now

Get dramatic results

Pick up these exciting titles from the brands you trust for gardening expertise—wherever books are sold.

Miracle·Gro